THE GREAT BRITISH BAKE OFF

THE GREAT BRITISH BAKE OFF®

GET BAKING

for friends & family

sphere

CONTENTS

FOREWORD

A NOTE FROM PAUL

For Sandi, Noel, Prue and myself it is a privilege and a lot of fun being part of *The Great British Bake Off*, and it's fantastic to be able to open up the show's recipe box to bring you this celebration of the latest two series so that you can try the bakes for yourself.

I have been around baking all my life and at the heart of the baking community is a desire to share, so it is fitting that this book should be about giving you the opportunity to share some of these great *Bake Off* recipes with family, friends and colleagues.

The bakers' recipes in this book have not only gone through rigorous testing by each baker and got the seal of approval from their own families and friends, but they have also passed the intense scrutiny of Prue and myself and received a thumbs up from Noel and Sandi.

Since the beginning of *Bake Off*, I've judged more than 400 challenges. I love working with the behind-the-scenes team to come up with challenges that will help bakers to showcase their skills and creativity, and I hope that when you open up this book, taking a step inside the *Bake Off* tent, the recipes will inspire you, too.

A NOTE FROM PRUE

Baking, cooking and feeding people really is a joy and I want everyone to experience the pleasure and satisfaction of producing food to share with others.

For me, seeing what the bakers have produced this series and last has been so inspiring that I have been unable to resist making many of the recipes myself. So I'm delighted to see the recipes published as a book for all *Bake Off* fans and keen cooks everywhere to have a go.

Paul and I have enormous fun working with the *Bake Off* team thinking up the challenges for the series and there are wonderful bakes featured in this book, from the familiar and classic to the more unusual. It doesn't matter how good you are – or in the case of some of our celebrities on *Stand Up to Cancer Bake Offs*, how bad – you can dazzle with one of our Showstoppers Made Simple at your local charity bake sale or community event, or just to show off to family and friends.

I've always believed that baking should be fun, the bakes should be worth the calories and to bake is to share. Follow a delicious recipe from this book and, with a little effort and enthusiasm, you can create a bit of *Bake Off* magic for all.

MEET THE BAKERS

ANTONY, 29
LONDON
BANKER

BRIONY, 33
BRISTOL
FULL-TIME PARENT

DAN, 36
LONDON
FULL-TIME PARENT

Describing himself as a 'Bollywood baker', Antony grew up in India, where he learned to bake with his father. It is his father who remains his inspiration – thanks to him, Antony got serious about baking. Antony's adventurous attitude to flavour profiling is the result of a willingness to try new foods, his determination to ask probing questions of established bakers, and – in particular – his cultural roots and his travels around the world. His bold, inquisitive nature has enabled him to collect ideas and techniques that he is unafraid to use in his own creations, making his bakes at times unconventional and always interesting. He takes his research very seriously: he once tasted 50 choux buns during a single trip to Paris.

He says, *"Let's just say I went to a lot of bakeries and I had a choux bun and an éclair in each."*

Born and raised in Bristol, Briony is a self-taught baker, inspired by her nan's baking wisdom and motivated by her determination never to let anything defeat her. Using *YouTube* tutorials to help her learn specific techniques, Briony has been baking seriously since 2013. She is a whiz with puff pastry – a weekly favourite at home with her husband and daughter – and has created several wedding cakes and stunning, intricately decorated novelty cakes for both friends and family.

She says, *"Baking calms me and takes me to a happy place. I still get a real sense of achievement when a bake goes well!"*

For Dan, the pleasure of eating begins with what we see. A self-confessed perfectionist, Dan considers aesthetic one of the most important aspects of his bakes – he begins every creation with the aim of making it not just delicious, but also a thing of beauty. While that can cause stress during the cooking and making itself, he aims for well-thought-through results, with every bake created with a genuine and knowledgeable appreciation for the process. He is a full-time father to two small children, so home-baking is part of his everyday life. He sees it as a means to create family memories, as well as to foster family mealtimes.

He says, *"Anything creative is inherently satisfying to me. My father always made things with his hands, so I think it must be in my genes to find such pleasure in the process."*

IMELDA, 33
COUNTY TYRONE, NI
COUNTRYSIDE
RECREATION OFFICER

Imelda is one of four siblings and grew up in County Tyrone, Northern Ireland, where she learned to cook and bake from her mother, in their family home. Now juggling a busy job and family life, Imelda spends her evenings and weekends making soda breads, biscuits and treats for her father and son, and cakes that she takes into work to share with her colleagues. She lives surrounded by aunts, uncles and cousins, which means catering for friends and family at large sociable gatherings is just part of normal, everyday life.

She says, *"My wee granny always said there was a separate stomach for dessert; no matter how much dinner there'd been, there was always room for a sweet."*

JON, 47
NEWPORT, WALES
BLOOD COURIER

Welshman Jon loves nothing more than spending quality family time with his wife and four children and bakes in the kitchen as a way to relax after a hard day's work. He loves a showy bake – and a showy Hawaiian shirt, too – and loves wowing friends and family with his creations. Jon loves to research new ideas and experiment with different techniques to try to achieve something unique in his baking.

He says, *"People say if you make puff pastry, you haven't got a life – I love my life and I love making puff pastry!"*

KAREN, 60
WEST YORKSHIRE
IN-STORE SAMPLING
ASSISTANT

Karen began her love affair with baking during the 15 years in which she and her husband owned a house in France. Although she had baked with her mum since she was little, it was the local French pâtisserie that really inspired her. Now, she can knock up profiteroles, Religieuse buns, tartes au citron, and even foot-long éclairs to rival any French bakery. Karen is unafraid to experiment in her baking and has even been known to go into baking 'frenzies' whenever there is a party or a barbecue, baking everything she can think of and freezing as she goes.

She says, *"I once cooked a full, three-course Christmas lunch for 27 people in a caravan kitchen."*

KIM-JOY, 27
LEEDS
MENTAL HEALTH
SPECIALIST

Kim-Joy's birthday falls on World Baking Day, which she takes as the surest sign there can be that she was born to bake. Born in Belgium to an English father and Malaysian–Chinese mother, she grew up in London, studied in Bristol and now lives in Leeds with her partner. Her bustling, mixed-heritage background is reflected in her open attitude to all styles of baking, loving rustic baking just as much as she loves cutesy perfectionism. Her baking passion, though, is bread – she has turned her hand to pretty much every style and type of bread there is.

She says, *"A part of me can be seen in my cakes. I like colourful and cute items."*

LUKE, 30
SHEFFIELD
CIVIL SERVANT &
HOUSE/TECHNO DJ

Some of Luke's earliest memories are standing on a step ladder so that he could reach the worktop to help his Nan make scones. He has been baking independently since he was a mere ten years old, making Victoria sponges, fruit cobblers and chocolate cake for his family. Now, inspired by early morning cookery shows and his travels throughout Europe and North America, he has tried his hand at almost every baking discipline going. His minimal and clutter-free attitude to life is reflected in the things he creates – his bakes are clean and precise.

He says, *"Forget Paul Hollywood... my fiancée does not hold back when it comes to giving me her opinion on my bakes."*

MANON, 26
LONDON
IT PROJECT MANAGER

Born and raised in France, Manon learned to bake with her mother and grandmother, who made everything from scratch – from breads to desserts and biscuits. However, although she grew up in a foodie French family, it was in London that Manon found her passion for baking, arriving in the city to work as an au pair and being blown away by the style and variety of bakeries that the city has to offer. Now she takes inspiration not only from her French heritage, and her London discoveries, but also from her travels around the world. She creates bakes that are pretty and precise and have bags of personality.

She says, *"I love Baking, but I guess my heart will always go for Eating."*

**RAHUL, 30
SHEFFIELD
RESEARCH SCIENTIST**

**RUBY, 29
LONDON
PROJECT MANAGER**

**TERRY, 56
WEST MIDLANDS
RETIRED AIR STEWARD**

Rahul grew up in Kolkata, surrounded by his family, and moved to the UK on a university scholarship when he was 23. Once here, he discovered an abundance of new flavours and cuisines that have inspired his 'East-meets-West'-style of baking. As a research scientist, Rahul's instinct is to undertake every bake with a forensic attitude to research and an uncompromising attention to detail. He is fascinated by the science of baking, but also loves to ensure that his creations are beautiful, full of flavour and structurally elegant, too.

He says, *"When I came to the UK in 2010 I started to watch cooking and baking programmes and I thought maybe I could do something similar. Having never used an oven in my life before made the learning journey a long one – but also definitely more interesting!"*

Ruby's love of baking is the result of having become everyone's 'mother' when she went to university, taking seven male housemates under her wing, cooking and baking for them. Growing up as part of an Indian family, the youngest of four children, Ruby remembers childhood baking being about her mum making *jalebis*, an Indian sweet. Now Ruby loves to gather friends and family together to indulge in her cakes and pastries, as well as her infamous spicy minced lamb rolls. Her baking style is pretty boozy and she will always try to sneak a dash of something into whatever she is making.

She says, *"I'm not a girly girl, I like punchy flavours and I want my bakes to be a knockout."*

Terry's background as a prosthetic technician, as well as spoils from his own microbrewery and allotment, are all evident in his baking – particularly in the precision, science and flavour of his creations. The design and craftsmanship in Terry's bakes are a testament to his background in fine art. However, it is family that lies at the heart of Terry's baking journey. As a small child Terry learned to bake with his grandmother; and his dad taught him how to bake bread and make pastry when Terry was only ten years old. And it was his daughters who finally encouraged him to take the plunge and apply for *Bake Off*.

He says, *"My daughters have always been very willing participants in eating my bakes. Looking back at the photographs, I had two pudgy daughters and I think I fed them far too well."*

INTRODUCTION

Baking something delicious for loved ones is among life's simple pleasures – and eating it together is even better. *The Great British Bake Off: Get Baking for Friends and Family* celebrates the joy of a really good bake shared with friends, and offers simple, tasty recipes for every occasion.

Inspired by recipes from *The Great British Bake Off* and developed by the behind-the-scenes team, this baker's bible is packed with more than 100 mouthwatering cakes, biscuits, breads, pastries, savouries and puddings. It offers something for everyone, from children beginning their baking adventures to accomplished home cooks wanting to try something impressive for a party.

Take a step inside the tent and try your hand at Paul Hollywood and Prue Leith's Judges' Recipes. Or, why not have a go at some of the best signature bakes from series 8 and 9, in the Bakers' Recipes. Follow the step-by-step photographs in our Showstoppers Made Simple, or try some of the wonderful treats devised by the team behind the scenes of *Bake Off*.

Six simple chapters cover each type of bake, and if you need help with an essential recipe like shortcrust pastry or crème pâtissière, they're all gathered together at the end of the book for easy reference. To make things even simpler, all recipes are colour-coded to help you out when you need inspiration for a special celebration, when you're baking with your children, when you're entertaining friends and, of course, when you need a fresh idea for a family meal. There are recipes for vegans, vegetarians and those who are gluten- or dairy-free – so everyone can get stuck in. We have taken the hard work out of these recipes – all that is left is for you to enjoy making delicious food to share with your nearest and dearest. So, get baking!

For the latest *Bake Off* book news and giveaways, sign up to the newsletter at www.gbbobook.co.uk

KEY TO COLOUR-CODING

BAKING WITH CHILDREN
CELEBRATIONS
ENTERTAINING
FAMILY MEALTIMES
TEATIME TREATS
BAKER'S RECIPE
JUDGE'S RECIPE
SHOWSTOPPERS MADE SIMPLE
INSPIRED BY THE SHOW

KEY TO SYMBOLS

The recipes in this book use the following symbols to indicate suitability for special diets. Please always check the labels on your ingredients, too, in case of hidden allergens, or cross-contamination.

VEGETARIAN

VEGAN

GLUTEN-FREE

DAIRY-FREE

A BAKER'S KITCHEN

Everything you need to start – and some useful extras, too.

You really don't need a lot to start baking. With an oven, scales, a bowl and a baking sheet you can bake bread, biscuits, scones … . Add a couple of cake tins and a wooden spoon (plus plenty of muscle power), and you can whip up a cake. So, although the following list seems long, please don't be put off – you can build up your kitchen gradually, as you build up your skills.

BAKING BEANS
An essential to keep the base of a pastry case flat and the sides upright while you 'blind bake' (that is, without its filling). You can use ceramic beans repeatedly, but uncooked dried beans will work well, too. Just make sure you store them in a labelled jar afterwards as, once baked, they won't be suitable for eating.

BAKING PAPER AND LINERS
These make removing biscuits, pastries and cakes from tins and trays easier as they help prevent sticking. Choose non-stick baking paper (sometimes called parchment). Greaseproof is less sturdy and has a waxy coating that doesn't stand up as well to the heat of the oven. Reusable silicone liners are more expensive, but are easy to use, can be cut to fit the tins and trays you use most often, and can be wiped clean after use. They will last a long time with proper care, making them a good investment for frequent bakers.

BAKING SHEETS AND TRAYS
A baking sheet is flat with only one raised edge for gripping, making it good for bakes, such as biscuits, you might want to slide onto a cooling rack. A baking tray has a rim or shallow edge all the way around and is good for baking pies or tarts that might leak. Aim to have at least one heavy-duty baking sheet, and two or three trays or lightweight sheets to make batch-baking easier.

BAKING STONES
Baking stones and pizza stones will give your dough that perfect base. Remember to put your stone in the oven when you switch the oven on, so that the stone is thoroughly hot before you use it.

BAKING TINS
It's really important to use the tin that's specified in the recipe as the quantities and baking time have been calculated to work according to a specific tin size. A really solid, good-quality tin will withstand repeated baking without scorching or losing its shape. Make sure you clean and dry your tins thoroughly after use. Several of the recipes in the book call for specialist tins or moulds (such as the madeleines on p.101). However, the following will otherwise see you through nicely:

Loaf tins are essential for neat brick-shaped breads and cakes. They're available in a variety of sizes, but the most-used sizes are 450g (measuring about 19 x 12.5 x 7.5cm) and 900g (measuring about 26 x 12.5 x 7.5cm). Heavy-duty ones won't dent or warp and will give you a better crust than silicone.

Muffin or cupcake tins are what you need for small bakes. They are usually 6- or 12-hole. Non-stick and silicone versions will produce equally good results.

Sandwich tins are essential. Aim to own two 20–20.5cm-diameter sandwich tins, each 4–5cm deep. A third tin is useful for baking American-style layer cakes.

Springform (or springclip) tins are deep metal tins with a spring release that are useful for cakes, tortes, pies and pull-apart bread rolls because they won't damage a fragile bake.

Swiss roll tins are rectangular (usually 20 x 30cm or 23 x 33cm) and about 2cm deep.

Tart and tartlet tins, available with fluted and straight sides, give the most professional results when made from sturdy metal, such as silver anodised, which is also hard-wearing and easy to clean. Mince-pie tins (which are useful for jam tarts and mini-tart cases, not just for traditional Christmas bakes) are trays with 6 or 12 shallow hollows. Choose non-stick versions.

Traybake tins are square or rectangular and about 4cm deep, and used for brownies, shortbread, and all traybakes. Buy loose-bottomed tins to help you release your bakes easily.

BOWLS

For versatility, sturdiness and durablity, heatproof glass and stainless steel bowls are good choices for mixing and whisking, and melting ingredients over hot water, although plastic bowls are cheaper. Ceramic bowls look pretty but can be heavy. A very large bowl with a snap-on lid is very useful for mixing and rising bread doughs. Incidentally, make your bowls non-slip by resting them on a damp cloth as you mix.

COOLING/WIRE RACKS

A large wire rack with legs allows air to circulate around and underneath a bake as it cools, avoiding any sogginess. A wire grill-pan rack makes a good improvisation.

DOUGH SCRAPER

One of the cheapest and most useful pieces of equipment, the dough scraper helps to scoop, scrape and divide bread dough, and makes easy work of cleaning bowls and worktops.

ELECTRIC STAND MIXERS, PROCESSORS AND WHISKS

Lots of the recipes in the book call for a helping hand from an electric gadget, such as a stand mixer. Although these can make life easier, if you're new to baking, don't feel you have to rush out and buy expensive kit. Cakes and biscuits are often easily baked without a mixer, and in fact most of the recipes in the book can be made with muscle power – just remember to keep going (with a hand whisk, a wooden spoon, or your bare hands), until you reach the consistency described in the method. Find tips for baking by hand on pages 311–313.

A large capacity stand mixer is a good investment if you do a lot of baking. Use the whisk attachment for meringues, buttercreams and light sponge mixtures; the paddle or beater for heavier, mixtures, such as richer cakes, choux pastry, and savarin-type enriched doughs; and the dough hook for mixing, then kneading bread doughs. A spare bowl will help with multi-element sponges.

An electric hand mixer is a good, versatile choice if you want to make whisked mixtures, creamed sponges, meringues or mixtures whisked over heat.

A stick blender (which will often come with a whisk attachment) is good for smoothing out fruit sauces and crème pâtissière.

A food processor makes light work of making pastry as it's so quick at blending the fat and flour until it looks like fine crumbs. You can use the 'pulse' button to avoid overworking. It's also good for finely chopping nuts and herbs (a mini version is especially good for small quantities), or making pâtés and torrines.

HAND OR BALLOON WHISK

A wire hand whisk can be balloon shaped or flat, while a hand-held rotary whisk consists of a pair of beaters set in a metal frame. Any one of these is essential even if you have an electric version, too.

KNIVES

The better the knife, the easier it will be to perfect your knife skills. Stainless steel knives are easy to keep clean, but need to be sharpened regularly; carbon-steel knives are a bit more expensive, but easier to keep to sharp; and ceramic ones are harder still, but much lighter and won't require sharpening. Gather a sharp medium-sized knife, about 20cm long, a small, sharp knife (useful for pastry work, trimming edges, and making decorations) and a really good-quality large serrated bread knife (for sawing through crusts). An off-set palette knife (one with a kink near the handle) is essential for spreading icings and delicate mixtures where you need a smooth, precise result.

MEASURING EQUIPMENT

Baking is a science and, for perfect results, careful weighing and precision are essential.

Digital scales are particularly useful. As well as weighing tiny ingredients and switching easily between units, you can 'zero' ingredients you've already weighed and add others to the same bowl, knowing precisely how much you're adding (remember that 1ml of water is the same as 1g).

Measuring jugs, even if you have digital scales, are a must. Pick a heat-resistant and microwave-safe one that's easy to read and starts at 50ml (ideally) or 100ml, and goes up to 2 litres.

Measuring spoons do a far better job than everyday spoons (teaspoons, dessert spoons, tablespoons), which can vary in size and will give inconsistent results. All spoon measures in this book are level, not heaped or rounded, so use the back of a knife to skim off the excess.

METAL SPOON

A large, long-handled metal spoon is invaluable for folding wet ingredients into dry.

OVEN THERMOMETER

In the same way that measuring ingredients needs to be precise, so does oven temperature. Built-in oven thermostats can be inconsistent and will become less efficient with age. An oven thermometer is a great way to make sure your oven reaches the right temperature before you bake, as well as to identify the hot and cool spots to avoid an uneven bake. If you don't have a thermometer, know your oven – they are all different and you may find that you consistently need to increase or decrease the temperature or baking time to get the right results. Giving your oven a regular clean will help, too.

PASTRY BRUSH

Opt for a heat- and dishwasher-proof, medium-sized pastry brush. It's a must-have you'll use not only for glazing pastry and bread, but for tasks such as brushing down sugar crystals from the sides of a pan as you make caramel.

PIPING BAGS AND NOZZLES

The recipes in this book use both reusable and disposable piping bags. The latter permit you to snip off the end to pipe directly without a nozzle, and to use several bags at once without washing, but they aren't as ecologically sound as reusable nylon bags. Both come in various sizes.

Piping nozzles, made from metal or plastic, range from wide round tips for piping choux pastry and meringue, to star-shaped for icings, to fine writing tips for delicate work. Set the nozzle in the bag, then stand it in a jug or mug for support, then fill.

PASTRY CUTTERS

Pick a double-sided (plain on one side, fluted on the other) nest of metal cutters in different sizes. A pizza wheel-cutter is handy for cutting straight lines (such as the lattice strips you'll need for Prue's Mince Pies on p.234). Shaped cutters are infinite and lovely – but can be expensive.

ROLLING PIN

A fairly heavy wooden pin about 6–7cm in diameter and without handles will make the easiest work of rolling out pastry.

SIEVE

Every baker needs a sieve – to combine flour with raising agents; remove lumps from icing and sugars; and for straining and puréeing. Go for a large metal sieve that will sit over your largest mixing bowl for sifting tasks, and a smaller, tea-strainer-sized one for dusting your finished bakes.

SPATULA

A strong and flexible spatula is useful for mixing, folding and scraping with ease.

STORAGE CONTAINERS

Old-fashioned stainless steel tins or hard-wearing plastic containers with tight-fitting lids are perfect. Store bread in a bread bin, rather than plastic, to stave off mould. And don't forget to add a label with the date of baking.

SUGAR THERMOMETER/ COOKING THERMOMETER

Essential for sugar work (and deep-frying), a sugar thermometer will ensure your sugar reaches the correct temperature if, for example, you're making caramel or nougat, or tempering chocolate – among other baking tasks. Pick one that's easy to read and can clip on to the side of the pan. A thermometer with a probe will help you to measure the internal temperatures of your bakes (and other cooking) for doneness, too.

TIMER

A digital kitchen timer with seconds as well as minutes (and a loud bell) is essential – don't rely on just your oven timer. Set for a minute or two less than the suggested time in your recipe (especially if you are uncertain of your oven) – you can always increase the oven time.

WOODEN SPOON

Cheap, heat-resistant, and safe on non-stick pans, a wooden spoon mixes, beats, creams and stirs – the essentials of good baking. You can even use the handle to shape brandy snaps and tuiles and make little indentations for sweet fillings. Just remember to keep your sweet and savoury spoons separate – as wood will absorb strong flavours.

ZESTER

A long-handled zester is the best and quickest way to remove the zest from citrus fruits (use unwaxed citrus fruits for zesting). Pick one that's sturdy and easy to hold.

A BAKER'S LARDER

Most of the bakes in this book use ingredients that you'll find in major supermarkets. Keep the following in your store cupboard and you'll be ready to get baking whenever the mood takes you. As a rule of thumb: the best-quality ingredients tend to give the best results.

BAKING POWDER, BICARBONATE OF SODA, AND CREAM OF TARTAR

Chemical raising agents, all these ingredients increase the lightness and volume of cakes and small bakes, and some types of biscuit and pastry. Always use the amount given in the recipe and check the date stamps, too, as raising agents will lose their potency over time. If you've run out of baking powder, you can easily make your own: for 1 teaspoon of baking powder combine ½ teaspoon of cream of tartar with ¼ teaspoon of bicarbonate of soda.

BUTTER AND OTHER FATS

Most of the recipes in this book use unsalted butter, as it has a delicate flavour, adds a good, even colour (perhaps because it contains less whey than salted), and allows you to season your bake to taste yourself, as relevant. Store butter tightly wrapped in the fridge, well away from strong flavours. When relevant, a recipe will tell you whether to use butter chilled (from the fridge), at room temperature, or softened. Diced butter is cut into small cubes, which enables you to add small amounts at a time and makes the butter easier to combine.

Lard, from pigs, gives a short, flaky texture to traditional hot-water crust pastry so that it bakes to a crisp, golden finish. White solid vegetable fat is a good alternative.

Dairy-free spreads, made from vegetable and sunflower oils, make good substitutes in most recipes that require softened or room-temperature butter, but always check the label to make sure it's good for baking beforehand. Some are made specifically for baking and you can use them straight from the fridge. They give good results, but may lack that buttery flavour. Avoid spreads designed for use on bread/crackers – they contain too much water and not enough fat to make good baking ingredients.

Solid coconut oil is a good option for dairy-free and vegan recipes, but isn't a like-for-like butter substitute.

Suet, from cows, gives a light, soft pastry rather than a very crisp or flaky one. Suet is more solid than butter or lard and melts much more slowly, forming tiny pockets in the dough as it cooks.

Vegetable oil often pops up in bakes these days, with sunflower oil giving the best results as it's light and mildly flavoured.

CHOCOLATE

Chocolate is a must in baking – from chocolate collars and spheres to drizzles and sauces, it features in many of the recipes in this book.

Dark chocolate, with around 70% cocoa solids, is the kind most used in these recipes as it gives a good balance of flavour – chocolate with a higher percentage (75% and above) may be too bitter and dry for general baking. Some recipes use 54% dark, which is a little sweeter.

Milk chocolate has a much milder and sweeter flavour – choose a good-quality favourite, and expect the best results from milk chocolate with good amounts of cocoa solids.

White chocolate doesn't contain any cocoa solids, just cocoa butter. Look out for brands with 30% or more cocoa butter as a measure of quality. White chocolate sets less firmly than dark or milk chocolate owing to the higher fat content, and melts at a lower temperature, so take care as it easily scorches and becomes unusable.

COCOA POWDER

A dark, unsweetened powder made from pure cocoa liqueur with nearly all the cocoa butter removed, cocoa powder is very bitter, strongly flavoured and gives a powerful hit. Never substitute with drinking chocolate, which contains milk powder and sugar, as well as cocoa powder itself.

CREAM

For best results, chill cream thoroughly before whipping (in really hot weather chill the bowl and whisk, too).

Buttermilk, sometimes labelled 'cultured buttermilk', is low-fat or non-fat milk plus a bacterial culture to give it an acidic tang. It is often used along with bicarbonate of soda to add lightness as well as flavour to scones and cakes.

Crème fraîche is a soured cream with a creamy, tangy flavour. It won't whip, but you can use it for fillings, toppings and serving.

Double cream contains at least 48% butterfat. It also whips well and has a richer flavour than whipping cream. The extra-rich type of double cream is designed for spooning, rather than whipping or making ganache.

Lactose-free and soya-based dairy-free creams can give varied results, and are usually unsuitable for whipping.

Single cream contains 18% butterfat and is good for adding to sauces and fillings, for adding richness to rubbed-in mixtures, or for pouring over desserts and pastries.

Soured cream has only 18% butterfat. It is made by introducing a bacterial culture to cream, giving a naturally sour tang.

Whipping cream contains at least 36% butterfat and is designed to whip well without being overly rich.

DRIED FRUIT

Keep stores of dried fruit out of direct sunlight and tightly sealed in containers. Vine fruit, such as raisins, sultanas and currants, have a long shelf-life, but will always be best bought when you need them. Soft-dried apricots, as well as dried figs, cranberries, blueberries, sour cherries, and dates, can replace vine fruits in many recipes. They add sweetness and moisture to cakes and breads, which is useful if you want to reduce refined sugar.

EGGS

When it comes to eggs, size really does matter. Unless otherwise stated, all the recipes in this book use medium-sized eggs. If the eggs are too small, a sponge may not rise properly and look thin or dry; too big and a pastry or bread dough may be too wet or soft to handle.

For baking, use eggs at room temperature, so take them out of the fridge 30–60 minutes before you start cooking. If you forget, pop them into a bowl of lukewarm water for a couple of minutes.

Spare egg whites will keep for 3–4 days in a sealed container or jar in the fridge, or for up to a month in the freezer (defrost overnight in the fridge before using; yolks can't be frozen).

EXTRACTS AND FLAVOURINGS

Avoid synthetic flavourings as much as you can – they often have an aftertaste that will spoil your hard work. Here's a guide to the best to use.

Almond extract may be pricey, but most recipes need only a few drops. Avoid anything marked 'flavouring'.

Ground spices are best when you use them fresh, but if you're storing them, do so in screw-topped jars, rather than open packets, to prolong their flavour.

Vanilla is usually the most expensive flavouring used in baking, although you need to use only small amounts of the real thing. Vanilla extract – labelled 'pure' or 'natural' – costs more than vanilla essence, which might contain artificial flavourings. Vanilla bean paste is made from the seeds of the pods and has a thicker texture and more concentrated flavour. Best of all, though, are vanilla pods, which you can split to scrape out the tiny seeds to flavour custards, crème pâtissière and fillings. Don't throw away the pods: rinse and dry carefully, then put them in a jar of caster sugar to make vanilla sugar.

FLOUR

Whether made from wheat or other grains, flour has to be the most valued ingredient in the baker's larder. Avoid poor-quality, out-of-date or stale flour, as this will affect the result and taste of the final bake. Always buy the best and freshest flour you can afford.

Cornflour is a finely milled white powder added to biscuits to give a delicate crumb, and used to thicken custard and crème pâtissière.

Cornmeal is bright yellow and made from the ground kernels of the corn or maize plant (making it naturally gluten-free). Sold as polenta, it gives a sandy texture to pastry and shortbread and is good for sprinkling under and on top of soft doughs to prevent sticking and to give a crisp, crunchy crust.

Gluten-free flours are wheat-free mixtures of several ingredients, including rice, potato, tapioca, maize, chickpea, broad bean, white sorghum or buckwheat – depending on the brand. Ready-mixed gluten-free flours sometimes suggest adding xanthan gum (a powder sold in small tubs) to improve the texture and crumb of your bake – check the packet and, if your flour mix doesn't already include it, add 1 teaspoon xanthan gum per 150g gluten-free flour. Some gluten-free flours need a little more liquid than wheat flour doughs, so you can't substitute them exactly, but it is well worth experimenting.

Plain flour is a type of wheat flour used for pastry-making, pancakes and rich fruit cakes, for example, and has no added raising agents.

Rye flour has a deep, dark flavour that works well in breads, particularly sourdoughs. It's low in gluten, which makes it harder to knead than wheat flours, and the dough rises less well. Available as wholegrain and a finer 'light' rye, which has had some of the bran sifted out, it is useful for crackers and adding to wheat flour for savoury pastry recipes.

Self-raising flour has added baking powder and is most often used in sponge-cake recipes to give a light, risen texture. If you run out of self-raising flour you can easily make your own: add 4 teaspoons of baking powder to every 225g plain flour, sifting them together a couple of times. Sponge self-raising flour is more expensive than regular self-raising, but is slightly 'softer' and silkier, as it is more finely milled.

Semolina flour is a slightly gritty, pale yellow flour made from durum wheat, and often used for pasta and Italian-style breads (as well as semolina pudding).

Speciality wheat flours are created from wheat varieties that are specifically grown to make flour for baking ciabatta, pizza bases, and baguettes.

Spelt flour comes from the same family as wheat, but has a slightly different genetic make-up and a richer and more nutty flavour – it is good for most recipes that call for flour, except very delicate biscuits and sponges.

Stoneground flour means that the grain (wheat, rye, spelt and so on) is milled between large stones instead of steel rollers, giving a coarser texture and fuller flavour.

Strong flour is made from wheat with a higher proportion of protein to starch than the flours used for cakes and pastry, which is crucial to bread-making. As you knead the dough, the protein develops into strands of gluten that expand around the gases produced by the yeast and enable the dough to rise. Strong bread flour has 12–16% protein, ideal for most breads. Extra-strong or Canadian strong flour has even more (15–17%), which is good for bagels or larger loaves.

Wholemeal or wholegrain flours are made from the complete wheat kernel, making them far more nutritious than white flours (which are made using 75% of the cleaned wheat kernel, and have most of the wheat bran and wheatgerm removed). The small specks of bran in these flours mean that they give a dough that rises less well than one made with all white flour. Wholemeal plain flour has been milled to make it lighter and more suitable for making pastry and cakes.

NUTS
Buy nuts in small quantities to use up quickly (always before the use-by date) – the high oil content means that once opened, nuts can quickly turn rancid. If you're storing them, do so in an airtight container in a cool, dark place.

Almonds are incredibly versatile – ground, chopped, flaked (toasted and untoasted) and whole (blanched or unblanched). To blanch (remove the skins) yourself, put the nuts in a small pan, add water to cover and bring to the boil. Remove the pan from the heat and drain, then slip the nuts out of their casings. Dry on kitchen paper.

Hazelnuts are usually ready-blanched (without their brown papery skins) or ground.

Pistachios are easy to find shelled and unsalted, but they usually come with their papery skins attached. To reveal the deep-green colour of the nuts, carefully tip them into a pan of boiling water. Remove from the heat, leave for 1 minute, then drain. Transfer the nuts to a clean, dry tea towel and rub gently to loosen the skins, then peel if necessary.

Walnuts and pecans, usually halved or chopped, are interchangeable in most baking recipes as they share a similar texture and appearance (walnuts are slightly more bitter). Gently toasting walnuts and pecans in a medium-heat oven gives them a much deeper, richer flavour.

SUGAR
Different sugars combine and interact with other ingredients in different ways, affecting the end results of the bake. Always use the sugar the recipe specifies. Sugar doesn't have a shelf life and will keep indefinitely in an airtight container in a cool, dark place.

Brown muscovado sugars come as soft light muscovado, soft dark muscovado, and Demerara. These add a stronger, warmer caramel or butterscotch flavour and darker colour to bakes, but they can make them more moist and heavy. They are good in rich fruity cakes, gingerbreads, parkins, and spice cakes. Press out any lumps with the back of a spoon before using.

Caster sugar comes as both refined white and unrefined golden. White provides sweetness with a neutral colour and flavour that is, for example, perfect for white meringues or very pale sponges. Unrefined golden caster sugar has a slight caramel, rich flavour. Use it when having a warmer colour in your final bake is not an issue. The fine grains of caster sugar break down easily during beating or creaming with butter for sponges, melt quickly for lemon curd, and disappear in pastry mixtures.

Granulated sugar, available as white or golden, has bigger grains that take longer to dissolve, giving pastry a visibly spotty appearance, and producing heavier cakes than caster sugar. Keep it for making sugar syrups and caramel.

Icing sugar is also available as refined (white) and unrefined (golden). Again, the unrefined version has a pale caramel colour and flavour. Use white icing sugar for icings, fillings and frostings that need to be very pale or that are to be coloured with food colouring. Sift before use.

SYRUP AND TREACLE
Golden syrup and sticky, thick black treacle add a rich, toffee-ish flavour, as well as sweetness, to bakes. They can be difficult to measure, so warm the measuring spoon in a mug of just-boiled water before scooping, or stand the syrup or treacle tin in a bowl of boiled water for a few minutes to loosen the stickiness. Maple syrup has a lighter texture than golden syrup, but a distinctive flavour that works particularly well with nuts, and, of course, over pancakes.

YEAST
Yeast is a living organism that makes bread doughs rise. It needs moisture, gentle warmth and flour (or sugar) to stimulate its growth and the production of carbon dioxide, which expands the dough. The recipes in this book use dried, finely powdered yeast. This type is available in 7g sachets or in tubs as fast-action, easy-blend, or instant dried yeast. Always add the yeast powder to the flour, never to the liquid. If you add it with the salt, do so on opposite sides of the bowl, as salt (and too much sugar) retards its growth. (And hot water kills it.) If you use too much yeast in a bake the dough will be lively, but the baked loaf may have a strong aftertaste and will stale more quickly. If you use too little, the dough will take longer to rise and prove, but it will have a deeper flavour and will most likely keep better.

CHAPTER ONE

CAKES

A much-loved centrepiece of many family gatherings, the cake sits at the heart of baking with very good reason. All you need is weighed-out, good-quality ingredients, a spoon, a bowl, some baking paper and a tin, and a delicious crowd-pleaser is within your grasp.

The cakes in this chapter are round, shaped, naked, decorated, whole, sandwiched, and topped and flavoured in so many different ways; the three things they have in common are that they are delicious, achievable and completely user-friendly. Start with the simpler Sticky Apple Cake or the Morello Cherry & Almond Squares and, as your confidence grows, have a go at the irresistible Hot Chocolate Birthday Cake, the Fresh Orange Cake (perfect for spring and summer celebrations) or the Boston Cream Pie (for a little taste of Stateside baking).

There are three impressive Showstoppers in this chapter – the Chocolate Collar Cake (the ultimate chocolate-lover's treat), the Sticky Toffee Apple Caramel Cake (three layers of glorious stickiness), and the 'One in Melon' Cake (it's simpler than it seems!). With our easy-to-follow methods, none of these incredible bakes is out of reach – so go on and make something to impress your loved ones.

HOT CHOCOLATE BIRTHDAY CAKE

This warmly spiced cake is reminiscent of a cup of Mexican hot chocolate.

SERVES 12

75G COCOA POWDER

375G CASTER SUGAR

375ML BOILING WATER

200G UNSALTED BUTTER

3 LARGE EGGS

335G PLAIN FLOUR

1½ TSP BAKING POWDER

1½ TSP BICARBONATE OF SODA

2 TSP GROUND CINNAMON

½ TSP GROUND NUTMEG

¼ TSP GROUND CAYENNE (OPTIONAL)

FOR THE FILLING

225G UNSALTED BUTTER, SOFTENED

450G ICING SUGAR, SIFTED

75G COCOA POWDER, SIFTED

½ TSP GROUND CINNAMON

4–5 TBSP WHOLE MILK

FOR THE DECORATION

300ML DOUBLE CREAM

HANDFUL OF VEGETARIAN MINI MARSHMALLOWS

10G 70% DARK CHOCOLATE, GRATED

GROUND CINNAMON, FOR DUSTING

YOU WILL NEED

20CM ROUND CAKE TINS X 3, GREASED, THEN BASE-LINED WITH BAKING PAPER; LARGE PIPING BAG FITTED WITH A LARGE STAR NOZZLE

STEP 1 Heat the oven to 180°C/160°C fan/350°F/ Gas 4. Put the cocoa powder, 150g of the caster sugar and the boiling water in a jug and whisk together until the sugar has dissolved. Set aside to cool slightly.

STEP 2 Cream the butter and remaining caster sugar together until pale and fluffy, then add the eggs, one at a time, beating well between each addition.

STEP 3 Sift the flour, baking powder, bicarbonate of soda, cinnamon, nutmeg and cayenne, if using, together in another bowl. Add ⅓ of the flour mixture to the creamed butter and sugar, and beat well to combine. Repeat twice more, using ⅓ of the flour mixture each time and beating well between each addition.

STEP 4 Fold in the cocoa and sugar mixture until fully combined. Divide the cake batter equally between the 3 lined tins and bake for 25–30 minutes, until risen and a skewer inserted into the centre comes out clean.

STEP 5 Remove the cakes from the oven, leave to cool in the tins for 5 minutes, then turn out onto wire racks. Peel off the paper and leave to cool completely.

STEP 6 To make the filling, whisk all the ingredients together, until light and aerated (it should look like bubbles in hot chocolate). Divide the mixture into 3 equal portions, using 2 portions to sandwich the cakes together and the third to cover the top and sides.

STEP 7 To decorate the cake, whip the cream to firm peaks, then spoon it into a large piping bag fitted with a large star nozzle. Pipe swirls of cream over the top of the cake, then sprinkle with mini marshmallows and the grated chocolate, and dust with cinnamon.

JUDGE'S RECIPE
LE GÂTEAU VERT

This green cake was artist Claude Monet's favourite birthday cake.

SERVES 8-10

FOR THE PISTACHIO MARZIPAN

300G PISTACHIO KERNELS

225G ICING SUGAR

1 LARGE EGG WHITE, WHISKED

1 TSP PISTACHIO ESSENCE

FOR THE GÉNOISE SPONGE

50G PISTACHIO KERNELS

75G PLAIN FLOUR

125G CASTER SUGAR

4 LARGE EGGS

25G UNSALTED BUTTER, MELTED

GRATED ZEST OF
1 UNWAXED LEMON

FOR THE CRÈME AU BEURRE

300G SPINACH

100G PISTACHIO KERNELS

1 TBSP KIRSCH

150G UNSALTED BUTTER, SOFTENED

80G CASTER SUGAR

2 LARGE EGG YOLKS

FOR THE DECORATION

1 QUANTITY OF POURING
FONDANT (SEE P.305), MADE
INSTEAD WITH 3-4 TBSP SPINACH
WATER (SEE METHOD) AND
½ TSP PISTACHIO ESSENCE

25G PISTACHIO KERNELS

EDIBLE FLOWERS, TO DECORATE

YOU WILL NEED

23CM ROUND CAKE TIN, GREASED,
THEN BASE-LINED WITH BAKING
PAPER; MUSLIN SQUARE

STEP 1 Make the marzipan. Grind the pistachios in a food processor. Add the icing sugar and grind until fine, then tip into a mixing bowl. Add the egg white and pistachio essence and combine. Turn out onto a worktop dusted with icing sugar and knead until smooth. Wrap in cling film to rest.

STEP 2 Heat the oven to 180°C/160°C fan/350°F/Gas 4. Make the génoise. Finely grind the pistachios and flour in a food processor. Place the sugar and eggs in a large bowl and whisk until thick and pale. Fold in the flour mixture, the butter and the lemon zest.

STEP 3 Pour the mixture into a cake tin and bake for 20–30 minutes, until risen and springy to the touch. Set aside to cool for 5–10 minutes, then turn out onto a wire rack to cool completely.

STEP 4 Make the crème au beurre. Bring 125ml of water to the boil in a large pan. Add the spinach and wilt for 2–3 minutes. Transfer to a blender and blitz to a purée.

STEP 5 Drain the purée through a piece of muslin, squeezing out all the spinach water into a bowl. You should have 160–170ml. Set aside.

STEP 6 Grind the pistachios in a blender. Add the kirsch, 1 tablespoon of the spinach water and 50g of the butter. Blitz to a paste and set aside.

STEP 7 Put the sugar and 100ml of the spinach water into a pan. Dissolve the sugar gently, then boil for 2–3 minutes, until the syrup is clear and forms a thread when pulled between 2 teaspoons.

STEP 8 Whisk the egg yolks in a stand mixer, then pour in the syrup in a thin stream, whisking all the time. Whisk until the mixture is thick and cold, then add the remaining 100g of softened butter, and whisk in the pistachio paste.

STEP 9 Slice the sponge into three equal layers. Spread the bottom layer with ⅓ of the crème au beurre, then the middle layer with another ⅓, then top with the final sponge. Spread a thin buttercream layer over the top and sides.

STEP 10 Roll out the marzipan and use to cover the whole cake. Stand the cake on a wire rack and pour over the fondant icing. Leave to drip for 2–3 minutes, then transfer to a cake stand. Press the chopped pistachios around the base of the cake, then decorate with edible flowers.

BREAKFAST MUFFINS

A perfect way to start the day, these muffins make for a tasty, on-the-go breakfast.

MAKES 12

175G SELF-RAISNG FLOUR

100G WHOLEMEAL SELF-RAISING FLOUR

½ TSP BAKING POWDER

1 TSP GROUND CINNAMON

100G PORRIDGE OATS, PLUS EXTRA FOR SPRINKLING

25G CHOPPED ALMONDS

100G LIGHT MUSCOVADO SUGAR

100ML MAPLE SYRUP

175ML WHOLE MILK

150ML NATURAL YOGURT

75ML SUNFLOWER OIL

125G BLUEBERRIES

1 SMALL EATING APPLE, SKIN ON, GRATED

YOU WILL NEED

12-HOLE MUFFIN TRAY LINED WITH PAPER MUFFIN CASES

STEP 1 Heat the oven to 200°C/180°C fan/400°F/ Gas 6. Put the flours, baking powder, cinnamon, oats, almonds and sugar into a mixing bowl and combine. In a large jug, whisk together the maple syrup, milk, yogurt and oil. Pour the liquid mixture onto the dry ingredients and gently mix until all the ingredients are just combined.

STEP 2 Add the blueberries and grated apple to the bowl and gently fold through until they are evenly distributed.

STEP 3 Divide the mixture equally between the muffin cases. Sprinkle the top of each muffin with a few oats, then bake for about 20 minutes, until the muffins are risen and golden with the characteristic cracked crust.

STEP 4 Remove the muffins from the oven and leave to cool in the tray. Once the muffins are cool enough to handle, transfer to a wire rack to cool completely.

BAKER'S RECIPE

BONFIRE NIGHT GINGER CAKE WITH CINDER TOFFEE

This ginger cake, with stem ginger inside and a salted caramel Swiss meringue buttercream, is decorated with cinder toffee. The spicy warmth of ginger, with the crunch and caramel flavour of cinder toffee, makes it the perfect autumn treat.

SERVES 12

200G UNSALTED BUTTER, AT ROOM TEMPERATURE

200G DARK BROWN SUGAR

100G GOLDEN SYRUP

30G TREACLE

275G SELF-RAISING FLOUR

1 TBSP GROUND GINGER

1 TSP GROUND CINNAMON

PINCH OF SALT

5 LARGE EGGS

10 BALLS OF STEM GINGER, CUT INTO 1CM DICE

4 TBSP STEM GINGER SYRUP

100G CRYSTALLISED GINGER, ROUGHLY CHOPPED, TO DECORATE

FOR THE CINDER TOFFEE

100G CASTER SUGAR

90G GOLDEN SYRUP

1 TSP GROUND GINGER

1½ TSP BICARBONATE OF SODA

FOR THE CARAMEL SAUCE

180G CASTER SUGAR

180ML DOUBLE CREAM

1 TSP SEA SALT

FOR THE SWISS MERINGUE BUTTERCREAM

3 LARGE EGG WHITES

225G CASTER SUGAR

200G UNSALTED BUTTER, AT ROOM TEMPERATURE, DICED

175G SALTED BUTTER, AT ROOM TEMPERATURE, DICED

6 BALLS STEM GINGER, VERY FINELY CHOPPED

FOR THE DRIPPING SAUCE

25G SOFT DARK BROWN SUGAR

½ TBSP GOLDEN SYRUP

25G UNSALTED BUTTER

5CM PIECE OF GINGER, PEELED AND GRATED

25ML DOUBLE CREAM

¼ TSP SEA SALT FLAKES

YOU WILL NEED

20CM LOOSE-BOTTOMED ROUND CAKE TINS X 3, GREASED, THEN BASE-LINED WITH BAKING PAPER; SUGAR THERMOMETER; 2 BAKING TRAYS LINED WITH SILICONE SHEETS; SHALLOW CONTAINER; MUSLIN CLOTH; MEDIUM PIPING BAG FITTED WITH A MEDIUM STAR NOZZLE; MEDIUM DISPOSABLE PIPING BAG

STEP 1 For the sponge, heat the oven to 180°C/160°C fan/350°F/Gas 4. Put the butter, sugar, golden syrup and treacle into the bowl of a stand mixer fitted with the beater attachment, and beat on medium speed for 3–5 minutes, until soft and creamy.

STEP 2 In a separate bowl, sift together the flour, ground ginger, ground cinnamon and salt.

STEP 3 Add the eggs, one at a time, to the creamed mixture, beating after each addition. If the mixture starts to curdle, add 1 tablespoon of the flour mixture with each egg.

STEP 4 Fold the flour mixture and stem ginger cubes into the creamed mixture. Divide the batter evenly between the 3 lined tins and level with a palette knife. Bake for 25–30 minutes, or until risen and a skewer inserted into the centre comes out clean.

STEP 5 Remove from the oven and leave to cool in the tins for 5 minutes, then turn out onto a wire rack and leave to cool completely.

RECIPE CONTINUES OVERLEAF »»

STEP 6 For the cinder toffee, put the sugar, golden syrup and ground ginger into a large pan. Place over a medium heat and cook, stirring, until the sugar dissolves.

STEP 7 Increase the heat and cook until the temperature on a sugar thermometer reaches 155°C/311°F. Immediately remove from the heat and stir in the bicarbonate of soda. Be careful as the mixture will bubble and might splatter. Pour the cinder toffee into one of the lined baking trays and leave to cool and set hard, about 30 minutes.

STEP 8 For the caramel sauce, put the sugar into a medium pan. Add 3 tablespoons of water and stir with your fingers until the mixture feels like wet sand.

STEP 9 Place over a medium heat and cook, without stirring, until the sugar has dissolved. Increase the heat and boil to a dark caramel, swirling the pan occasionally. This time, do not stir.

STEP 10 Remove from the heat and whisk in the cream (take care as it might splatter). Add the salt, then pour the mixture into the other lined baking trays and leave to cool. Transfer to the fridge and chill for 30 minutes.

STEP 11 For the Swiss meringue buttercream, place the egg whites and sugar in a heatproof bowl set over a pan of gently simmering water and whisk until the mixture reaches 52–53°C/125–127°F on a sugar thermometer.

STEP 12 Remove from the heat and transfer to the bowl of a stand mixer fitted with a whisk attachment. Whisk on high speed until the meringue is cool to touch. Once cool, whisk in the unsalted and salted butter, a cube at a time, whisking continuously until the mixture thickens. Add the cooled caramel sauce and mix well to combine.

STEP 13 Divide the buttercream equally between 2 bowls. Stir the chopped stem ginger into one of the bowls. Chill until required.

STEP 14 For the dripping sauce, put the sugar, syrup and butter into a medium pan. Place the grated ginger in a piece of muslin and wring out the juice into the pan. Place the pan over a medium heat and bring to the boil, stirring until the sugar has melted. Stir in the cream and salt and boil for 2 minutes. Remove from the heat, then pour into a shallow container and leave to cool. Chill for about 30 minutes until cold.

STEP 15 To assemble, place one of the sponges on a cake stand. Drizzle over 2 tablespoons of the stem ginger syrup, then cover with half of the stem ginger buttercream. Place a sponge on top and drizzle with the remaining stem ginger syrup, then top with the remaining stem ginger buttercream. Top with the remaining sponge.

STEP 16 Place ½ of the remaining icing (without the chopped stem ginger) in a medium piping bag fitted with a medium star nozzle. Use the other ½ to cover the top and sides of the cake, then freeze for 10 minutes.

STEP 17 Break the cinder toffee into small and large pieces. Pour the dripping sauce into a medium disposable piping bag. Remove the cake from the freezer, then snip the end off the piping bag and drizzle the sauce over the top and down the sides of the cake.

STEP 18 Pipe rosettes of buttercream around the top of the cake, then decorate the middle with large shards of cinder toffee. Put smaller pieces of toffee around the base. Finally, scatter the crystallised ginger over the top, to decorate.

RUNEBERG CAKES

Eaten in Finland on 5th February to celebrate the life of poet John Ludvig Runeberg, these cakes are traditionally made using Finnish dark sugar cookies, but the recipe is a great way to use up any stale biscuits.

MAKES 12

200G UNSALTED BUTTER, SOFTENED

100G DARK BROWN SOFT SUGAR

100G CASTER SUGAR

3 EGGS

100G PLAIN FLOUR

2 TSP BAKING POWDER

1 TSP GROUND CARDAMOM

1 TSP GROUND CINNAMON

100G GROUND ALMONDS

200G CRUSHED GINGERNUTS OR OTHER BISCUITS

100ML WHOLE MILK

3 TBSP QUICK & EASY RASPBERRY JAM (SEE P.307)

FOR THE SUGAR SYRUP

50G CASTER SUGAR

2 TBSP RUM OR COGNAC

FOR THE TOPPING

150G ICING SUGAR

4 TBSP QUICK & EASY RASPBERRY JAM (SEE P.307)

YOU WILL NEED

12-HOLE MUFFIN TIN, GREASED, OR 12 SILICONE CUPCAKE MOULDS LINED WITH CUPCAKE CASES; SMALL DISPOSABLE PIPING BAG

STEP 1 Heat the oven to 200°C/180°C fan/400°F/ Gas 6. To make the cakes, cream the butter and sugar together in a bowl until pale and creamy. Beat in the eggs, one at a time, and fully combine.

STEP 2 Sift together the flour, baking powder, cardamom and cinnamon, then fold the dry mixture into the butter mixture until fully combined.

STEP 3 Fold in the ground almonds and the crushed biscuits, then stir in the milk and combine. Spoon the batter into the muffin tin or cupcake moulds until each hollow is ⅔ full.

STEP 4 Make an indentation in the top of each cupcake and divide the 3 tablespoons of jam equally between them. Bake for 20 minutes, or until deep golden brown, then remove from the oven and leave to cool in the tin or moulds for 5 minutes, then transfer the cakes to a wire rack to cool completely.

STEP 5 Make the syrup. Put the sugar in a small pan with 100ml of water and place over a high heat. Stir, until the sugar dissolves, then stir in the rum or Cognac. Pour the syrup over the cakes and leave to cool completely.

STEP 6 Make the topping. Mix the icing sugar in a small bowl with 2 tablespoons of water. Spoon the icing into a small disposable piping bag, snip the end and pipe broad circles around the edge of the top of each cupcake. Divide the jam into 12 portions and spoon into the middle on the top of each cake.

CAKES FROM THE ARCHIVES

STICKY TOFFEE APPLE CARAMEL CAKE

All the elements of a sticky-toffee pudding plus toffee apples in one cake!
The sponge layers are made with dates, spices and pieces of dried apple.

SERVES 16

FOR THE SPONGE LAYERS

125G MEDJOOL DATES, STONED AND FINELY CHOPPED

5 TBSP CLOUDY APPLE JUICE

325G UNSALTED BUTTER, SOFTENED

250G LIGHT MUSCOVADO SUGAR

5 EGGS, BEATEN

300G SELF-RAISING FLOUR

1/4 TSP BAKING POWDER

2 TBSP GROUND CINNAMON

2 TSP GROUND MIXED SPICE

60G DRIED APPLE RINGS OR SLICES, FINELY CHOPPED

FOR THE CARAMEL BUTTERCREAM

175G GOLDEN CASTER SUGAR

175G DOUBLE CREAM

175G UNSALTED BUTTER, SOFTENED

100G ICING SUGAR, SIFTED

125G FULL-FAT CREAM CHEESE

1½ TSP VANILLA EXTRACT

FOR THE TOFFEE APPLES

2 BRAMLEY APPLES, PEELED

175G GOLDEN CASTER SUGAR

YOU WILL NEED

20.5CM ROUND CAKE TINS X 3, GREASED, THEN BASE-LINED WITH BAKING PAPER; MELON BALL CUTTER (OPTIONAL); BAKING SHEET LINED WITH BAKING PAPER

STEP 1 Put the dates and apple juice in a small pan and cook over a low heat, stirring frequently, for 10 minutes, until thick and soft. Remove from the heat and mash the contents to make a coarse, thick purée. Leave to cool.

STEP 2 Heat the oven to 180°C/160°C fan/350°F/ Gas 4. Put the butter into a large bowl and beat for 2–3 minutes until very light. Add the sugar and beat again for about 5 minutes, until light and fluffy.

STEP 3 Gradually add the eggs, beating well after each addition. Sift the flour, baking powder and ground spices into the bowl and fold in. Add the cooled date mixture and the dried apple and combine.

STEP 4 Divide the mixture equally between the 3 cake tins. Bake for about 20–22 minutes, until well risen, golden and springy. Cool in the tins for 5 minutes, then turn out onto a wire rack to cool completely.

STEP 5 Make the caramel buttercream. Put the sugar and 3 tablespoons of water into a medium pan over a low heat, stirring occasionally. In a small pan heat the cream until almost boiling and set aside. Once the sugar has dissolved, turn up the heat and boil until the syrup turns caramel brown. Remove from the heat, and pour in the warmed cream.

STEP 6 Return the pan to a low heat and whisk for 1 minute, until smooth and thick. Pour into a heatproof bowl, leave to cool, then cover and chill for about 1 hour.

STEP 7 Beat the butter in a stand mixer for 2–3 minutes, until light. Add the icing sugar and mix for 5 minutes, until fluffy. Beat in the cream cheese, then the cold caramel and the vanilla extract. Cover and chill until spreadable.

STEP 8 To make the toffee apples, use the melon baller to cut out balls of apple (or, cut the apple into 1cm chunks). Pat dry and set aside. Put the sugar and 3 tablespoons of water into a medium pan, dissolve gently, then boil to a rich caramel. Remove from the heat and stir in the apple. Leave for 3 minutes, until the caramel has thickened, then remove the apple and set aside on the lined baking sheet.

STEP 9 To assemble: remove the paper from the sponges. Set 1 sponge top-side down on a serving plate. Spread with ⅓ of the buttercream, place ⅓ of the apples on top, then top with another sponge. Repeat with another ⅓ of the buttercream and apples, then cover with the final sponge, top-side down. Spread a thin layer of buttercream around the sides, and the remaining buttercream on top. Decorate with the remaining toffee apples. Leave overnight to firm up before serving.

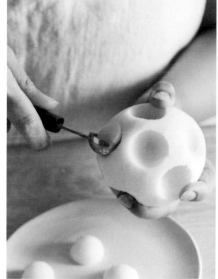

MORELLO CHERRY & ALMOND SQUARES

Morello cherries are smaller than eating cherries, with a tart flavour. Using dried Morello cherries intensifies the tang even more.

MAKES 16–25

200G CASTER SUGAR

200G UNSALTED BUTTER, SOFTENED

4 EGGS

½ TSP ALMOND EXTRACT

¼ TSP VANILLA EXTRACT

75G GROUND ALMONDS

175G SELF-RAISING FLOUR

½ TSP BAKING POWDER

100ML WHOLE MILK

275G WHOLE DRIED MORELLO CHERRIES

25G FLAKED ALMONDS

ICING SUGAR, FOR DUSTING

YOU WILL NEED

23CM SQUARE CAKE TIN, GREASED, THEN LINED WITH BAKING PAPER

STEP 1 Heat the oven to 170°C/150°C fan/325°F/ Gas 3. Beat together the sugar and butter until light and creamy.

STEP 2 Beat in the eggs, one at a time. Stir in the almond and vanilla extracts and combine fully.

STEP 3 Fold in the ground almonds, flour and baking powder, then stir in the milk. Separate out ½ of the dried cherries and fold them through the mixture.

STEP 4 Spoon the mixture into the prepared tin. Press the remaining cherries over the top, then sprinkle with flaked almonds.

STEP 5 Bake the cake for about 1 hour, or until the cake is firm to the touch and a skewer inserted into the centre comes out clean.

STEP 6 Remove from the oven and leave the cake to cool in the tin completely, then turn out onto a serving board and peel off the paper. Dust the top of the cake with icing sugar and cut into 16 or 25 squares to serve.

BAKER'S RECIPE

STEM GINGER CAKE WITH CREAM-CHEESE FROSTING & SALTED CARAMEL

Ginger cake laced with crystallised stem ginger, drizzled with salted caramel and topped with pears and a little gingerbread house!

SERVES 12

FOR THE POACHED PEARS

3 CONFERENCE PEARS, PEELED, STEM INTACT

40G DARK MUSCOVADO SUGAR

1 STAR ANISE

2 PIECES CINNAMON BARK

1 TBSP VANILLA PASTE

3 GREEN CARDAMOM PODS

FOR THE SPONGE

250G SLIGHTLY SALTED BUTTER

250G DARK MUSCOVADO SUGAR

120G TREACLE

375G PLAIN FLOUR

1 TBSP GROUND CINNAMON

4 TBSP GROUND GINGER

300ML WHOLE MILK

2 TSP BICARBONATE OF SODA

3 EGGS, BEATEN

100G CRYSTALLISED GINGER, ROUGHLY CHOPPED

FOR THE SALTED CARAMEL

120G CASTER SUGAR

115ML DOUBLE CREAM

½ TSP SALT

FOR THE BISCUIT DOUGH

75G SLIGHTLY SALTED BUTTER

50G DARK MUSCOVADO SUGAR

1 TSP MOLASSES

1½ TBSP BEATEN EGG

110G PLAIN FLOUR

¼ TSP BICARBONATE OF SODA

¾ TSP GROUND CINNAMON

1 TBSP GROUND GINGER

1 BOILED SWEET, CRUSHED

FOR THE FROSTING

100G UNSALTED BUTTER, AT ROOM TEMPERATURE

280G FULL-FAT CREAM CHEESE

600G ICING SUGAR

100G WALNUTS, CHOPPED

FOR THE ROYAL ICING

2 TBSP PASTEURISED EGG WHITE

100G ICING SUGAR

YOU WILL NEED

18CM ROUND CAKE TINS X 3, GREASED, THEN BASE-LINED WITH BAKING PAPER; BAKING SHEET LINED WITH BAKING PAPER; LARGE DISPOSABLE PIPING BAG; SMALL PIPING BAG FITTED WITH A NO.1 WRITING NOZZLE

STEP 1 For the poached pears, place the pears in a medium pan. Add the sugar, star anise, cinnamon, vanilla and cardamom, then add enough water to cover the pears. Place over a high heat and bring to the boil. Reduce the heat to low and simmer for 20 minutes, until the pears are tender but not soft. Remove from the heat, drain and leave the pears to cool. When cold, trim the bases so the pears stand up.

STEP 2 For the sponges, heat the oven to 180°C/160°C fan/350°F/Gas 4. Put the butter, sugar and treacle into a medium pan over a medium heat. Stir until the sugar has dissolved, then remove from the heat and set aside.

STEP 3 In a separate bowl, sift the flour, cinnamon and ginger together. Heat the milk in a small pan over a low heat until lukewarm. Remove from the heat, add the bicarbonate of soda and whisk until foamy.

STEP 4 Pour the warm butter mixture over the flour mixture and whisk together. Add the eggs and crystallised ginger, then whisk in the milk until smooth and just combined.

RECIPE CONTINUES OVERLEAF »»

STEP 5 Immediately divide the mixture equally between the 3 lined tins and level with a palette knife. Bake for 25–35 minutes, until risen and a skewer inserted into the centre comes out clean. Remove from the oven and cool in the tins for 5 minutes, then turn out onto a wire rack to cool completely.

STEP 6 For the salted caramel, put the sugar in a medium pan. Add 3 tablespoons of water and stir with your fingers until the mixture feels like wet sand. Place over a medium heat and cook, without stirring, to dissolve the sugar.

STEP 7 Increase the heat and boil to an amber caramel, swirling the pan occasionally. Do not stir. Remove from the heat and whisk in the cream (take care – it might splatter). Add the salt, then set aside to cool. Once cool, refrigerate until cold.

STEP 8 Make the biscuit dough. Put the butter, sugar and molasses in a stand mixer fitted with the beater. Cream together until smooth. Add the egg and combine. Add the flour, bicarbonate of soda, cinnamon and ginger and mix with a wooden spoon to form a soft dough. Wrap in cling film and chill for 20 minutes.

STEP 9 Heat the oven to 190°C/170°C fan/375°F/ Gas 5. Roll out the gingerbread dough on a lightly floured surface to ½cm thick.

STEP 10 Cut out shapes to make a ginger biscuit house (2 ends, 2 side walls, and 2 roof sides), measuring 4cm wide and 6cm high in total. Cut out a window and a door shape in one of the ends, then place all the house pieces on the lined baking sheet. Spoon the crushed boiled sweet in the window to make a pane.

STEP 11 Bake the biscuits for 6–8 minutes, until cooked through. Remove from the oven and, using the baking paper, slide onto a wire rack to cool and harden.

STEP 12 For the frosting, beat the butter and cream cheese together until just incorporated, then beat in the icing sugar until just thick and smooth. Spoon into a large disposable piping bag and snip to make a 2cm diameter hole in the end.

STEP 13 For the royal icing, lightly whisk the egg white until frothy. Then, add the icing sugar, a little at a time, stirring continuously with a wooden spoon, until you reach a piping consistency.

STEP 14 Spoon into a small piping bag fitted with a No.1 writing nozzle. When the biscuits are cooled, assemble the house using the royal icing as glue. Then, pipe an outline around the window and door, and pipe roof tiles on the top.

STEP 15 To assemble the cake, trim the sponges until level. Place one sponge on a cake stand and pipe over ⅓ of the frosting and sprinkle over ½ of the walnuts. Place the second sponge on top and pipe over another ⅓ of the frosting and sprinkle over most of the remaining walnuts, reserving a few for the top.

STEP 16 Place the last sponge on top and spread the top of the cake with the remaining frosting. Spoon some caramel over the frosting and smooth over with a palette knife, allowing some to drip down the sides. Arrange the pears and the biscuit house on top and sprinkle around the reserved walnuts to finish.

BAKER'S RECIPE

GILDED PEAR & CARDAMOM CAKE

This spiced sponge, layered with fruit compote and cardamom buttercream, is topped with a golden pear.

SERVES 16

6 PEARS, PEELED, CORED AND CUT INTO 3MM-THICK SLICES

250G FRESH OR FROZEN BLACKCURRANTS

250G BLUEBERRIES, PLUS EXTRA TO DECORATE

200G BLACKBERRIES, PLUS EXTRA TO DECORATE

500G SELF-RAISING FLOUR

500G UNSALTED BUTTER, SOFTENED

435G CASTER SUGAR

10 EGGS, LIGHTLY BEATEN

2 TSP GROUND CINNAMON

2 TSP FINELY GROUND GREEN CARDAMOM (ABOUT 20 PODS)

2 TSP BAKING POWDER

1 TSP LEMON JUICE

1 SMALL PEAR, TO DECORATE

1 SHEET OF EDIBLE GOLD LEAF

FOR THE BUTTERCREAM ICING

250G UNSALTED BUTTER, SOFTENED

500G ICING SUGAR, SIFTED, PLUS EXTRA FOR GILDING

ABOUT 2 TBSP WHOLE MILK

¼ TSP FINELY GROUND GREEN CARDAMOM (ABOUT 5 PODS)

1 TSP VANILLA EXTRACT

YOU WILL NEED

23CM SPRINGFORM TINS X 3, GREASED, THEN BASE-LINED WITH BAKING PAPER; CAKE-DECORATING PAINTBRUSH

STEP 1 Heat the oven to 190°C/170°C fan/375°F/ Gas 5. Put the pears into one bowl, and 100g each of the blackcurrants and blueberries and all of the blackberries into another. Toss each bowl of fruit in 1 tablespoon of flour

STEP 2 Beat together the butter and 375g of the sugar in a stand mixer until creamy. Gradually add the egg, beating after each addition and, on the fourth or fifth addition, add a tablespoon of the flour. Mix in the cinnamon and cardamom. Sift the remaining flour and the baking powder into the bowl and fold in. Divide the mixture into 3 equal portions.

STEP 3 Take ⅓ of 1 portion of the sponge mixture and spread it evenly over the base of 1 prepared tin. Scatter over ⅙ of the pear slices, then ⅙ of the berry mixture. Spread ½ the remaining sponge mixture from the same portion over the fruit. Add another fruit layer on top, then the rest of the portion of batter. Repeat twice with the remaining tins and bowls of sponge mixture.

STEP 4 Bake the cakes for 50–55 minutes, until golden, springy, and a skewer inserted into the centres comes out clean. Loosen the sponges, then unclip the tins and leave to cool on a wire rack.

STEP 5 Make the compote. Put the remaining 150g blackcurrants, 150g blueberries and 60g sugar, along with the lemon juice and 1 tablespoon of water into a pan over a low heat and simmer, stirring, until the juices run. Increase the heat and boil for a few minutes, until thick. Leave to cool.

STEP 6 Make the icing. Beat the butter in a bowl until creamy, then add ½ of the icing sugar, the milk, cardamom and vanilla, and finally the remaining icing sugar. Beat for 2–3 minutes, until light and spreadable. Add more milk, a little at a time, if needed.

STEP 7 Gild the pear. Mix 1 teaspoon of icing sugar with a few drops of water to make a paste and brush this onto one side of the pear. Carefully, place the sheet of gold leaf onto the pear and press it gently with a dry paintbrush.

STEP 8 To assemble, place 1 sponge (top-side down) on a cake board. Spread with a ¼ of the buttercream. Drizzle over 3 rounded tablespoons of the compote, then place the second sponge on top. Repeat, then place the third sponge on top (top-side up). Swirl the remaining buttercream over the top sponge. Decorate with berries and the gilded pear.

STICKY APPLE CAKE

For flavour, use a Bramley apple for grating, then use some showy pink-skinned apples for the topping.

SERVES 8–12

2 PINK-SKINNED APPLES, CORED, HALVED AND THINLY SLICED

JUICE OF 1 LEMON

1 BRAMLEY APPLE, PEELED, CORED AND GRATED

225G UNSALTED BUTTER, SOFTENED

175G LIGHT BROWN SOFT SUGAR

100ML MAPLE SYRUP

4 EGGS

2 TSP VANILLA EXTRACT

350G SELF-RAISING FLOUR

2 TSP BAKING POWDER

1 TSP GROUND CINNAMON

DEMERARA SUGAR, FOR SPRINKLING

YOU WILL NEED

30 X 23CM TRAYBAKE TIN, GREASED, THEN LINED WITH BAKING PAPER

STEP 1 Heat the oven to 180°C/160°C fan/350°F/Gas 4. Place the sliced pink-skinned apples in a dish and sprinkle them with lemon juice to stop them turning brown.

STEP 2 Put the grated apple, butter, soft brown sugar, maple syrup, eggs, vanilla extract, flour, baking powder and cinnamon in a bowl and beat together until smooth. Spoon the mixture into the lined tin and level with a palette knife.

STEP 3 Arrange the pink-skinned apple slices in 2 or 3 rows, depending on the size of your apples, on top of the cake batter. Sprinkle generously with Demerara sugar.

STEP 4 Bake for about 45 minutes, or until the cake is firm to the touch and a skewer inserted into the centre comes out clean.

STEP 5 Remove from the oven and leave the cake to cool in the tin for about 15 minutes, then turn out onto a wire rack, peel off the baking paper and leave to cool completely. Cut into squares or bars to serve.

CHOCOLATE FROM THE ARCHIVES

CHOCOLATE COLLAR CASTLE CAKE

This cake is a showstopper for story-lovers. The chocolate collar becomes the turrets of a fairytale castle and the cake is topped with a sugarcraft prince and princess, but you could easily substitute a kissable frog, a magical wizard or a gallant knight.

SERVES 12

FOR THE SPONGES

450G SELF-RAISING FLOUR

1 TSP BAKING POWDER

450G UNSALTED BUTTER, SOFTENED

450G CASTER SUGAR

7 EGGS

1 TSP VANILLA EXTRACT

2 TBSP ORGEAT SYRUP

CRYSTAL CANDY PINK RAINBOW DUST, TO SPRINKLE

FOR THE ALMOND CRÈME DIPLOMAT

75G CASTER SUGAR

3 EGG YOLKS

10G PLAIN FLOUR, SIFTED

10G CORNFLOUR, SIFTED

250ML WHOLE MILK

75G GROUND ALMONDS

1 TBSP WHITE RUM (OPTIONAL)

100ML WHIPPING CREAM, WHIPPED UNTIL THICK

FOR THE RHUBARB

400G RHUBARB, FINELY SLICED

75G CASTER SUGAR

1½ TSP VANILLA EXTRACT

1 TBSP WHITE RUM (OPTIONAL)

FOR THE MERINGUE BUTTERCREAM

225G CASTER SUGAR

2 EGG WHITES

350G UNSALTED BUTTER, AT ROOM TEMPERATURE, DICED

1 TSP VANILLA PASTE

FOR THE PRINCE & PRINCESS

50G EACH BLUE, VIOLET, SKIN-TONE AND YELLOW ROLLING FONDANT (SEE P.305)

BLACK FOOD-COLOURING GEL

FOR THE CHOCOLATE COLLAR

200G 70% DARK CHOCOLATE, BROKEN INTO PIECES

YOU WILL NEED

20CM ROUND CAKE TINS X 3, GREASED, THEN BASE-LINED WITH BAKING PAPER; BAKING TRAY; SHALLOW CONTAINER LINED WITH KITCHEN PAPER; SUGAR THERMOMETER; SMALL CAKE-DECORATING PAINTBRUSH; 70 X 18CM ACETATE SHEET, CUT IN THE SHAPE OF A TURRET; SHEET OF BAKING PAPER; PASTRY COMB; FAKE GRASS (OPTIONAL)

STEP 1 For the sponges, heat the oven to 180°C/160°C Fan/350°F/Gas 4. Sift the flour and baking powder together into a bowl. Place the butter and sugar in a stand mixer and beat until light and fluffy. Beat in the eggs one at a time, then the vanilla extract. Add the flour mixture and beat until smooth.

STEP 2 Divide the mixture between the 3 tins, smoothing the top of each. Bake for 20–25 minutes, until the cakes are firm to the touch and a skewer inserted into the centre comes out clean. Leave to cool in the tins for 5 minutes, then turn out onto a wire rack, remove the paper and leave to cool completely.

STEP 3 For the almond crème diplomat, whisk the sugar and egg yolks together until pale, then stir in the plain flour and cornflour. Heat the milk to just below boiling point, then gradually whisk into the sugar and egg mixture. Pour back into the pan, and whisk over a medium heat until thick. Stir in the almonds, and the rum (if using). Pour into a baking tray and cover the surface with cling film. Chill until firm, then fold in the whipped cream. Chill again until needed.

RECIPE CONTINUES OVERLEAF »»

STEP 4 For the rhubarb, place the rhubarb, sugar, vanilla, and rum (if using) in a pan and simmer over a low heat for 30 minutes. Drain, discarding the liquid. Tip out the rhubarb into a shallow container lined with kitchen paper and leave to cool completely.

STEP 5 For the meringue buttercream, boil the sugar and 75ml of water in a pan until it reaches 110°C/230°F on a sugar thermometer. Put the egg whites in a stand mixer fitted with the whisk attachment. Whisk until stiff, then gradually pour in the syrup, whisking all the time. Then, beat in the butter, a cube at a time, and lastly the vanilla paste. Leave to cool, then chill until ready to use.

STEP 6 For the prince and the princess, use violet and blue fondant for the bodies; skin-tone for the heads, arms and legs; blue and purple for the shoes; and yellow for the hair and 2 crowns. Use a paintbrush dipped in water to assemble the figures, then in a little black food-colouring gel to give them features.

STEP 7 To assemble the cake, brush the sponges with orgeat syrup. Place 1 sponge on a cake board, top-side down, and spread with ½ the almond crème diplomat and ½ the rhubarb. Repeat with another sponge and the remaining almond crème diplomat and rhubarb. Top with the third sponge, top-side down.

STEP 8 Spread the meringue buttercream around the sides and over the top of the cake and smooth with a palette knife. Sprinkle with the pink rainbow dust.

STEP 9 For the chocolate collar, melt the chocolate in a heatproof bowl set over a pan of barely simmering water. Remove it from the heat, leave it for 5–10 minutes to cool a little, then spread it over the turret-shaped acetate, placed on a sheet of baking paper. Pull the acetate towards you after spreading, so that you can see the turret shape (this will help to give your turrets clean lines).

STEP 10 Leave for a few minutes to set slightly, then, using a pastry comb, scrape the chocolate so that you can see lines of acetate through it.

STEP 11 Leave the collar to set until pliable, then slowly wrap it around the cake, sticking it to the buttercream. Leave until the chocolate is set, then carefully peel away the acetate. Place the cake on the fake grass, if using, and position the prince and princess on the top.

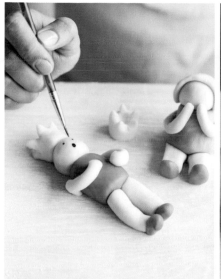

FRESH ORANGE CAKE

This is a super-easy, all-in-one cake that takes minutes to mix up and get in the oven.

SERVES 12

200G SELF-RAISING FLOUR

1 TSP BAKING POWDER

3 LARGE EGGS

200G UNSALTED BUTTER, SOFTENED

200G GOLDEN CASTER SUGAR

2 TBSP WHOLE MILK

GRATED ZEST OF 1 LARGE UNWAXED ORANGE

2 TSP SICILIAN ORANGE EXTRACT

12 MINI ORANGE JELLY SLICES, TO DECORATE

FOR THE FILLING

280G FULL-FAT CREAM CHEESE

50G UNSALTED BUTTER

500G ICING SUGAR, SIFTED

GRATED ZEST OF 1 LARGE UNWAXED ORANGE

YOU WILL NEED

20CM ROUND CAKE TINS X 2, GREASED, THEN BASE-LINED WITH BAKING PAPER; PIPING BAG FITTED WITH A 1CM ROUND NOZZLE

STEP 1 Heat the oven to 180°C/160°C fan/350°F/Gas 4. Sift the flour and baking powder together into a large bowl. Add the eggs, butter, sugar, milk, orange zest and orange extract and beat everything together until the mixture is smooth.

STEP 2 Spoon half the sponge mixture into each prepared tin and level the surface with a palette knife. Bake for 30–35 minutes, or until the cakes are firm to the touch and a skewer inserted into the centre comes out clean.

STEP 3 Remove from the oven and leave the cakes to cool in the tins for 5 minutes, then turn out onto a wire rack and peel off the paper. Leave to cool completely.

STEP 4 Meanwhile, make the filling. Beat the cream cheese and butter together in a bowl until just incorporated, then beat in the icing sugar and orange zest until thick and smooth.

STEP 5 Use ½ the filling mixture to sandwich the two sponges together, then spread ¼ of the remaining filling over the top. Spoon the remaining ¼ into a piping bag fitted with a 1cm round nozzle and pipe 12 evenly spaced blobs around the edge of the cake. Top each blob with an orange jelly slice.

ILLUSION CAKES FROM THE ARCHIVES

'ONE IN A MELON' CAKE

A real 'wow' of a cake, this beauty is four layers of sponge, coloured and flavoured to look and taste just like a watermelon, complete with chocolate chip 'seeds' and a green fondant 'rind'. To save time, we've used green ready-to-roll icing, but you could make the rolling fondant from scratch, if you prefer (see p.305).

SERVES 20

FOR THE SPONGE

620G BAKING MARGARINE, AT ROOM TEMPERATURE

620G CASTER SUGAR

11 EGGS, BEATEN

620G SELF-RAISING FLOUR

100G 70% DARK CHOCOLATE CHIPS

28G RED FOOD-COLOURING GEL

7 TBSP WATERMELON SYRUP

1KG READY-TO-ROLL GREEN FONDANT ICING

DARK GREEN FOOD-COLOURING GEL

FOR THE WHITE BUTTERCREAM

250G UNSALTED BUTTER, SOFTENED

400G ICING SUGAR, SIFTED

1 TBSP WATERMELON SYRUP

FOR THE RED BUTTERCREAM

165G UNSALTED BUTTER, SOFTENED

265G ICING SUGAR, SIFTED

1 TSP WATERMELON SYRUP

RED FOOD-COLOURING GEL

YOU WILL NEED

20CM ROUND CAKE TINS X 3, GREASED, THEN BASE-LINED WITH BAKING PAPER; 20.5CM HEMISPHERE MOULD, GREASED; BAKING SHEET; CAKE-DECORATING PAINTBRUSH

STEP 1 Heat the oven to 180°C/160°C fan/350°F/Gas 4. Beat the margarine and sugar in a mixer until light and creamy. Gradually beat in the eggs, adding a tablespoon of the flour with each of the last 4 pours of egg. Fold in the rest of the flour with a large metal spoon, followed by ⅔ of the chocolate chips.

STEP 2 Mix about ½ the red food colouring with 2 tablespoons of the syrup, then stir in a few tablespoons of the sponge batter. Add this to the rest of the batter and combine until there are no streaks.

STEP 3 Transfer equal amounts of the mixture into the 3 prepared tins and the hemisphere mould (place the mould on a baking sheet). Bake until a skewer inserted into the centre comes out clean, about 30–35 minutes for the sandwich sponges; 55–70 minutes for the hemisphere sponge. Remove from the oven and loosen the edges. Turn out the sponges to cool on a wire rack for 5 minutes; leave the hemisphere sponge to cool in its tin, then turn out.

STEP 4 Make the white buttercream. Beat the butter in a bowl until creamy, then gradually beat in the icing sugar, then the syrup. Cover and set aside. Repeat for the red buttercream, adding about ⅛ of a teaspoon of red colouring. Cover and set aside.

STEP 5 Brush the undersides of the warm sandwich sponges with watermelon syrup, then cool completely. Place 1 sponge, top-side down, on a cake board. Spread with ⅓ of the red buttercream and sprinkle over ⅓ of the remaining chocolate chips. Place the second sponge on top, top-side down, and repeat. Add the third sponge and repeat again. Set the hemisphere sponge on top and gently press down so the cake holds together. Chill for 20 minutes to firm up.

STEP 6 Using a bread knife, carve the bottom 2 sponge layers into the curve of a watermelon. Spread ½ the white buttercream over the whole cake. Chill for 15 minutes, then spread over the remaining buttercream to make a smooth and even top layer. Chill until very firm.

STEP 7 Roll out the fondant icing on a worktop dusted with icing sugar into a large disc to cover your cake. Drape the icing over the cake, then press and smooth out any pleats. Tuck the icing under the cake, then trim the excess. Use the tip of a knife to press the icing under the sponge to cover any gaps.

STEP 8 Mix a little dark-green food colouring with water and paint darker green stripes down the sides of the 'watermelon'. Allow to firm up for 4–5 hours before cutting.

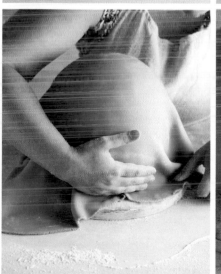

CHAPTER TWO

BISCUITS
AND
TRAYBAKES

Biscuits and traybakes are a wonderful starting point for the novice home cook, but everyone – from children to experienced bakers – will enjoy making and sharing the bakes in this chapter. They are quick to make, so you can transform a bowl of ingredients into something spectacular within a very short space of time, but they also lend themselves to many different flavours and decorative techniques.

From simple Chocolate Chip Granola Cookies to scones, shortbread, brownies, blondies and even Cappuccino-dipped Madeleines, this chapter has something for everyone to make and enjoy. If you're feeling adventurous, why not try our Cardamom & Vanilla Hanging Biscuit Decorations? For those of you keen to practise your piping skills, there are decorated matcha biscuits, piped with a gorgeous cherry-blossom design – it may sound challenging, but each step is broken down for you and there are pictures to guide you along the way.

Whether you love a bake that snaps or one that melts in the mouth, a short crumble or a soft gooey centre, you'll find something here to tempt your fancy. And remember to store your biscuits and traybakes in an airtight container to keep them fresh (for about three to five days in most cases) … if you can resist eating them all at once!

BAKER'S RECIPE

SALTED PEANUT MILLIONAIRE SHORTBREAD

This shortbread base is topped with salted caramel, roasted peanuts and homemade peanut butter, and finished with a layer of tempered dark chocolate.

MAKES 10–12

175G PLAIN FLOUR

90G RICE FLOUR OR GROUND RICE

¼ TSP FINE SEA SALT

85G CASTER SUGAR

175G UNSALTED BUTTER, CHILLED AND DICED

½ TSP VANILLA BEAN PASTE

250G 70% DARK CHOCOLATE, CHOPPED INTO SMALL PIECES

FOR THE PEANUT BUTTER

150G SHELLED UNSALTED PEANUTS

½ TSP FINE SEA SALT

1 TSP RUNNY HONEY

1–2 TSP PEANUT OIL

FOR THE SALTED CARAMEL

90ML DOUBLE CREAM

½ TSP VANILLA BEAN PASTE

30G LIQUID GLUCOSE

185G CASTER SUGAR

100G SALTED BUTTER, AT ROOM TEMPERATURE, DICED

YOU WILL NEED

BAKING PAPER; 10- OR 12-BAR (EACH BAR ABOUT 3 X 7CM) SILICONE MOULD TRAY; RULER; BAKING TRAY; SUGAR THERMOMETER

STEP 1 Put the flours, salt and sugar into a processor and pulse to combine. Add the butter and vanilla and blitz to combine to a dough.

STEP 2 Turn out the dough onto a large sheet of baking paper, gently knead it into a ball, then shape it into a brick. Place another sheet of baking paper on top and, using a rolling pin, roll into a 1cm-thick rectangle at least the size of your mould tray. Use a sharp knife and a ruler to cut bar shapes. Press the bars into each hollow in the mould tray. Prick with a fork, then chill for 15 minutes. Heat the oven to 180°C/160°C fan/350°F/Gas 4.

STEP 3 Bake the bars for 14–16 minutes, until golden at the edges. Meanwhile, start making the peanut butter. Tip the peanuts into a baking tray and dry-roast on the oven shelf beneath the shortbread, for 10–12 minutes, until golden, then remove and allow to cool. Take the shortbread out of the oven, place the tray on a wire rack and cool.

STEP 4 Continue making the peanut butter. Put 100g of the roasted peanuts, and the salt, honey and oil in a processor and blitz to a paste. Set aside. Put the reserved peanuts in the processor and chop up.

STEP 5 To make the caramel, slowly heat the cream and vanilla in a small pan until almost boiling. Meanwhile, warm a medium pan over a medium–low heat. Add the glucose and 60g of the sugar and heat gently, swirling the pan, until dissolved and a light straw colour.

STEP 6 Add the remaining sugar and heat for 15–25 minutes, stirring occasionally, until dissolved. Remove from the heat, then add the heated cream. Return the pan to a low heat and stir continuously, until melted and smooth. Remove from the heat.

STEP 7 Stir in the butter, then mix in 2 tablespoons of the peanut butter and the chopped peanuts. Spoon 1 rounded tablespoon of the peanut caramel on top of each shortbread bar (still in the mould tray) and spread evenly. Chill until set.

STEP 8 Melt 165g of the chocolate in a bowl over a pan of simmering water until it reaches 45°C/115°F on a sugar thermometer. Stir in the remaining chocolate to melt. Pour this over the caramel-topped shortbread bars and spread evenly. Chill for about 1 hour, until firm. Pop out of the moulds to serve.

BLUEBERRY OATIES

In just the time it takes to heat the oven, you can whip up a batch of these easy fruity buns for an instant teatime treat. There's no need for extra jam or butter, kids (and everyone) will love them just as they are.

MAKES 9

200G PLAIN FLOUR

2 TSP BAKING POWDER

1/2 TSP BICARBONATE OF SODA

1/8 TSP SALT

3 1/2 TBSP DEMERARA SUGAR

80G UNSALTED BUTTER, CHILLED AND DICED

50G PORRIDGE OATS

85G BLUEBERRIES

1/2 TSP LEMON JUICE

ABOUT 200ML SINGLE CREAM

1 TBSP PORRIDGE OATS, FOR SPRINKLING

YOU WILL NEED

BAKING SHEET LINED WITH BAKING PAPER; ROUND-BLADED KNIFE

STEP 1 Heat the oven to 200°C/180°C fan/400°F/ Gas 6. Sift the flour, baking powder, bicarbonate of soda and salt into a mixing bowl.

STEP 2 Stir 2 tablespoons of the sugar into the bowl. Quickly rub in the butter using your fingertips to make very coarse crumbs, then add the oats and blueberries and mix in with your hands.

STEP 3 Using a round-bladed knife mix in the lemon juice with enough of the cream or creamy milk to make a very soft and sticky dough.

STEP 4 With a large spoon, spoon 9 bun-like mounds of mixture, spaced well apart, on the lined baking sheet. Mix together the remaining sugar and the oats in a small bowl and sprinkle the mixture over the top of each bun.

STEP 5 Bake the buns in the oven for about 25 minutes, until golden brown and just firm. Remove from the oven and transfer to a wire rack for 5–10 minutes to cool slightly. Best eaten warm.

DECORATED MATCHA BISCUITS

With their delicate cherry-blossom piping, these iced matcha biscuits
have all the 'wow' factor of a showstopper, but take less than half the time
of a full-on decorated-biscuit challenge!

MAKES 20

LAVENDER POLENTA SHORTBREAD FINGERS

Adding polenta to the plain white flour in these shortbread fingers makes for a light and crumbly texture; a pinch of lavender gives a gentle flavour and aroma. You'll find culinary lavender on supermarket shelves among the herbs and spices. Use it sparingly – a little goes a long way.

MAKES 16

- 100G CASTER SUGAR, PLUS 1 TBSP TO FINISH
- GOOD PINCH OF CULINARY LAVENDER, PLUS EXTRA TO FINISH
- 225G UNSALTED BUTTER, SOFTENED
- 200G PLAIN FLOUR
- 100G POLENTA
- ¼ TSP SEA SALT FLAKES

YOU WILL NEED

- A 20.5CM BROWNIE TIN OR SHALLOW SQUARE CAKE TIN, GREASED, THEN BASE-LINED WITH BAKING PAPER

STEP 1 Heat the oven to 180°C/160°C fan/350°F/ Gas 4. Put the sugar and lavender into a mixing bowl. Use your fingertips to rub them together for a few minutes to release the oil (and its flavour) from the lavender. Add the soft butter and beat well with a wooden spoon until very light and creamy.

STEP 2 Mix the flour, polenta and salt in another bowl, then add to the creamed mixture. Work in using a wooden spoon. As soon as the mixture starts to form small clumps, use your hand to bring all the ingredients together into larger clumps, making sure you catch everything on the base of the bowl.

STEP 3 Tip the mixture into the prepared tin and give it a shake to evenly distribute. Use the back of a soup spoon or the flat base of a tumbler dipped in flour to gently press down and flatten the surface, until the mixture looks nice and even, and the corners of the tin are well-filled.

STEP 4 Place in the oven and bake for 25–30 minutes or until the edges of the shortbread are turning golden brown. Remove from the oven, place the tin on a wire rack and carefully loosen the shortbread from the edges of the tin with a palette knife. Then cut into 16 fingers with a sharp knife while still in the tin.

STEP 5 Mix together the extra sugar and lavender for finishing, and scatter the mixture over the shortbread. Leave the fingers until cold, then remove from the tin.

TIP Try adding the zest of a small unwaxed lemon, or a teaspoon of vanilla bean paste instead of the lavender.

FUDGY ESPRESSO VEGAN BROWNIES

This egg- and dairy-free chocolate-fudge brownie is made with store-cupboard ingredients. Turn the brownies into a quick dessert with a bowl of fresh berries and a side of Fresh Raspberry Sauce or Bitter Chocolate Sauce (see p.307).

MAKES 25

- 50G COCOA POWDER
- 175G PLAIN WHITE FLOUR OR WHITE SPELT FLOUR
- 1 TSP BAKING POWDER
- 1/4 TSP SEA SALT FLAKES
- 175G GOLDEN CASTER SUGAR
- 125ML LIGHT OLIVE OIL OR SUNFLOWER OIL
- 150ML WARM COFFEE OR WATER
- 1 1/2 TBSP CIDER VINEGAR
- 100G 70% DARK CHOCOLATE CHIPS OR CHOPPED DARK CHOCOLATE
- 50G PECAN OR WALNUT HALVES
- ICING SUGAR, FOR DUSTING (OPTIONAL)

YOU WILL NEED

20.5CM SQUARE BROWNIE TIN OR SHALLOW SQUARE CAKE TIN, OILED WITH SUNFLOWER OIL, THEN BASE-LINED WITH BAKING PAPER

STEP 1 Heat the oven to 180°C/160°C fan/350°F/ Gas 4. Sift the cocoa powder, flour and baking powder into a mixing bowl, then stir in the salt and sugar.

STEP 2 Gently whisk the oil and warm coffee or water in a measuring jug, then whisk in the vinegar.

STEP 3 Pour the liquid mixture into the bowl with the dry ingredients and stir well until thoroughly combined. Add the chocolate chips or chopped chocolate, and stir until evenly distributed.

STEP 4 Transfer the mixture to the prepared tin, spreading it evenly, and making sure the corners are properly filled. Scatter the nuts over the top, then bake for 25 minutes, or until a skewer inserted at a mid-point between the sides and the centre of the brownie comes out just clean (you're aiming for a squidgy brownie, rather than a dry one).

STEP 5 Remove from the oven, place the tin on a wire rack and leave the brownie to cool completely before cutting it into 16 squares in the tin. Dust with icing sugar before serving, if you wish.

CHOCOLATE CHIP GRANOLA COOKIES

Adding homemade low-sugar granola to such a traditional snack means more crunchy texture, same chocolate treat. For the best flavour use good-quality chocolate chips that have about 70% cocoa solids.

MAKES 16

110G UNSALTED BUTTER, SOFTENED

100G CASTER SUGAR

70G LIGHT MUSCOVADO SUGAR

1 EGG

½ TSP VANILLA EXTRACT

135G PLAIN FLOUR

¼ TSP FINE SEA SALT

¾ TSP BAKING POWDER

90G 70% DARK CHOCOLATE CHIPS

70G HOMEMADE LOW-SUGAR GRANOLA (SEE P.308)

YOU WILL NEED

2 BAKING SHEETS LINED WITH BAKING PAPER

STEP 1 Heat the oven to 170°C/150°C fan/325°F/ Gas 3. Put the softened butter and both sugars into a mixing bowl. Beat, scraping down the sides from time to time, until lighter in colour and creamy in texture.

STEP 2 Break the egg into a small bowl, add the vanilla and beat with a fork just until combined. Incorporate into the butter mixture, little by little, beating well after each addition.

STEP 3 Sift in the flour, salt and baking powder. Mix until just combined, with no visible flour streaks, then add the chocolate chips and granola and mix until thoroughly combined.

STEP 4 Using 1 tablespoon of mixture for each cookie, spoon the mixture into heaps spaced widely apart on the lined sheets, so that you have 8 cookies on each sheet (they will spread significantly during cooking).

STEP 5 Bake the cookies for about 10–12 minutes, until a light gold colour with darker edges. Rotate the sheets after 7 minutes for an even bake, and then watch the cookies carefully, as overbaking will give a crisp rather than chewy texture.

STEP 6 Remove from the oven and place the baking sheets on a wire rack. Leave the cookies to firm up for 5 minutes before removing them from the sheets and placing them directly on a wire rack to cool completely.

BAKER'S RECIPE
BLACK FOREST SLICE

A riff on a Black Forest gâteau, this is an everyday version of the classic celebration cake.

SERVES 16

175G PLAIN FLOUR

25G COCOA POWDER

1 TSP ESPRESSO POWDER

1 TSP BAKING POWDER

175G UNSALTED BUTTER

200G LIGHT BROWN SOFT SUGAR

1 TSP VANILLA EXTRACT

3 LARGE EGGS

200G CHERRIES, PITTED AND QUARTERED

1 QUANTITY OF CRÈME CHANTILLY (SEE P.306)

25G 70% DARK CHOCOLATE

16 CHERRIES IN KIRSCH, DRAINED

FOR THE CHOCOLATE DECORATIONS

75G 54% DARK CHOCOLATE

1G PURE COCOA BUTTER POWDER

FOR THE SYRUP

2 TBSP CASTER SUGAR

2 TBSP KIRSCH

YOU WILL NEED

25CM SQUARE CAKE TIN, GREASED, THEN BASE-LINED WITH BAKING PAPER; COOKING THERMOMETER; SMALL PIPING BAG FITTED WITH A NO.2 WRITING NOZZLE; BAKING SHEET LINED WITH A SHEET OF ACETATE OR BAKING PAPER; MEDIUM PIPING FITTED WITH A LARGE STAR NOZZLE

STEP 1 Heat the oven to 200°C/180°C fan/400°F/Gas 6. Sift the flour, and cocoa, espresso and baking powders into a bowl, and set aside.

STEP 2 Put the butter and sugar into the bowl of a stand mixer fitted with the beater attachment and cream together until light and fluffy.

STEP 3 Add the vanilla extract, then add the eggs, one at a time, beating well after each addition. With the mixer on the slowest speed, add the flour mixture, then add the pitted and quartered cherries.

STEP 4 Scrape the cake batter into the prepared cake tin and level. Bake for 20 minutes, or until a skewer inserted into the centre comes out clean. Remove from the oven and leave to cool in the tin for 10 minutes, then turn out on a wire rack to cool completely.

STEP 5 For the chocolate decorations, first temper the chocolate. Melt the chocolate in a heatproof bowl set over a pan of simmering water until it reaches 45°C/113°F on a cooking thermometer.

STEP 6 Remove from the heat and cool to 34°C/93°F, then add the cocoa butter powder, stirring until the chocolate reaches 31°C/88°F.

STEP 7 Pour the tempered chocolate into the piping bag, fitted with the writing nozzle, and pipe 16 decorative shapes onto the acetate or baking paper. Leave for at least 30 minutes, to set.

STEP 8 For the syrup, pour the kirsch and sugar into a small pan and heat gently over a low heat, stirring, until the sugar dissolves. Remove from the heat. Pierce the cooled cake all over with a cocktail stick and brush the kirsch syrup over the cake.

STEP 9 Place ⅓ of the crème Chantilly into the piping bag fitted with the star nozzle and set aside.

STEP 10 Turn the cake top-downwards and spread the remaining Chantilly over. Finely grate the dark chocolate evenly over the cream, then cut the cake into 16 squares.

STEP 11 Pipe a swirl of cream in the middle of each square and top with a kirsch-soaked cherry and a chocolate decoration.

BAKER'S RECIPE

CHERRY & CHOCOLATE OATMEAL BISCUITS

This modern version of a traditional Irish oatmeal biscuit includes glacé cherries and a half-coat of white chocolate.

MAKES 30–32 BISCUITS

225G SALTED BUTTER

100G GOLDEN CASTER SUGAR

100G MEDIUM OATBRAN

150G PORRIDGE OATS

100G WHOLEWHEAT FLOUR

1 TSP GROUND NUTMEG

150G GLACÉ CHERRIES, CHOPPED

FOR THE DECORATION

200G WHITE CHOCOLATE

75G DESICCATED COCONUT

YOU WILL NEED

6CM ROUND CUTTER; 2 BAKING SHEETS DUSTED WITH FLOUR; BAKING PAPER

STEP 1 Heat the oven to 180°C/160°C fan/350°F/ Gas 4. Beat the butter and sugar together in a large mixing bowl with an electric hand mixer, until just combined.

STEP 2 Fold in the oatbran, oats, flour, nutmeg and cherries with a wooden spoon, then, using your hands, bring the dough together.

STEP 3 Turn out the dough onto a lightly floured worktop and flatten into a large disc. Wrap in cling film and chill for 15 minutes.

STEP 4 On a lightly floured worktop, gently roll out the dough to 0.75cm thick. Using a 6cm round cutter, cut out 24 discs and place 12 discs on each baking sheet.

STEP 5 Bake the biscuits for 10 minutes, then increase the oven temperature to 200°C/180°C fan/400°F/ Gas 6 and bake for a further 8–10 minutes, or until crisp and golden.

STEP 6 Remove the sheets from the oven and transfer the biscuits to a wire rack. Leave to cool completely.

STEP 7 To decorate, melt the white chocolate in a bowl set over a pan of simmering water. Tip the desiccated coconut into a separate, small bowl.

STEP 8 Remove the bowl of white chocolate from the heat and dip in 1 cooled biscuit, dipping halfway up the biscuit, to coat only one half. Allow the excess to run off, then dip the same half into the desiccated coconut. Place on a sheet of baking paper and leave to set.

STEP 9 Repeat with the remaining biscuits, until all the biscuits are half-coated in chocolate and coconut.

COFFEE & AMARETTO KISSES

These walnut-topped finger biscuits have two fillings: a bitter-chocolate ganache, and a coffee-amaretto buttercream.

MAKES 15

250G SALTED BUTTER, VERY SOFT

50G ICING SUGAR

30G CORNFLOUR

250G PLAIN FLOUR

1 TBSP INSTANT ESPRESSO COFFEE POWDER

½ TSP VANILLA EXTRACT

60G 70% DARK CHOCOLATE, MELTED (SEE P.311), TO DECORATE

35G WALNUT PIECES, FINELY CHOPPED, TO DECORATE

FOR THE GANACHE

75G 70% DARK CHOCOLATE, FINELY CHOPPED

150ML DOUBLE CREAM

10G SALTED BUTTER, SOFTENED

FOR THE BUTTERCREAM

60G UNSALTED BUTTER, SOFTENED

120G ICING SUGAR, SIFTED

1 TBSP INSTANT ESPRESSO COFFEE POWDER

1 TBSP AMARETTO LIQUEUR

YOU WILL NEED

2-3 BAKING SHEETS LINED WITH BAKING PAPER; RULER; LARGE PIPING BAG FITTED WITH A LARGE STAR NOZZLE; LARGE PIPING BAG FITTED WITH A 1.5CM ROUND NOZZLE; 3 SMALL DISPOSABLE PIPING BAGS

STEP 1 Heat the oven to 190°C/170°C fan/375°F/Gas 5. Draw 30 7cm-long lines on the underside of the paper lining your baking sheets, to use as a piping guide.

STEP 2 Put the butter in a mixing bowl and beat until creamy. Sift in the icing sugar, cornflour, flour and coffee. Add the vanilla, then combine to a soft dough.

STEP 3 Transfer half the mixture to the piping bag with the large star nozzle, and the other half to the bag with the round nozzle. Pipe 15 biscuits each 7cm long with each bag, piping along the lines you've drawn on the baking paper.

STEP 4 Bake the biscuits for 13–15 minutes, until golden. Rotate after 10 minutes for an even bake. (You may need to bake in 2 batches.) Remove from the oven and cool on the baking sheets on a wire rack, until firm.

STEP 5 Meanwhile, make the ganache. Put the chocolate in a heatproof bowl. Heat the cream in a pan until almost boiling, then pour it over the chocolate. Leave for 1 minute, then stir to melt the chocolate. Stir in the butter. Cover and chill for 10 minutes, until cool but still fluid.

STEP 6 Now make the buttercream. Beat the butter in a mixing bowl until light and fluffy. Stir in half the icing sugar, beat to combine, then add the remaining icing sugar and ¾ of the coffee and all the liqueur. Beat until light and fluffy. Taste, and add more coffee or liqueur as needed. Transfer to a small piping bag.

STEP 7 Remove the ganache from the fridge, beat with a wooden spoon for 3–4 minutes, until fluffy and thick, and transfer to a second small piping bag.

STEP 8 To assemble, remove the biscuits from the cooling rack. Arrange the plain biscuits, underside up, on a board. Snip the end of the buttercream piping bag. Pipe a 1.5cm dot of buttercream on the centre of each. Repeat with ganache on either side of the buttercream (you could use a star nozzle for variation, if you prefer). Set a ridged biscuit, underside down, on top of each to sandwich.

STEP 9 To decorate, put the melted chocolate in the third small piping bag. Snip the end and pipe a streak of chocolate along the top of each finger, scatter over the nuts and leave to set. Transfer to a serving platter.

BAKER'S RECIPE
INDIAN BURFI-TOPPED TRAYBAKE

A traybake topped with the sweetness of coconut burfi.

MAKES 16

FOR THE JAM

100G DRAINED CANNED PINEAPPLE

150G JAM SUGAR

JUICE AND GRATED ZEST
OF 1 UNWAXED LEMON

FOR THE PASTRY

225G PLAIN FLOUR

180G UNSALTED BUTTER, DICED

50G CASTER SUGAR

1 EGG, BEATEN

FOR THE FRANGIPANE

175G UNSALTED BUTTER

175G CASTER SUGAR

4 EGGS, BEATEN

150G GROUND ALMONDS

25G PLAIN FLOUR

½ TSP CARDAMOM ESSENCE

FOR THE COCONUT BURFI

300G CASTER SUGAR

150G DESICCATED COCONUT

4 TBSP MILK POWDER

100G 70% DARK CHOCOLATE,
TO DECORATE

3 SHEETS OF SILVER LEAF,
TO DECORATE

YOU WILL NEED

SUGAR THERMOMETER;
SHALLOW CONTAINER; 20 X 30CM
TRAYBAKE TIN, GREASED, THEN
LINED WITH BAKING PAPER;
SMALL PIPING BAG FITTED
WITH A NO.2 WRITING NOZZLE

STEP 1 Make the jam. Tip the pineapple into the bowl of a food processor and blitz to a pulp. Pour the pulp into a small pan with the sugar and the lemon zest and juice.

STEP 2 Bring to the boil over a low heat, until the sugar has melted. Increase the heat and boil for 4–5 minutes, until the temperature on a sugar thermometer reaches 105°C/221°F. Remove from the heat and pour into a shallow container. Leave to cool and set.

STEP 3 Make the pastry. Put the flour in a bowl and rub in the butter with your fingertips until the mixture resembles fine crumbs. Stir in the sugar, add the egg and 1 tablespoon of water, if needed, mixing to form a soft dough.

STEP 4 Roll out the dough on a lightly floured worktop and use it to line the tin. Refrigerate for 15 minutes. Heat the oven to 180°C/ 160°C fan/350°F/Gas 4.

STEP 5 Make the frangipane. Cream the butter and sugar together until pale and fluffy. Add the eggs, ground almonds, flour, and cardamom essence and mix together to combine. Set aside until needed.

STEP 6 To assemble, spread the pineapple jam in a smooth layer over the pastry and spoon the frangipane over the top. Level out and bake for 40–45 minutes, until golden and a skewer inserted in the centre comes out clean. Remove from the oven and leave in the tin on a wire rack to cool.

STEP 7 Make the coconut burfi. Tip the sugar into a pan with 350ml of water. Bring to the boil, stirring, until the sugar dissolves. Boil for 5–10 minutes to a syrup consistency, then remove from the heat and stir in the coconut and the milk powder.

STEP 8 Leave the coconut to soak up the syrup, until the mixture is sticky and moist, but not wet. Spread the coconut burfi over the cooled frangipane, then chill until set and hardened, about 1 hour.

STEP 9 To decorate, melt the chocolate in a bowl set over a pan of simmering water. Spoon into a piping bag fitted with a writing nozzle. Cut the tray bake into 16 slices, then drizzle chocolate from the piping bag over each slice. Decorate each slice with slivers of silver leaf.

BAKER'S RECIPE

YORKSHIRE GINGERNUTS WITH LIME

This Yorkshire-inspired gingernut becomes a sandwich biscuit with a zesty lime filling. There's a zing of lime in the biscuit, too – first you get the citrus, then a few seconds later the ginger hits you.

MAKES 24

100G UNSALTED BUTTER

25G GOLDEN SYRUP

1 EGG

350G SELF-RAISING FLOUR

100G SOFT LIGHT BROWN SUGAR

100G LIGHT MUSCOVADO SUGAR

1 TSP BICARBONATE OF SODA

12G GROUND GINGER

10G MIXED SPICE

FINELY GRATED ZEST OF 3 UNWAXED LIMES

JUICE OF 1 LIME

FOR THE FILLING

25G UNSALTED BUTTER, SOFTENED

100G FULL-FAT CREAM CHEESE

300G ICING SUGAR

FINELY GRATED ZEST OF 1 UNWAXED LIME

JUICE OF ¼ LIME

YOU WILL NEED

4 BAKING SHEETS LINED WITH BAKING PAPER; LARGE PIPING BAG FITTED WITH A 0.5CM ROUND NOZZLE

STEP 1 Heat the oven to 180°C/160°C fan/350°F/Gas 4. Put the butter and golden syrup together in a medium pan over a low heat, stirring occasionally, until the butter melts. Remove from the heat and leave to cool a little, then add the egg and stir to combine.

STEP 2 Sift the flour into a large bowl. Add the light brown sugar, light muscovado sugar, bicarbonate of soda, ground ginger and mixed spice and make a well in the centre. Pour the warm buttery mixture into the well, along with the lime zest and juice, then mix together with a wooden spoon until the mixture starts to combine.

STEP 3 Bring the dough together with your hands and shape into a ball, but don't knead it.

STEP 4 Divide the dough into 48 pieces, each weighing approximately 15g, and roll each piece of dough into a ball between your hands. Place 12 balls, evenly spaced apart, on each baking sheet and gently flatten each ball with the base of a glass or the palm of your hand, making sure all the balls are identical in size.

STEP 5 Put 2 baking sheets in the oven at a time to bake the biscuits for 15 minutes, until golden around the edges but soft in the middle. The biscuits will harden up once cooled. Remove from the oven and leave to cool on the tray for 2 minutes before placing on wire racks to cool and completely harden.

STEP 6 To make the filling, beat the butter, cream cheese, icing sugar, and lime zest and juice together until soft and fluffy, but firm enough to pipe.

STEP 7 Spoon the filling into a large piping bag fitted with a 0.5cm round nozzle. Turn half the biscuits undersides upwards, and pipe on the filling. Sandwich each with the remaining 24 biscuits (undersides downwards), gently squeezing together to spread the filling to the edge of each biscuit.

INSPIRED BY THE SHOW

CAPPUCCINO-DIPPED MADELEINES

The light, delicate texture of these small, butter-rich sponge cakes comes from whisking eggs with sugar. Dipped in a white chocolate and coffee glaze, they are perfect for an elegant tea party, or even as part of a dessert buffet. As there's no standard size shell-shaped mould, the mixture may give a few more or fewer madeleines.

MAKES ABOUT 36

140G UNSALTED BUTTER, DICED

155G PLAIN FLOUR

1 TSP VERY FINELY GROUND COFFEE BEANS

GOOD PINCH OF SALT

4 EGGS

140G CASTER SUGAR

ICING SUGAR, FOR DUSTING

FOR THE COATING

200G GOOD-QUALITY WHITE CHOCOLATE, FINELY CHOPPED

2 TBSP WHOLE MILK

2 TSP STRONG LIQUID COFFEE

YOU WILL NEED

METAL OR SILICONE MADELEINE MOULD TRAY, BRUSHED WITH MELTED BUTTER, CHILLED, THEN BRUSHED AGAIN; BAKING PAPER

STEP 1 Heat the oven to 190°C/170°C fan/375°F/ Gas 5. Gently melt the butter in a small pan over a low heat, then set aside and leave to cool. Sift the flour, ground coffee and salt into a bowl, and set aside.

STEP 2 Break the eggs into a large mixing bowl and whisk for a few seconds. Add the sugar and whisk again for 4–5 minutes, until the mixture is very thick, pale and mousse-like, and the whisk leaves a ribbon-like trail when lifted.

STEP 3 Sprinkle the flour mixture over the egg-and-sugar mousse and fold in with a large metal spoon. Drizzle over the melted butter, then fold that in, too, until you can't see any more streaks.

STEP 4 Using about 2–3 rounded teaspoons of mixture for each madeleine, spoon the mixture into the prepared moulds, until each mould is about ¾ full. Then, bake in the oven for 10–13 minutes, until golden, and the sponge springs back when gently pressed. (You will probably need to bake the madeleines in batches.)

STEP 5 Stand the tray on a wire rack and leave the madeleines to cool and firm up for 3–5 minutes, then tip out onto the rack and leave to cool completely. (To bake the next batch of sponge mixture, wipe out the warm moulds with kitchen paper, brush with melted butter, chill for 2 minutes and re-butter. Repeat steps 4 and 5 until you have used all the mixture.)

STEP 6 Once the madeleines have cooled, make the coating. Melt the white chocolate with the milk very gently. Stir until smooth, then stir in the coffee. Remove from the heat, then dip the rounded end of each madeleine into the mixture, leaving the flat end uncoated. Leave to set, rounded side up, on baking paper.

STEP 7 Dust the uncoated ends of the madeleines with icing sugar just before serving. These are best eaten within 3 days.

CARDAMOM & VANILLA BISCUIT HANGING DECORATIONS

These biscuit decorations are perfect for creating bunting or garlands for a birthday party or naming ceremony, or for hanging on the Christmas tree. You can make as many or as few of the biscuits as you need for your creations – any leftover biscuit dough will freeze for use another time. Just remember to adjust the quantities of boiled sweets and royal icing appropriately, too.

MAKES ABOUT 50-60 BISCUITS

FOR THE BISCUITS

200G UNSALTED BUTTER, AT ROOM TEMPERATURE

100G SALTED BUTTER, AT ROOM TEMPERATURE

180G CASTER SUGAR

ZEST OF 3 ORANGES

½ TSP ORANGE EXTRACT

1 TSP CARDAMOM EXTRACT

1 TSP VANILLA EXTRACT

2 EGGS

500G PLAIN FLOUR

1½ TSP BICARBONATE OF SODA

5 TSP GROUND CARDAMOM

8 BLACK CARDAMOM PODS, SEEDS REMOVED AND CRUSHED

2 X 200G PACKETS OF BOILED MINT SWEETS

2 X 200G PACKETS OF BOILED FRUIT SWEETS

FOR THE ROYAL ICING

250G ICING SUGAR, SIFTED

2 TBSP PASTEURISED EGG WHITE

1 TSP CARDAMOM ESSENCE

YOU WILL NEED

2 SHEETS OF BAKING PAPER; 4 BAKING SHEETS LINED WITH BAKING PAPER; 6.5CM ROUND CUTTER; 6CM SQUARE CUTTER; 3CM ROUND CUTTER (OR YOUR CHOICE OF LARGE AND SMALL CUTTERS); COCKTAIL STICK; STRING, WIRE OR RIBBON; SMALL DISPOSABLE PIPING BAG

STEP 1 Place the butters into the bowl of a stand mixer fitted with the beater attachment and beat for 1 minute, until soft. Add the sugar and orange zest, and the orange, cardamom and vanilla extracts and beat until light. Add the eggs, one at a time, beating after each addition.

STEP 2 Place the flour, bicarbonate of soda and ground cardamom in a large bowl. Sift the dry mixture over the creamed butter mixture, then add the seeds and mix to form a dough.

STEP 3 Divide the dough into 4 equal pieces, wrap in cling film and chill for at least 30 minutes. (If you aren't using all the dough, freeze the spare portions.) Roll each chilled dough piece between 2 sheets of baking paper to 5mm thick.

STEP 4 Remove the top layer of paper and use the larger cutters to stamp out shapes. Remove the middle of each shape with the smaller round cutter. Re-roll the trimmings as necessary. Place the biscuits on the baking sheets and chill for 30 minutes.

STEP 5 Heat the oven to 170°C/150°C fan/325°F/Gas 3. Using a cocktail stick, make a small hole for threading at the top of each biscuit. Bake the biscuits for 4 minutes (you can do this in batches), then remove from the oven and place a boiled sweet in the middle of each shape.

STEP 6 Return the biscuits to the oven and bake for a further 5–8 minutes, until the sweets melt to fill the holes and the biscuits are golden brown, and slightly soft (they'll harden as they cool).

STEP 7 Remove from the oven and check the holes: if they have filled in during cooking, use the cocktail stick to re-pierce them while the biscuit is still warm and soft. Cool the biscuits on the baking sheets for 5–10 minutes, then transfer to a wire rack to cool completely.

STEP 8 To make the royal icing, put the icing sugar into a bowl. Put 2 tablespoons of pasteurised egg white into a separate large bowl, then add the icing sugar 2 tablespoons at a time, whisking between each addition, until the mixture is fairly stiff and very white. Add the cardamom essence, then just enough water for a piping consistency.

STEP 9 Fill the disposable piping bag with royal icing. Snip the end and pipe around each biscuit 'window', then around each edge. Leave for 10 minutes to dry.

STEP 10 Thread string, wire or ribbon through the holes. To make bunting or a garland, thread downwards through 1 biscuit, then upwards through the next, and so on. Or, to make hanging decorations, thread singly, or in groups of 3.

BAKER'S RECIPE

AMARSPRESSI BISCUITS

Definitely one for macaroon fans! These crunchy, piped biscuits are made with whisked egg whites, ground almonds, semolina and a touch of amaretto, all sandwiched together with a creamy, Italian-style filling flavoured with coffee and grated chocolate.

MAKES 8

140G GROUND ALMONDS

140G GOLDEN CASTER SUGAR

30G SEMOLINA

2 EGG WHITES

1 TBSP AMARETTO LIQUEUR

1 TBSP FLAKED ALMONDS, TO DECORATE

FOR THE CREAM FILLING

125G FULL-FAT MASCARPONE CHEESE

½ TSP VERY FINELY GROUND COFFEE BEANS

4–5 TSP INSTANT ESPRESSO COFFEE POWDER

4–5 TSP ICING SUGAR, PLUS EXTRA TO DUST (OPTIONAL)

15G 70% DARK CHOCOLATE, GRATED

YOU WILL NEED

2 BAKING SHEETS LINED WITH BAKING PAPER; 2 LARGE PIPING BAGS EACH FITTED WITH A 1.25CM ROUND NOZZLE

STEP 1 Heat the oven to 190°C/170°C fan/375°F/ Gas 5. Using a pencil, draw 8 circles of 6cm diameter on the undersides of the baking paper lining each of your baking sheets (giving 16 circles in total).

STEP 2 Mix the ground almonds, sugar and semolina in a bowl. Set aside. Put the egg whites in the bowl of a stand mixer and whisk to form stiff peaks. Tip in the almond, sugar and semolina mixture and fold in. When combined, fold in the amaretto. Transfer the mixture to a large piping bag fitted with a 1.25cm round nozzle.

STEP 3 To make the biscuits, hold the piping nozzle fairly close to the baking paper. Pipe a thin line around the edge of one of the drawn circles. Don't stop when you reach the beginning of the circle – continue to create an even spiral that ends in the centre. Finish by quickly pulling up the bag to give a tiny peak. Repeat for the remaining 15 circles.

STEP 4 Use a wet finger to neaten the ragged edges and central peak. Then place a flaked almond in the middle of each biscuit.

STEP 5 Bake the biscuits for 15 minutes, or until light golden, rotating the baking sheets after 10 minutes for an even bake. Remove the trays from the oven and leave the biscuits to cool slightly and firm up before transferring to a wire rack to cool completely.

STEP 6 To make the cream filling, spoon the mascarpone into a mixing bowl, stir to loosen, then add both the ground coffee beans and the coffee powder and stir again. Cover and chill for about 10 minutes to allow the flavours to infuse.

STEP 7 Sift the icing sugar into the bowl with the coffee-cream filling, then add the chocolate and stir to combine. Taste and add more coffee or icing sugar as needed. Transfer the mixture to the second large piping bag fitted with a 1.25cm nozzle.

STEP 8 Match the biscuits in pairs of the same size, shape and colour. Turn one of each pair bottom up and pipe on a large mound of the flavoured cream. Top with the other biscuit and press together to spread the cream evenly between the biscuits. Dust with icing sugar to serve, if you wish.

BAKER'S RECIPE

TURRON & ORANGE TRAYBAKE

Turron, a type of nougat, and orange marmalade give this traybake a Spanish twist.

MAKES 16

FOR THE PASTRY

175G PLAIN FLOUR

PINCH OF SALT

75G UNSALTED BUTTER, DICED

GRATED ZEST OF 1 UNWAXED ORANGE

25G GOLDEN CASTER SUGAR

1 EGG, BEATEN

FOR THE GANACHE

250ML DOUBLE CREAM

30G SALTED BUTTER

250G 54% DARK CHOCOLATE

CANDIED ORANGE PEEL STRIPS

FOR THE SPONGE

150G UNSALTED BUTTER, SOFTENED

150G GOLDEN CASTER SUGAR

4 EGGS, BEATEN

200G GROUND ALMONDS

1 TSP ALMOND EXTRACT

100G HOMEMADE VALENCIAN ORANGE MARMALADE (SEE P.307)

FOR THE TURRON

280G CASTER SUGAR

5 TBSP RUNNY HONEY

1 LARGE EGG WHITE

100G TOASTED FLAKED ALMONDS

YOU WILL NEED

20 X 30CM TRAYBAKE TIN, GREASED, THEN LINED WITH BAKING PAPER; SUGAR THERMOMETER

STEP 1 First, make the pastry. Sift the flour and salt into a bowl, add the butter and rub in with your fingertips until the mixture resembles fine crumbs. Stir in the orange zest and sugar. Add the beaten egg and 1–2 tablespoons of water and mix to a dough. Shape into a flat rectangle, wrap in cling film and chill for 15 minutes.

STEP 2 Make the ganache. Pour the cream into a pan. Add the butter and heat until melted and warm, but not boiling. Remove from the heat, add the chocolate and melt for 2 minutes, then beat with a wooden spoon until glossy. Set aside to cool.

STEP 3 Roll out the pastry on a lightly floured worktop to a 20 x 30cm rectangle. Use this to line the base of the tin. Chill for 10 minutes.

STEP 4 To make the sponge, heat the oven to 180°C/160°C fan/350°F/Gas 4. Beat the butter and sugar together for 3–5 minutes, until fluffy. Beat in the eggs, then fold in the ground almonds and almond extract. Spoon into the tin and level off. Bake for 40–45 minutes, until golden brown and a skewer inserted into the centre comes out clean. Remove from the oven and cool on a wire rack.

STEP 5 For the turron, tip the sugar into a medium pan. Add the honey and 2 tablespoons of water. Cook over a medium heat, stirring, until the sugar dissolves, then increase the heat and boil until the temperature reads 120°C/ 248°F on a sugar thermometer.

STEP 6 Place the egg white in the bowl of a stand mixer fitted with a whisk attachment and whisk to soft peaks. With the motor running, pour in the hot syrup in a slow, steady stream and continue whisking on high until the mixture is thick and the bowl is cool to the touch. Fold in the almonds.

STEP 7 When the traybake is cool, spread the marmalade over the sponge, then spread the turron over the marmalade and level with a palette knife. Chill for 10 minutes. Finally pour over the chocolate ganache and spread to the edges. Leave to set in the fridge until the ganache is firm and set, about 2 hours.

STEP 8 Remove the traybake from the tin and cut into 16 equally sized rectangles. Top each with 1 or 2 strips of candied orange peel.

TEATIME TREATS
FRESH BERRY RICOTTA DROP SCONES

A mixture of ricotta and natural yogurt makes the lightest-ever drop scones. Mixing in a combination of raspberries and blackberries works well, but feel free to use your own favourite berry combo, if you prefer.

MAKES 12–14

135G RICOTTA CHEESE

135ML LOW-FAT NATURAL YOGURT

3 EGGS

FINELY GRATED ZEST OF 1 SMALL UNWAXED LEMON, OR 1/2 TSP VANILLA BEAN PASTE

85G SELF-RAISING FLOUR

1 TBSP CASTER SUGAR, PLUS EXTRA FOR DUSTING

100G MIXED RASPBERRIES AND BLACKBERRIES, OR BERRIES OF CHOICE

25G UNSALTED BUTTER

STEP 1 Put the ricotta and yogurt into a mixing bowl. Add the eggs and the lemon zest or vanilla paste, and whisk together until very smooth.

STEP 2 Sift the flour and sugar into the bowl and gently whisk in to make a smooth, thick batter. Add the berries and gently fold in with a large metal spoon.

STEP 3 Set a non-stick frying pan over medium heat. Melt a little of the butter in the hot pan and, when it starts to look foamy, gently swirl the pan to coat the base.

STEP 4 Add 2 tablespoons of the batter to the pan – this is your test scone. Cook for about 2 minutes, then gently slide a palette knife under one side of the drop scone and peek underneath. If the underside looks golden brown, flip over the drop scone. Gently press the top surface with a palette knife to slightly flatten the bumpy mixture and cook for another 2 minutes or so, until the underside is golden.

STEP 5 Remove the drop scone from the pan, adjust the heat, if necessary, then add more butter to the pan and cook the remaining mixture in batches of 3 or 4, using 2 tablespoons of mixture for each drop scone. Set aside each batch to keep warm.

STEP 6 When all the scones are cooked, transfer them to a warmed serving plate, dust lightly with sugar and eat immediately.

HONEY & PISTACHIO CREAMS

This glamorous version of the much-loved thumbprint biscuit is flavoured with ground cardamom and finished with a swirl of pistachio cream. You can make both the dough and the filling in a processor, although you shape the dough with your hands.

MAKES 16

225G SELF-RAISING FLOUR

GOOD PINCH OF SALT

5 CARDAMOM PODS, SEEDS REMOVED AND FINELY GROUND

85G CASTER SUGAR

125G UNSALTED BUTTER, CHILLED AND DICED

2 EGG YOLKS

1 TBSP RUNNY HONEY

1 TBSP WHOLE MILK

½ TSP VANILLA EXTRACT

25G PISTACHIO KERNELS, FINELY CHOPPED, PLUS 16 KERNELS TO DECORATE

ICING SUGAR, FOR DUSTING

FOR THE PISTACHIO CREAM

75G PISTACHIO KERNELS

2 TBSP RUNNY HONEY

1 TSP SUNFLOWER OIL

45G UNSALTED BUTTER, VERY SOFT

YOU WILL NEED

LARGE BAKING SHEET LINED WITH BAKING PAPER

STEP 1 Heat the oven to 180°C/160°C fan/350°F/Gas 4. Put the flour, salt, ground cardamom and sugar into a processor and pulse to combine. Add the butter and blitz until the mixture resembles fine crumbs.

STEP 2 Mix the egg yolks, honey, milk and vanilla in a small bowl, then pour into the processor and blitz for 1 minute, until you have a soft dough. If the mixture seems very sticky, work in a little flour; if it feels stiff, work in more milk.

STEP 3 Turn out the dough onto a floured worktop and divide into 16 equal pieces. Use your hands to roll and shape each into a ball. Dip the balls, one at a time, into the chopped pistachios, lightly coating ½ of each ball. Space the balls well apart, pistachio side up, on the lined baking sheet. Bake for 10 minutes.

STEP 4 Remove from the oven and use the handle of a wooden spoon to make a 2cm-wide shallow hollow in the centre of each bun. Bake for 5–7 minutes more, until golden brown. Remove from the oven and leave to firm up for 5 minutes then transfer to a wire rack to cool completely.

STEP 5 Once the buns are cool, make the pistachio cream filling. Put the pistachios, honey and oil into a processor and blitz to a smooth paste. Add the soft butter and blitz for a few seconds, until the mixture is very creamy.

STEP 6 To assemble the thumbprints, spoon a large blob of the filling into the centre of each bun, then decorate with a pistachio kernel and dust with icing sugar.

TIP To make classic jam thumbprints, don't dip the dough in the chopped pistachios. Instead, shape and bake, then as soon as the buns come out of the oven spoon or pipe about 1 teaspoon of Quick & Easy Raspberry Jam (see p.307) into the centre of each bun. Leave to cool.

(V)

STEM GINGER SPELT SCONES

Combining wholemeal and white spelt flours with tangy, mildly acidic, buttermilk gives the best of both worlds: real flavour with that all-important light and open texture. Ground ginger and small chunks of stem ginger add spicy warmth.

MAKES 8

50G WALNUT PIECES

125G WHITE SPELT FLOUR

125G WHOLEMEAL OR WHOLEGRAIN SPELT FLOUR

1 TBSP BAKING POWDER

¼ TSP FINE SEA SALT

1 TSP GROUND GINGER

50G GOLDEN CASTER SUGAR OR DEMERARA SUGAR

65G UNSALTED BUTTER, CHILLED AND DICED

2 LUMPS (ABOUT 40G) STEM GINGER, DRAINED

125ML BUTTERMILK (OR, SEE TIP), PLUS EXTRA IF NEEDED

1 EGG

1 TBSP GINGER SYRUP FROM THE STEM GINGER JAR

1–2 TBSP DEMERARA SUGAR, FOR SPRINKLING

YOU WILL NEED

ROUND-BLADED KNIFE; BAKING SHEET LINED WITH BAKING PAPER

STEP 1 Heat the oven to 220°C/200°C fan/425°F/ Gas 7. Tip the walnuts into a baking dish and lightly toast in the oven for 4–5 minutes, or until fragrant and slightly darker. Leave to cool.

STEP 2 Combine both flours in a mixing bowl. Add the baking powder, salt, ground ginger and sugar and mix well with your hand. Add the butter, tossing the pieces in the flour to lightly coat. Using just the tips of your fingers, rub the butter into the flour, until the mixture resembles fine crumbs.

STEP 3 Chop the walnuts a little smaller, then chop up the stem ginger into similar-sized chunks and mix both into the flour mixture. Make a well in the centre.

STEP 4 Place the buttermilk in a measuring jug and break in the egg. Add the ginger syrup and combine with a fork. Pour into the well in the dry mixture. Using a round-bladed knife, work the mixtures together to make a damp, shaggy-looking dough. If the dough seems dry or stiff, work in more buttermilk, 1 tablespoon at a time.

STEP 5 Turn out the dough onto a lightly dusted worktop. Gently knead the dough for a few seconds, just until it comes together. Don't worry if it's slightly rough-looking.

STEP 6 Working quickly, lift the ball of dough onto the prepared baking sheet and gently pat it out to a disc about 20cm in diameter. Flour a kitchen knife and deeply score the disc into 8 segments. Sprinkle with demerara sugar and bake for about 20–25 minutes, until golden and firm.

STEP 7 Remove from the oven and gently cut along the score markings without separating the segments completely, then transfer to a wire rack and cool for a few minutes. Serve in slices, warm, with butter and marmalade, or split and toasted the following day.

TIP If you don't have buttermilk, you can use 2 tablespoons of plain (unsweetened) yogurt made up to 125ml with semi-skimmed milk.

Bread is baking alchemy at its finest – with just flour, water, yeast and salt, anyone can make a delicious loaf.

The judges' recipe for Naan with Garlic Ghee is a lovely challenge for fans of Indian cuisine. If you're inspired to try some other flatbreads, we have Rice-flour Dosas, Spiced Lamb Lahmacun and Campfire Frying-pan Flatbreads to tempt you. You can top and stuff flatbreads with a vast array of vegetables, meats, cheeses and sauces – they are wonderful for family get-togethers and fun for children to make for themselves and have a hand in assembling their own fillings.

If you like bread with an unusual flavour, then look no further than the best recipes from series 8. The Stuffed Smoked Paprika Loaf is a meal in itself, and the Orange Plaited Brioche is not only fragrant, but also stunningly beautiful – a perfect centrepiece for a family gathering.

So flour your work surface, prep your ingredients and get ready to be fully – and joyfully – immersed in the world of bread. Get baking!

BAKER'S RECIPE
TANGY CITRUS STICKY CHELSEA BUNS

These Chelsea buns have a tangy lemon twist.

MAKES 12

450ML WHOLE MILK

60G UNSALTED BUTTER, DICED

650G STRONG WHITE BREAD FLOUR

100G WHOLEMEAL FLOUR

15G SALT

1½ TSP FAST-ACTION DRIED YEAST

2 LARGE EGGS

ZEST AND JUICE OF 1 UNWAXED LEMON

125G ICING SUGAR

40G UNSALTED BUTTER, MELTED

1 EGG, BEATEN WITH A DASH OF MILK, TO WASH

FOR THE FILLING

1 SWEET-CURED LEMON, PEEL REMOVED AND CHOPPED (OPTIONAL; SEE P.308)

100G MIXED CHOPPED PEEL

100G MIXED DRIED FRUIT

50G CHOPPED DRIED APRICOTS

50G CHOPPED DRIED DATES

120G SOFT LIGHT BROWN SUGAR

1 TSP MIXED SPICE

1 TSP GROUND CINNAMON

FOR THE GLAZE

50ML LEMONADE

125G GRANULATED SUGAR

RIND OF 2 UNWAXED LEMONS

70G SWEET-CURED LEMON PULP (OPTIONAL)

YOU WILL NEED

LARGE BAKING SHEET LINED WITH BAKING PAPER

STEP 1 Put the milk in a pan with the butter over a low heat and warm until the butter has melted. Set aside. Place the flours into the bowl of a stand mixer fitted with a dough hook. Add the salt on one side and the yeast on the other. Crack the eggs into the warm milk mixture and combine.

STEP 2 With the mixer on a slow speed, add half the milk mixture. Then, slowly add just enough of the remaining milk mixture to form a soft, but not sticky dough. Discard any remaining milk mixture and increase the mixer speed to medium. Mix for 5 minutes more.

STEP 3 Tip the dough onto a lightly floured worktop and knead until smooth. Place into a clean bowl, cover with cling film and leave to rise for 1–2 hours, or until doubled in size.

STEP 4 Meanwhile, make the filling. Place all the peel and dried fruit in a bowl. Mix to distribute evenly and set aside. In a small bowl mix the sugar with the mixed spice and cinnamon. Set aside.

STEP 5 Put the lemon zest and juice in a mixing bowl. Whisk in the icing sugar, 1 tablespoon at a time, until you have a dripping consistency. Set aside.

STEP 6 Place the dough on a lightly floured worktop. Knock it back and roll it out to a 50 x 30cm rectangle, 4–6mm thick. With a short end nearest you, tack it down.

STEP 7 Brush the melted butter over the dough, then spread over the sugar and spice mixture, then the dried fruit. From the far end, tightly roll up the dough. Brush along the tack line with a little egg wash, then trim the ends. Cut into 12 equal slices.

STEP 8 Place the slices, with a small gap between each, on a baking sheet. Cover with a tea towel and prove for 45–60 minutes, until doubled in size. Heat the oven to 200°C/180°C fan/400°F/Gas 6.

STEP 9 Brush the buns all over with the egg wash, then bake for 30 minutes, until risen and golden.

STEP 10 Make the glaze. Put all the glaze ingredients in a small pan. Bring to a rolling boil for 5 minutes, to form a syrup. Allow to cool.

STEP 11 Cool the cooked buns for 2 minutes, then brush with the glaze. Cool for 5 minutes more, then slide the baking paper with the buns onto a wire rack to cool completely. Finally, drizzle all over with lemony icing.

BAKER'S RECIPE

ORANGE PLAITED BRIOCHES

Rich and buttery, yet light and delicate, brioche is so soft it needs chilling before shaping – the results make the wait well worth it. Served with apricot jam or blue cheese, this recipe is ideal for a special brunch.

MAKES 4

75ML WHOLE MILK

FINELY GRATED ZEST OF 3 SMALL UNWAXED ORANGES

400G STRONG WHITE BREAD FLOUR

2 TSP FAST-ACTION DRIED YEAST

30G CASTER SUGAR

5G SALT

5 EGGS, BEATEN

170G UNSALTED BUTTER, SOFTENED

2 EGG YOLKS, BEATEN WITH 2 TSP WATER

2 TBSP PEARL SUGAR (OPTIONAL)

YOU WILL NEED

1-2 LARGE BAKING SHEETS LINED WITH BAKING PAPER

STEP 1 Warm the milk with the grated orange zest in a small pan until it just feels comfortable to the touch. Set aside. Place the flour into a large mixing bowl, then mix in the yeast with your hand, until combined. Work in the sugar and salt and make a well in the centre.

STEP 2 Pour the warm milk and the beaten eggs into the well. Draw the flour into the liquid (you can use the dough hook of a mixer on the slowest speed), to make a very soft dough. Work the dough in the bowl for 5 minutes. Then, beat and slap it with your hand until smooth and elastic.

STEP 3 In a bowl, work the butter, little by little, into the dough, until thoroughly incorporated. Beat for 4 minutes, then cover the bowl with cling film and prove for 1 hour, or until doubled in size. Punch down the risen dough, cover again and chill for at least 2 hours, until very firm.

STEP 4 Turn out the dough onto a floured worktop and knead it to deflate. Divide it into 4 equal portions. Take 1 portion and pat it out with your fingers to a rectangle 10 x 15cm. Cut it lengthways into 4 strips, then, using your hands, roll each strip into a neat 19cm-long sausage.

STEP 5 Set the 4 sausages vertically in front of you. Pinch them together at the top. Begin with the strand on the far right. Bring that strand over the one next to it, then under the next. Then, bring the strand on the far left under the strand you've just moved (now next to it). Repeat using the farthest right strand (over, then under), then again move the one on the left under.

STEP 6 Repeat until all the dough strands are plaited, then pinch the ends together and tuck them neatly under the plait. Gently transfer to a lined baking sheet. Repeat the rolling and plaiting with the remaining dough.

STEP 7 Loosely cover the baking sheets with cling film and leave on the worktop to prove for about 1 hour, or until doubled in size and the plaits have retained their shape.

STEP 8 Heat the oven to 200°C/180°C fan/400°F/ Gas 6. Uncover the plaits and brush lightly with the beaten egg yolk, then brush again. For sweet brioche, sprinkle with pearl sugar. Bake for 20–24 minutes, until rich golden brown, rotating the sheets after 15 minutes for an even bake. Transfer to a wire rack and leave to cool before slicing.

BAKER'S RECIPE

COCONUT KALA CHANA BREADS

These round loaves are stuffed with chickpeas, coconut milk, and spices. Serve warm from the oven with curry.

MAKES 4

500G STRONG WHITE BREAD FLOUR

2 TSP FAST-ACTION DRIED YEAST

1 TBSP CURRY POWDER

8G SALT

40ML OLIVE OIL OR RAPESEED OIL, PLUS EXTRA FOR WORKING

ABOUT 320ML LUKEWARM WATER

1 TBSP NIGELLA SEEDS

FOR THE FILLING

2 TSP RAPESEED OIL

1 TBSP MUSTARD SEEDS

1 ONION, FINELY CHOPPED

2 GARLIC CLOVES, CRUSHED

½ TSP TURMERIC

¼ TSP GARAM MASALA

¼ TSP GROUND CUMIN

2 TSP CURRY POWDER

1 TSP JAGGERY OR DEMERARA SUGAR

100G DESICCATED COCONUT (UNSWEETENED)

30G SULTANAS

1 X 400G CAN KALA CHANA OR CHICKPEAS, DRAINED AND RINSED

200ML COCONUT MILK

SEA SALT, TO TASTE

YOU WILL NEED

LARGE BAKING SHEET LINED WITH BAKING PAPER

STEP 1 Place the flour into a large mixing bowl, or the bowl of a stand mixer, and mix in the yeast with your hand. When combined, mix in the curry powder and salt, then make a well in the centre. Pour in the oil and work in the flour, using your hand or the dough hook of the mixer (on the slowest speed). Gradually add lukewarm water until the dough is soft but not sticky.

STEP 2 Turn out the dough onto a lightly oiled worktop and knead for 10 minutes (or leave in the mixer and knead using the dough hook for 7 minutes on a slow speed), until the dough is smooth and elastic. Return the dough to the bowl (if necessary), then cover with cling film and leave to prove for about 1 hour, until doubled in size.

STEP 3 Meanwhile, make the filling. Heat the oil in a deep frying pan, add the mustard seeds and when they start to pop turn down the heat and stir in the onion. Cook gently for about 10 minutes, until the onion is soft and translucent. Stir in the garlic, turmeric, garam masala, cumin and curry powder and cook for 3–4 minutes.

STEP 4 Stir in the remaining ingredients, except the salt, then cook over a low heat for 10 minutes, until thick and fairly dry. Season with salt to taste. Transfer to a heatproof bowl and leave to cool.

STEP 5 Uncover the risen dough and punch it down. Turn out onto a lightly floured worktop, sprinkle with the nigella seeds and knead to distribute. Divide the dough into 4 equal portions.

STEP 6 Take 1 portion of dough and flatten it to a 17cm disc. Spoon 75g of the cooled filling into the centre. Gather up the edges and pinch to seal in the filling. Turn over the parcel and shape into a round bun, then flatten lightly. Transfer to the baking sheet. Repeat with the remaining dough portions. Cover and set aside the remaining filling. Loosely cover the buns with cling film and prove for about 1 hour, or until doubled in size.

STEP 7 Heat the oven to 220°C/200°C fan/425°F/Gas 7. Uncover the buns and bake for about 20 minutes, until golden brown, rotating the sheet after 15 minutes for an even bake. Transfer to a wire rack and cool slightly before serving. Reheat the remaining filling to serve alongside.

TIERED KOROVAI

The korovai, originating from Russia and other countries of eastern Europe, is a shaped bread traditionally made for weddings and other celebrations. This simplified version uses the classic decorations of birds, plaits and flowers – all made using a special bread dough.

MAKES 30 SLICES

FOR THE BREAD CIRCLES

260ML WHOLE MILK

1 TBSP VANILLA PASTE

1 TBSP ALMOND EXTRACT

500G STRONG WHITE
BREAD FLOUR

10G SALT

4 TSP FAST-ACTION DRIED YEAST

1 EGG

100G UNSALTED BUTTER,
SOFTENED

100G APRICOT JAM, WARMED
WITH 2 TBSP ALMOND LIQUEUR

FOR THE FILLING

150G UNSALTED BUTTER

150G LIGHT MUSCOVADO SUGAR

300G DRIED APRICOTS, CHOPPED
INTO SMALL PIECES AND SOAKED
IN 200ML ALMOND LIQUEUR

200G DRIED CHERRIES

100G FLAKED ALMONDS

FOR THE DECORATION DOUGH

200G PLAIN FLOUR

½ TSP VANILLA PASTE

60G CASTER SUGAR

40G UNSALTED BUTTER,
SOFTENED

12 CLOVES

1 EGG, BEATEN

TO FINISH

200G CASTER SUGAR

A FEW FLOWERS, TO DECORATE

YOU WILL NEED

2 BAKING SHEETS LINED WITH
BAKING PAPER; 2 PROVING BAGS;
COOKING THERMOMETER

STEP 1 First, start the bread circles. Warm the milk with the vanilla paste and almond extract in a small pan over a medium heat. Do not let it boil – it should be warm, not hot.

STEP 2 Place the flour in a stand mixer fitted with a dough hook. Put the salt at one side and the yeast at the other. Add the egg and butter. Combine on a slow speed and, with the mixer running, pour in the warm milk mixture and mix to form a soft, sticky dough. Increase the speed and mix for 5 minutes, until smooth. Transfer to a bowl and cover with cling film. Leave to rise for 1 hour, or until doubled in size.

STEP 3 Meanwhile, make the filling. Cream the butter and sugar together with an electric hand whisk, until pale and fluffy. Drain the apricots and mix into the creamed mixture with the cherries and flaked almonds.

STEP 4 Tip out the risen dough onto a lightly floured worktop and divide into 2 pieces, ⅓ and ⅔. Roll out the largest piece into a rectangle about 36 x 24cm with the long edge facing you. Cover the dough with ⅔ of the filling.

STEP 5 Roll up the dough like a Swiss roll, keeping it tight and neat. Working from the middle outwards, gently squeeze and roll the dough until it measures about 50cm.

STEP 6 Using a large knife, cut along the middle of the length of the roll, leaving the halves joined at one end. Twist the strands, shape into a circle, join the ends, and place on a baking sheet.

STEP 7 Roll the remaining dough into a 19 x 24cm rectangle. Spread over the remaining filling, then roll up. Stretch out as before, until it measures 40cm long. Cut, twist and shape into a circle as before. Place on the other baking sheet. Place each sheet into a proving bag and leave for about 1 hour, until risen.

STEP 8 Heat the oven to 220°C/200°C fan/425°F/ Gas 7. Remove the bread circles from the proving bags and bake on the baking sheets for 10 minutes, then cover with foil and bake for a further 20–25 minutes, until the dough reaches 90°C/194°F on a cooking thermometer.

STEP 9 Remove from the oven and place the circles on a wire rack to cool. While still warm, brush with the liqueur-laced apricot jam. Lower the oven temperature to 180°C/ 160°C fan/350°F/Gas 4.

RECIPE CONTINUES OVERLEAF »»

STEP 10 Make the dough for the decorations. Place the flour, vanilla paste and sugar in a bowl. Add the butter and rub in until it resembles fine crumbs. Add 75ml of water and mix to a firm dough. Turn out onto a floured worktop and knead until smooth.

STEP 11 To make the heart decorations, take a little dough and roll it into 12 ropes approximately 10cm in length. Using 3 ropes at a time, plait and form into 4 heart shapes. Place on a lined baking sheet.

STEP 12 To make the birds, roll 12 dough ropes, each 7cm long. Lie 1 rope horizontally and place another over it at right angles. Wrap the horizontal dough around the vertical dough and cross over. Shape the head and use 2 cloves for the eyes. Use a sharp knife to score the tail and wings. Place on a lined baking sheet. Repeat to make 6 birds in total.

STEP 13 To make the flowers, roll out 6 strips of dough, each 30cm long. Flatten each strip so that each is 1.5cm wide. From one of the short ends, tightly roll up each dough strip to form a rosebud shape. Place on a lined baking sheet.

STEP 14 Brush all the decorations with beaten egg and bake for 10–15 minutes, until light golden brown and cooked through. Remove from the oven and transfer to a wire rack to cool.

STEP 15 To assemble the korovai, gently heat the caster sugar in a small pan with 60ml of water until it bubbles and turns a light golden brown, about 8–10 minutes. Remove the caramel from the heat. Place the largest ring onto your serving plate, sit the smaller ring on top. Using the caramel as glue, stick the decorations onto the dough circles. Decorate with a few fresh flowers.

NAAN BREAD WITH GARLIC GHEE

Unlike traditional naan that is leavened with yeast and cooked in a clay oven, this recipe uses baking powder and is cooked under a hot grill, making it possible to have naan on the table in a fraction of the time.

MAKES 8

450G PLAIN FLOUR

1 TSP SALT

1 TSP BAKING POWDER

200ML WHOLE MILK

100ML NATURAL YOGURT

1 EGG

1 TBSP CASTER SUGAR

SMALL BUNCH OF CORIANDER, CHOPPED, TO SERVE

FOR THE GARLIC GHEE

250G SALTED BUTTER

4 GARLIC CLOVES, PEELED AND FINELY CHOPPED

YOU WILL NEED

MUSLIN SQUARE; HEAVY-BASED METAL BAKING SHEET

STEP 1 Mix the flour, salt and baking powder together in a bowl.

STEP 2 In a jug whisk together the milk, yogurt, egg and caster sugar.

STEP 3 Make a well in the centre of the flour and pour in the milk mixture. Mix together with one hand, to a soft, sticky dough.

STEP 4 Turn out the dough onto a lightly oiled worktop. Knead for 5 minutes, until smooth, then place the dough into a lightly oiled bowl, cover and leave to rest for 30 minutes.

STEP 5 To make the ghee, melt the butter in a small pan over a low heat so that it is only just bubbling. Leave to simmer for 20 minutes – this gives the ghee its nutty flavour and golden colour – carefully skimming the foam as it rises to the surface. (Take care to remove just the foam and not the clarified butter.)

STEP 6 Remove the pan from the heat and pass the butter through a sieve lined with a square of muslin into a clean bowl. Skim off any remaining small bits of foam and stir in the chopped garlic. Set aside.

STEP 7 Tip the dough onto a lightly floured worktop and divide into 8 equal pieces. Shape 1 piece into a ball, flatten it, then roll it into a teardrop shape about 3–5mm thick, 20cm long and 12cm at its widest point. Repeat for the remaining dough pieces.

STEP 8 Lay a heavy-based metal baking sheet on a grill pan and heat under a hot grill for 5 minutes. One at a time, lay the naan on the hot baking sheet and grill for 1–2 minutes, until the naan bubbles up. (Keep a close eye on it, as it will burn easily as it puffs.)

STEP 9 Remove the naan from the grill, brush with garlic ghee, and set aside to keep warm. Repeat with the remaining naans, then sprinkle with chopped coriander to serve.

CINNAMON BRIOCHE BREAD

The light, fluffy crumb and rich, buttery flavour of this brioche is the result of a baker's patience: it needs to rise overnight, but it's worth the wait. This version has a cinnamon swirl running through it.

MAKES 1 LARGE LOAF

400G STRONG WHITE BREAD FLOUR

1 TSP SALT

2 TSP FAST-ACTION DRIED YEAST

2 TBSP CASTER SUGAR

4 EGGS, BEATEN

3 TBSP WHOLE MILK

150G UNSALTED BUTTER, AT ROOM TEMPERATURE, DICED

1 TBSP MELTED UNSALTED BUTTER

50G ICING SUGAR MIXED WITH 1 TBSP GROUND CINNAMON

1 EGG YOLK, TO GLAZE

YOU WILL NEED

900G LOAF TIN, GREASED, THEN LINED WITH BAKING PAPER

STEP 1 Put the flour, salt, yeast, sugar, eggs and milk in the bowl of a stand mixer fitted with a dough hook. Mix on a slow speed for 3 minutes, until the ingredients have been incorporated and you have a sticky dough.

STEP 2 Increase the mixer speed to medium, and add the butter a few cubes at a time, making sure each addition is fully incorporated before adding the next. Continue until you have added all the butter, and the dough has lost its stickiness and is shiny and silky smooth, about 15 minutes.

STEP 3 Transfer the dough to a large greased bowl and cover with cling film. Leave to rise for 2 hours, then refrigerate for at least 12 hours and up to 24 hours.

STEP 4 When you're ready to make the brioche, tip the chilled dough out onto a lightly floured worktop and roll into a rectangle approximately 20 x 45cm. With the long side facing you, brush the surface of the dough with melted butter, then sift over the cinnamon and sugar mixture.

STEP 5 Take a short end and roll up the dough into a sausage shape. Trim the ends to neaten. Cut the roll of dough in half down the length, exposing the filling and leaving you with 2 strips side by side with the cut-side facing up.

STEP 6 Pinch the two lengths together at one end, then twist the dough, left over right, all the way to the bottom, keeping the cut side up. Pinch the free ends together and place the twist in the prepared tin. Loosely cover with cling film and leave to prove for 2–3 hours, or until doubled in size.

STEP 7 Heat the oven to 170°C/150°C fan/325°F/ Gas 3. Gently brush the top of the brioche with egg yolk. Bake for 25–30 minutes, until risen and golden brown and a skewer inserted into the centre comes out clean. (Keep your eye on the brioche: if after 20 minutes it is getting too brown, cover with foil and then return it to the oven for the remainder of the cooking time.) Remove from the oven.

STEP 8 Leave to cool in the tin for 5 minutes, then remove from the tin and transfer to a wire rack to cool completely.

PEAK DISTRICT CHELSEA BUNS

Bakewell meets Chelsea in these flavoured buns.

MAKES 12

500G STRONG WHITE BREAD FLOUR

40G CASTER SUGAR

2½ TSP FAST-ACTION DRIED YEAST

10G SALT

60G UNSALTED BUTTER, SOFTENED

250ML WARM SEMI-SKIMMED MILK

3 LARGE EGGS

100G HOMEMADE MARZIPAN, COLOURED RED (SEE P.308)

1 TBSP AMBER SUGAR CRYSTALS

FOR THE FILLING

75G UNSALTED BUTTER, SOFTENED

75G CASTER SUGAR

1 EGG

75G GROUND ALMONDS

15G PLAIN FOUR

1 TSP ALMOND EXTRACT

2 TBSP DRIED CRANBERRIES, SOAKED OVERNIGHT IN 2 TBSP KIRSCH

1 TBSP GROUND CINNAMON

1 TSP GROUND MACE

FOR THE DECORATION

250G FONDANT ICING SUGAR

1 TBSP KIRSCH

RED FOOD-COLOURING PASTE

GREEN FOOD-COLOURING PASTE

12 MIXED GLACÉ CHERRIES

50G FLAKED ALMONDS, TOASTED

RED EDIBLE GLITTER

YOU WILL NEED

26CM SPRINGFORM TIN, GREASED; 3 SMALL DISPOSABLE PIPING BAGS

STEP 1 For the dough, place the flour, sugar, yeast and salt in a large mixing bowl. Rub the softened butter into the flour, then make a well in the centre and add the milk and beat in 2 of the eggs. Mix together to form a soft dough.

STEP 2 Tip the dough onto a lightly floured worktop and knead well for 7–10 minutes, until the dough is smooth and elastic. Place in an oiled bowl, cover with cling film and leave to rise for 1 hour, or until doubled in size.

STEP 3 Roll the coloured marzipan into balls the size of hazelnuts. Set aside for decoration.

STEP 4 For the filling, cream the butter and sugar together until pale and fluffy. Add the egg, ground almonds, flour, almond extract and soaked cranberries and mix together. Set aside.

STEP 5 Tip the dough out onto a lightly floured worktop. Roll it into a 40 x 30cm rectangle. Spread the filling over, then sprinkle over the cinnamon and mace.

STEP 6 Lay dough with the short end closest to your body, and, taking hold of the far edge, roll it up as tightly as you can. Trim the ends and cut into 12 equal slices. Arrange the slices in the tin in a circular pattern. Leave for 20–30 minutes, until risen.

STEP 7 Heat the oven to 190°C/170°C fan/375°F/ Gas 5. Beat the remaining egg and use to brush the risen slices, then sprinkle over the amber sugar crystals. Bake for 30–40 minutes, until risen and golden. Remove from the oven and turn out onto a wire rack.

STEP 8 To decorate, sift the icing sugar into a large bowl and add the kirsch. Mix to a stiff pouring consistency, adding some water if necessary. Divide the icing into thirds. Leave ⅓ white, colour ⅓ green and colour the remaining ⅓ red. Spoon each colour into its own disposable piping bag.

STEP 9 Snip the ends off the piping bags and pipe the coloured icing in lines over the buns, then scatter with the glacé cherries, balls of red marzipan and toasted flaked almonds. Finally, sprinkle with red edible glitter.

TEATIME TREATS

IRISH HALLOWE'EN TEA BREAD

This Irish celebration loaf is traditionally stuffed with charms that portend your fortune for the coming year. A coin in your slice brings good luck; a ring, a proposal; a pea, a loveless 12 months! This recipe is a simple, tasty, moist, fruit tea bread. Serve without butter if you're dairy-free.

MAKES 1 LARGE LOAF

300ML STRONG BLACK TEA

200G SULTANAS

200G RAISINS

50G MIXED PEEL

225G SELF-RAISING FLOUR

1/2 TSP MIXED SPICE

1/4 TSP GROUND CINNAMON

1/4 TSP GROUND NUTMEG

1/2 TSP SALT

175G LIGHT MUSCOVADO SUGAR

1 LARGE EGG, BEATEN

YOU WILL NEED

900G LOAF TIN, OILED WITH SUNFLOWER OIL, THEN LINED WITH BAKING PAPER

STEP 1 Pour the tea into a jug and add the sultanas, raisins and mixed peel. Cover and leave the fruit to soak overnight to absorb the tea and plump up.

STEP 2 Heat the oven to 160°C/140°C fan/315°F/ Gas 3. Put the flour with all the spices and the salt in a large mixing bowl and stir well to combine. Add the sugar and stir again, making sure you break up any lumps in the sugar.

STEP 3 Add the soaked fruit and any remaining soaking liquid to the dry mixture, then add the beaten egg, and stir until all the ingredients are thoroughly combined.

STEP 4 Tip the mixture into the prepared tin, smooth the surface and bake for 1–1¼ hours, until the loaf is risen and golden and a skewer inserted into the centre comes out clean.

STEP 5 Remove from the oven and leave to cool in the tin for 5 minutes. Then, remove from the tin and place on a wire rack to cool completely. Serve in slices, and spread with butter, if you wish.

STUFFED SMOKED PAPRIKA LOAF

Simplified here from a 'handbag' as the original showstopper, into a round loaf, this focaccia-like bread is flavoured and coloured with smoked sweet paprika and ground coriander. Stuffed with chorizo, Manchego cheese, spicy chipotle paste and onions, it's delicious eaten warm with salad.

MAKES 1 LARGE, FILLED LOAF

FOR THE DOUGH

500G STRONG WHITE BREAD FLOUR

2 TSP FAST-ACTION DRIED YEAST

8G SALT

2 TSP SWEET SMOKED PAPRIKA

1 TSP GROUND CORIANDER

70ML OLIVE OIL

300ML LUKEWARM WATER

FOR THE FILLING

200G CHORIZO, SKINNED AND CHOPPED INTO SMALL PIECES

1 RED ONION, FINELY CHOPPED

2 GARLIC CLOVES, CRUSHED

1 TBSP DEMERARA SUGAR

1 TBSP SWEET SHERRY

2 TSP CHIPOTLE PASTE

125G MANCHEGO CHEESE, CUT INTO SMALL PIECES

YOU WILL NEED

20CM, DEEP SPRINGFORM TIN, GREASED; BAKING SHEET

STEP 1 Make the dough. Put the flour into a large bowl and stir in the yeast with your hand to combine. Mix in the salt, paprika and coriander. Make a well in the centre and pour in the olive oil, followed by the lukewarm water.

STEP 2 Using your hand, work everything together to a very soft and slightly sticky dough. Turn out onto a lightly oiled worktop and knead for about 10 minutes, until the dough is stretchy, pliable and slightly firmer. Place in an oiled bowl. Cover the bowl with cling film and leave in a warm place for about 1 hour, until almost tripled in size.

STEP 3 Make the filling. Put the chorizo into a cold, non-stick frying pan and set over a low heat. Cook until the fat runs and the chorizo starts to colour. Leaving the fat in the pan, transfer the chorizo to a heatproof bowl. Pour all but 1 tablespoon of the fat from the pan into small heatproof bowl and set aside.

STEP 4 Add the chopped onion and garlic to the pan and cook gently, stirring frequently, for 10 minutes, until softened, then turn up the heat and cook for 2–3 minutes, stirring, until the onions start to caramelise.

STEP 5 Stir in the sugar, add the sherry and stir to dissolve any stuck-on bits. Simmer for 1–2 minutes, until the mixture looks sticky. Remove from the heat and stir in the chipotle paste, then add to the chorizo and mix well. Leave to cool.

STEP 6 Turn out the dough onto a lightly floured worktop and divide in ½. Oil your hands, then shape and flatten one ½ into a 22cm disc and press it into the base of the oiled tin, and about 1.5cm up the sides (it will be springy, so be patient). Spoon the chorizo mixture evenly over, then scatter the Manchego on top.

STEP 7 Knock back the remaining dough a little, then shape into a 19cm disc, and use it to cover the filling. Press down to expel any air, then pinch the edges to seal. Make 3 slits in the loaf, then cover with lightly oiled cling film. Leave for 1 hour, until the dough reaches the top of the tin. Heat the oven to 220°C/200°C fan/425°F/Gas 7.

STEP 8 Uncover the dough and brush the top of the loaf with the reserved chorizo fat. Place the tin on a baking sheet and bake for 30 minutes, or until golden.

STEP 9 Remove the tin from the oven, stand it on a wire rack, unclip the sides, and remove the loaf. Leave to cool for about 20 minutes before serving in wedges.

ENTERTAINING

BRAZILIAN CHEESE BREAD

These gooey cheese dough balls are a traditional Brazilian snack. Handling gluten-free dough takes practice – it lacks elasticity and behaves more like a pastry. Make sure the dough is firm enough to handle, but not dry.

MAKES ABOUT 16

100ML WHOLE MILK

50ML SUNFLOWER OIL

325G TAPIOCA FLOUR

½ TSP SALT

1 EGG, BEATEN

75G FINELY GRATED PARMESAN CHEESE, PLUS A LITTLE EXTRA FOR SPRINKLING

75G GRATED MOZZARELLA CHEESE

YOU WILL NEED

2 BAKING SHEETS LINED WITH BAKING PAPER

STEP 1 Heat the oven to 200°C/180°C fan/400°F/ Gas 6. Put the milk, oil and 25ml of water in a small pan and heat until the liquid just comes to the boil.

STEP 2 Meanwhile, place the tapioca flour and salt into the bowl of a stand mixer fitted with the paddle attachment. Pour the hot milk mixture onto the tapioca flour and mix on a slow speed. Once the liquid has been incorporated, increase the speed, until you have a mixture the consistency of a thick paste.

STEP 3 With the mixer running on a slow speed, gradually add the beaten egg and mix until fully incorporated. Gradually add the cheeses, a little at a time, and mix until just combined. The dough should be sticky, but not runny, and the sides of the bowl should be clean. Leave to rest for 5 minutes.

STEP 4 With wet hands, take a little mixture at a time and shape each piece into a ball the size of a table-tennis ball. Repeat until you have used up all the mixture. Place the balls spaced out on the prepared baking sheets and sprinkle with a little extra Parmesan, if you wish.

STEP 5 Bake for 20–25 minutes, until the balls are risen and golden. Remove from the oven and leave to cool on the sheets for 5 minutes, then transfer to a wire rack to cool completely. Serve warm.

INSPIRED BY THE SHOW

CAMPFIRE FRYING-PAN FLATBREADS

Using a few store-cupboard ingredients, you can knock up these versatile flatbreads in no time. The trick is getting the dough to the right consistency – not too wet, but not stiff – and mastering the cooking. Don't have the pan too hot or leave the flatbreads in for too long. Best of all, you can cook them in the great outdoors!

MAKES 8

250G PLAIN FLOUR

1 TSP SALT

2 TBSP SUNFLOWER OR LIGHT OLIVE OIL

180–200ML WARM WATER

YOU WILL NEED

HEATPROOF KITCHEN TONGS

STEP 1 Mix the flour and salt together in a large bowl. Add the oil and mix using your fingertips until the mixture resembles fine crumbs.

STEP 2 Add ¾ of the water and with one hand mix to incorporate the flour. Add just enough of the remaining water to bring the mixture together, leaving the sides of the bowl clean. You should have a soft and sticky dough.

STEP 3 Turn out the dough onto a lightly floured worktop and knead for about 3–5 minutes, until it becomes soft and smooth. Divide the dough into 8 pieces (each weighing about 50g) and roll each piece into a ball. Wrap each ball in cling film to stop it drying out while you work.

STEP 4 Take 1 ball of dough, unwrap it and roll it out into a 2mm-thick disc. Set aside and cover while you repeat with the remaining balls of dough, until you have 8 dough discs.

STEP 5 To cook the flatbreads, heat your frying pan over a medium—high heat. Then, without oiling the pan, add 1 flatbread. Air bubbles will begin to appear on the surface – just press them down with tongs.

STEP 6 After 1–2 minutes turn over the flatbread and cook the other side for 30 seconds to 1 minute. The flatbread should be soft and have brown speckled marks across the surface.

STEP 7 Remove from the pan and wrap in a clean tea towel to keep warm and soft, while you cook the remaining flatbreads. These breads are delicious served with curries and dips, and as wraps with various fillings.

IRISH QUICK BREAD

Stout porter was the Victorian name for strong porter, later shortened to stout. Combined with the treacle, it brings a rich, malty flavour to this quick and easy bread. It's delicious spread with a little butter or pâté, or topped with cream cheese, smoked salmon and a few snipped chives.

MAKES 1 LARGE LOAF

150G WHOLEMEAL
SELF-RAISING FLOUR

100G SELF-RAISING FLOUR

1 TSP SALT

100G UNSALTED BUTTER, DICED

100G PORRIDGE OATS

100G FINE OATMEAL

2 TBSP TREACLE

150ML STOUT

200ML BUTTERMILK

YOU WILL NEED

900G LOAF TIN, GREASED, THEN
LINED WITH BAKING PAPER

STEP 1 Heat the oven to 200°C/180°C fan/400°F/ Gas 6. Mix the flours and salt together in a large bowl. Use your fingertips to rub in the butter, until the mixture resembles fine crumbs. Stir in the oats and oatmeal until fully combined.

STEP 2 In a separate small bowl, mix the treacle with the stout, then add the wet mixture to the flour mixture. Stir to combine, then add enough buttermilk, a little at a time, to form a wet paste.

STEP 3 Transfer the mixture to the prepared loaf tin. Smooth the surface using a knife and bake for 1 hour, until the loaf is crisp and golden. Remove from the tin to test the base – if it sounds hollow when tapped, the loaf is ready.

STEP 4 Put the loaf back in the tin to cool for 5 minutes, then remove from the tin and transfer onto a wire rack to cool completely.

SPICED LAMB LAHMACUN

If you haven't tried this Turkish-style pizza before, you are in for a treat: it is a delicious combination of spiced lamb spread on a flatbread and finished with parsley and lemon juice.

MAKES 4

375G STRONG WHITE BREAD FLOUR

1 TSP SALT

1 TSP FAST-ACTION DRIED YEAST

2 TBSP OLIVE OIL

FOR THE TOPPING

250G LAMB MINCE

1 ONION, ROUGHLY CHOPPED

2 GARLIC CLOVES

1 GREEN PEPPER, DESEEDED AND ROUGHLY CHOPPED

1 ROASTED RED PEPPER, FROM A JAR

1/2 TSP SALT

1/4 TSP CHILLI FLAKES

TO SERVE

1 TSP SUMAC

2 TBSP CHOPPED FLAT-LEAF PARSLEY

1 TBSP POMEGRANATE SEEDS

1 LEMON, CUT INTO WEDGES

YOU WILL NEED

HEAVY-BASED BAKING SHEET OR BAKING/PIZZA STONE

STEP 1 Mix the flour, salt and yeast together in a large bowl. Add the oil and 100–125ml of water, then use one hand to start to combine the ingredients into a dough. Little by little, add a further 100–125ml of water, mixing thoroughly between each addition, until you have incorporated all the flour and formed a soft dough.

STEP 2 Tip out the dough onto a lightly floured worktop and knead for 5–10 minutes, until it becomes smooth. Place the dough into a clean bowl, cover with cling film and leave to rise for 1–2 hours, or until doubled in size.

STEP 3 Meanwhile, place all the topping ingredients in a food processor and pulse until you have a chunky paste.

STEP 4 Heat the oven to 220°C/200°C fan/425°F/ Gas 7 and place a heavy-based baking sheet or a baking stone inside the oven to heat up. Tip out the dough onto a lightly floured worktop and divide it into 4 equal pieces. Roll out each piece into a rough disc, 22cm in diameter.

STEP 5 Divide the topping into 4 equal portions. Spread 1 portion over 1 dough disc, making sure you take the filling all the way to the edges. (It can help to do this on pieces of baking paper, to make it easier to move the lahmacuns to the baking tray to cook.) Repeat with the remaining dough discs and filling.

STEP 6 Carefully place the covered discs on the heated tray (you may need to do this in batches) and bake for 10–12 minutes, until the dough is risen and golden brown.

STEP 7 To serve, dust the surface of each lahmacun with a little sumac, sprinkle with chopped parsley and pomegranate seeds, and finish with a good squeeze of lemon. Enjoy the lahmacuns on their own or with salad.

ALMOND CHALLAH

Sweet-tasting almond paste runs through each strand of this challah plait. Be sure to use almond paste, and don't be tempted to buy marzipan. Paste contains 50 percent almond, whereas shop-bought marzipan contains only 20–25 percent (the rest is glucose and sugar, which will burn when baked).

MAKES 1 LOAF

450G STRONG WHITE BREAD FLOUR

1 TSP SALT

2 TBSP CASTER SUGAR

1½ TSP FAST-ACTION DRIED YEAST

25G UNSALTED BUTTER, AT ROOM TEMPERATURE, DICED

2 EGGS, BEATEN, PLUS 1 EGG TO GLAZE

2 TBSP WHOLE MILK

175ML WARM WATER

250G ALMOND PASTE

WARMED APRICOT JAM, TO FINISH

2 TBSP FLAKED ALMONDS, TOASTED, TO DECORATE

YOU WILL NEED

LARGE BAKING SHEET LINED WITH BAKING PAPER

STEP 1 Put the flour, salt, sugar, yeast, butter, eggs and milk in the bowl of a stand mixer fitted with a dough hook. Add half the warm water, then mix on a slow speed until all the ingredients are combined.

STEP 2 Slowly add enough of the remaining water to form a rough, wet dough, then increase the speed to medium and mix for about 5 minutes, until the dough becomes soft and smooth. Transfer to a clean, oiled bowl, cover with cling film and leave for about 2 hours, or until the dough has doubled in size.

STEP 3 Tip out the dough onto a lightly floured worktop and knead to knock out any air. Divide the dough into 3 equal pieces. Roll each into a rectangle measuring 8 x 25cm.

STEP 4 Divide the almond paste into 3 equal pieces and use your hands to roll each piece into a sausage shape 20cm long. Place one almond-paste sausage onto the centre of each dough strip. Fold the dough around the almond paste to completely encase it.

STEP 5 Lay the 3 filled strips of dough vertically on the worktop in front of you. Pinch the 3 pieces together at the top to join them. Lift the strand on the far right over the middle strand, then lift the left strand over the middle. Continue plaiting until you get to the end. Tuck the end underneath.

STEP 6 Lift the plait onto the prepared baking sheet. Cover loosely with cling film and leave to prove for 1 hour, or until the dough has doubled in size and feels springy when lightly pressed. Towards the end of the proving time, heat the oven to 200°C/180°C fan/400°F/Gas 6.

STEP 7 Brush the loaf with beaten egg and bake for 20–25 minutes, until golden brown and cooked through – the base of the loaf should sound hollow when tapped. Remove from the oven and leave to cool a little on the sheet. Brush with apricot jam while still warm and scatter over the toasted flaked almonds. Transfer the loaf to a wire rack to cool completely. Serve in slices.

RICE-FLOUR DOSA

Paper-thin rice pancakes from southern India, dosa are traditionally made using soaked rice and urad dal, blended to a smooth paste and left to ferment. Using rice and gram flour speeds up the process. Getting the temperature of the pan just right can take a little practice – don't worry, the first dosa always sticks.

MAKES 9

- 100G RICE FLOUR
- 50G GRAM FLOUR
- ½ TSP FENUGREEK POWDER
- ½ TSP SALT
- SUNFLOWER OIL, FOR FRYING

STEP 1 Mix the rice and gram flours in a medium bowl with the fenugreek powder. Gradually add 300ml of water and mix to form a thick, smooth, lump-free batter. Cover and leave to ferment for at least 6 hours, or overnight.

STEP 2 The fermented batter will be thick and have a few bubbles on the surface. Add the salt and stir – the consistency should be slightly thicker than pancake batter, so add a little water if it is too thick.

STEP 3 Heat a large frying pan over a medium heat. Pour a little oil onto a piece of kitchen paper and wipe the surface of the pan. Use a large spoon or ladle to pour the batter into the centre of the pan, then spread it out using a circular motion with the back of the spoon or ladle, until the pancake is as thin as possible.

STEP 4 Cook the dosa until the underside is golden – it will take about 30 seconds to 1 minute, depending on how hot you have your pan. Then, turn the dosa over using a palette knife and cook for up to 1 minute on the other side. Remove the cooked dosa to a plate and keep warm.

STEP 5 Repeat until you have used up all the batter, now and again wiping the pan with oil between dosa, and occasionally removing the pan from the heat to cool it a little if it gets too hot. Serve the dosa warm or cold with a dry curry and chutneys.

INSPIRED BY THE SHOW

POTATO, RYE & CARAWAY BREAD

This versatile bread is perfect served in hunks with a soup, or sliced for a sandwich. The potato adds moisture, while the caraway gives a warming hint of aniseed. Leaving the potatoes in their skins to cook will make the mash easier to work with.

MAKES 1 LOAF

300G POTATOES (SUCH AS MARIS PIPER OR DESIRÉE), SKIN ON, LEFT WHOLE

1 TSP SALT

300G STRONG WHITE BREAD FLOUR

150G RYE FLOUR

1½ TSP FAST-ACTION DRIED YEAST

25G UNSALTED BUTTER, AT ROOM TEMPERATURE, DICED

1 TSP CARAWAY SEEDS

YOU WILL NEED

POTATO RICER; LARGE BAKING SHEET LINED WITH BAKING PAPER; ROASTING TIN

STEP 1 Bring a large pan of salted water to the boil and cook the potatoes whole and unpeeled, until tender (cooking time depends on the size of your potatoes). Drain the potatoes in a colander and leave them until they are cool enough to handle, then remove the skins. Mash the flesh through a ricer into a bowl, then cool completely.

STEP 2 Put the salt, flours, yeast, butter, caraway seeds and cooled potato into a large mixing bowl. Add 140ml of water, and bring everything together with your hands. Add water, a little at a time (up to about another 170ml), to bring the ingredients together and form a soft dough.

STEP 3 Tip out the dough onto a lightly floured worktop and knead until smooth. Transfer to a clean, oiled bowl, cover with cling film and leave to rise for 2 hours, or until doubled in size.

STEP 4 Turn out the dough onto a lightly floured worktop and knead to knock out any air. Shape the dough into a rectangle (about 30 x 25cm) with the long side facing you. Fold the short ends into the middle, then roll towards you from the farthest edge, so that the seam runs underneath.

STEP 5 With your hands on either end of the roll, gently rock the dough to form a bloomer shape. Place the loaf onto the prepared baking sheet, loosely cover with cling film and leave to prove for about 1 hour, or until doubled in size and the dough feels springy when you press it lightly.

STEP 6 Towards the end of the proving time, heat the oven to 220°C/200°C fan/425°F/Gas 7, and place a roasting tin in the base of the oven to heat up.

STEP 7 With wet hands, gently rub the surface of the dough, then dust with flour. Make 3 slashes across the top, and place, on the baking sheet, in the oven. Pour a jug of water into the roasting tin before you close the oven door. (The water will create steam, giving the bread a crisp crust.)

STEP 8 Bake for 25 minutes, then lower the heat to 200°C/180°C fan/400°F/Gas 6 and bake for a further 10 minutes, until the crust is deep, crisp and golden. Remove the bread from the oven, leave to cool a little on the sheet, then transfer to a wire rack to cool completely.

CHAPTER FOUR

PUDS
AND
DESSERTS

Puddings and desserts are the ultimate in comfort baking. They smell and taste wonderful and lend themselves to ... well, anytime really. The mouthwatering recipes in this chapter span the whole range from comforting and homely treats to more ambitious desserts to impress at a dinner party.

For starters, why not try the Piña Colada Meringue Roulade or the Apricot Meringue Torte which is filled with pillows of apricot cream. Or, if hot puds and desserts are more your thing, then you will love the Chocolate Soufflé Crêpes and Hungarian Apple Pie. If it's a sense of awe you want to create, then flick through to the stunning Melting Chocolate Ball – a Showstopper Made Simple with lashings of 'wow' factor (and of caramel sauce).

If you feel you missed out on the best bakers' recipes from Series 8, then we have a delicious selection for you to make and share. Work your way up from Lemon & Blackcurrant Drizzle Steamed Pudding and Mango Fruit Hat Pudding to a Rainbow Meringue Centrepiece. It may seem that the closest you could ever get to an entremet is gazing longingly at one in a pâtisserie shop window. But you can follow in the footsteps of last year's finalists with their recipes for an Ode to the Honeybee or White Chocolate & Yuzu Entremet and make your dessert dreams come true.

BAKER'S RECIPE
MANGO FRUIT HAT PUDDING

This light sponge is flavoured with lime and ginger, surrounded by fresh mangoes and decorated with crunchy caramelised coconut. The tropical theme continues with coconut custard to serve.

SERVES 8

170G UNSALTED BUTTER, SOFTENED

170G LIGHT MUSCOVADO SUGAR

1 TSP GROUND MIXED SPICE

1 LARGE RIPE MANGO, PEELED, STONED AND FLESH CUT INTO LONG 5MM-THICK SLICES

1 SMALL RIPE MANGO, PEELED, STONED AND FLESH CUT INTO 1CM CHUNKS

1 TBSP RUNNY HONEY

FINELY GRATED ZEST OF 2 UNWAXED LIMES

2 TSP STEM GINGER, FINELY CHOPPED

1/2 TSP VANILLA EXTRACT

2 EGGS, BEATEN

100G SELF-RAISING FLOUR

1/2 TSP BAKING POWDER

75G STALE WHITE BREADCRUMBS

FOR THE COCONUT CUSTARD

200ML WHOLE MILK

200ML COCONUT MILK

1 VANILLA POD, SPLIT, SEEDS SCRAPED AND POD RESERVED

3 EGG YOLKS

2 TSP CORNFLOUR

25G CASTER SUGAR

FOR THE CARAMELISED COCONUT

50G CASTER SUGAR

20G FLAKED COCONUT CHIPS

YOU WILL NEED

1-LITRE PUDDING BASIN; GREASED BAKING PAPER CUT INTO A 27CM DISC; KITCHEN FOIL CUT INTO A 27CM DISC; KITCHEN STRING; BAKING SHEET, WELL OILED WITH SUNFLOWER OIL

STEP 1 Mix 50g of the butter, 50g of the sugar and the mixed spice in a small bowl, until combined, then spread thickly over the inside base and sides of the pudding basin. Press the mango slices into the buttery coating in a sunburst pattern and spoon the mango chunks into the base. Drizzle the honey on top.

STEP 2 Place an upturned saucer or small plate on the base of a large, deep pan and fill about 1/3 full with hot water. Cover and set over a medium heat. Fold the 27cm greased baking-paper disc (greased side down) so it has a 3cm crease in the centre. Turn by 90 degrees and fold again, to create a cross. Repeat with the 27cm foil disc.

STEP 3 Put the remaining butter and sugar into a mixing bowl and beat with an electric whisk until creamy. Beat in the lime zest, ginger and vanilla extract. Add the eggs one by one, beating well after each addition.

RECIPE CONTINUES OVERLEAF ⟫

STEP 4 Sift in the flour and baking powder, add the breadcrumbs, and fold everything together. Spoon evenly into the basin without dislodging the mango – don't worry if the slices poke out above the level of the batter.

STEP 5 Cover the top of the basin with the baking paper (greased side down), then the foil, and secure with string around the rim. Tie a doubled length of string across the top of the basin to make a handle.

STEP 6 Put the basin into the pan, on top of the saucer, and add more hot water so it reaches about ⅓ up the sides of the basin. Cover, and simmer gently for 2 hours. Check regularly and top up with hot water, if necessary.

STEP 7 Meanwhile, make the coconut custard. Pour both milks into a medium pan. Add the vanilla seeds and pod and heat slowly until the mixture just comes to the boil, then remove from the heat. Put the yolks, cornflour and sugar into a heatproof bowl and mix until smooth.

STEP 8 Slowly whisk in the hot milk mixture, then tip everything back into the pan, discarding the vanilla pod. Stir over a medium–low heat, until the custard thickens to coat the back of a spoon. Pour into a warm jug.

STEP 9 To make the caramelised coconut, tip the sugar into a large pan. Set the pan over a medium–low heat. As soon as the sugar starts to melt around the edges, draw the liquid in towards the centre with a wooden spoon and leave until you have a dark golden caramel.

STEP 10 Remove from the heat and mix in the flaked coconut chips to coat, then spoon onto the oiled baking sheet. Leave until set, then break into shards.

STEP 11 Lift the pudding out of the pan. Remove the covering, loosen the edges with a palette knife, and let stand for 10 minutes, then turn out onto a warm serving plate. Decorate with the coconut shards and serve with the custard on the side.

ODE TO THE HONEY BEE ENTREMET

This entremet has four layers, each with a distinct flavour: an orange-blossom almond sponge, a set lemon curd, a caramelised honey set custard, and finally a gelée topping made with puréed blackberries.

SERVES 12

FOR THE SPONGE

80G UNSALTED BUTTER, DICED

115G CASTER SUGAR

75G GROUND ALMONDS

35G PLAIN FLOUR

4 EGG WHITES

GOOD PINCH OF SALT

FINELY GRATED ZEST OF
1 UNWAXED LEMON

FINELY GRATED ZEST OF
1 UNWAXED ORANGE

1/2 TSP ORANGE BLOSSOM WATER

1/4 TSP VANILLA BEAN PASTE

BLACKBERRIES, TO DECORATE

ICING SUGAR, FOR DUSTING

FOR THE LEMON SET CURD

200ML LEMON JUICE
(ABOUT 5 LEMONS)

4G AGAR-AGAR

2 EGGS

200G CASTER SUGAR

200G UNSALTED BUTTER, AT
ROOM TEMPERATURE, DICED

FOR THE HONEY SET CUSTARD

6G LEAF GELATINE
(ABOUT 3 LEAVES)

125G ORANGE BLOSSOM HONEY

1/2 TSP VANILLA PASTE

325ML DOUBLE CREAM,
AT ROOM TEMPERATURE

90ML WHOLE MILK,
AT ROOM TEMPERATURE

4 EGG YOLKS

1/4 TSP SALT

1 TBSP CASTER SUGAR

FOR THE BLACKBERRY GELÉE

6G LEAF GELATINE (ABOUT
3 LEAVES)

350G BLACKBERRIES

2 TBSP LEMON JUICE

55G UNSALTED BUTTER, AT
ROOM TEMPERATURE, DICED

125G CASTER SUGAR

2 EGGS

YOU WILL NEED

22CM SPRINGFORM TIN,
GREASED, THEN BASE-LINED
WITH BAKING PAPER; 22CM THIN
CARD CAKE BASE; WIDE STRIP
OF ACETATE; STICKY TAPE

STEP 1 Heat the oven to
180°C/160°C fan/350°F/
Gas 4. Melt the butter in a
small pan and leave to bubble
gently over a medium–low
heat, until it turns a nut-
brown colour. Set aside to
cool to room temperature.

STEP 2 Sift half the sugar, all
the ground almonds, and the
flour into a bowl. In a separate
bowl, whisk the egg whites,
with the salt, until they form
soft peaks. Whisk in the
remaining sugar, a little at
a time, until the meringue
stands in stiff peaks.

STEP 3 Sprinkle the flour
mixture and the grated lemon
and orange zests on top and
start to fold in by hand. When
the flour is half-combined,
trickle in the melted butter,
the orange blossom water and
the vanilla bean paste, and
fold again to fully combine.

STEP 4 Spoon the mixture
into the cake tin and bake
for 20–25 minutes, until
golden brown. Transfer to
a wire rack, unmould the cake
from the tin and leave to cool.

STEP 5 Clean the cake tin
and press the card base into
the bottom. Cut a wide strip
of acetate to fit inside the rim,
like a collar, and secure with
tape. Remove the paper from
the sponge, turn the sponge
top downwards and place
on the card base, pressing
it down firmly. Tighten the
acetate to fit, if necessary.

STEP 6 To make the lemon
set curd, pour the lemon juice
into a medium pan, sprinkle
over the agar-agar, and place
the pan over a medium–low
heat. Bring to the boil without
stirring, then simmer for 8
minutes, to dissolve the flakes.

RECIPE CONTINUES OVERLEAF »»

STEP 7 Meanwhile, break the eggs into a heatproof bowl, add the sugar and whisk for 2–3 minutes, until smooth, then whisk in the lemon mixture. Return to the pan and stir over a medium–low heat, just until it thickens to coat the back of a spoon. Remove from the heat.

STEP 8 Stir in the butter, a little at a time, then strain the curd into a bowl. Leave to cool to room temperature, stirring as it thickens. Spoon the curd on top of the sponge and chill for 4–5 hours, until set.

STEP 9 Make the honey set custard. Soften the gelatine in water. Put the honey into a medium pan, add the vanilla paste and set over a medium–low heat. Simmer, stirring occasionally, until the honey thickens and darkens. Remove from the heat and hand whisk in the cream and milk. Return to the heat and whisk until smooth and hot. Remove from the heat.

STEP 10 Put the egg yolks into a heatproof bowl, add the salt and sugar, and whisk for 2–3 minutes, until smooth.

STEP 11 Whisk in the hot honey cream, then pour the mixture back into the pan. Return to a medium–low heat and stir until the custard thickens to coat the back of the spoon. Remove the pan from the heat.

STEP 12 Lift the gelatine out of the water, squeeze out the excess, and stir into the hot custard to dissolve. Strain the custard into a jug. Leave to cool and thicken, stirring frequently, then pour on top of the lemon curd. Chill to set.

STEP 13 To make the gelée, soak the gelatine as before. Put the blackberries and lemon juice into a medium pan over a medium heat. Stir as the berries release their juice and the mixture comes to a boil, then simmer, stirring frequently, for about 10 minutes, until the berries are very soft. Remove from the heat and mash to a thick purée, then add the butter and sugar and stir until melted.

STEP 14 Beat the eggs in a heatproof bowl, then whisk in the hot blackberry purée. Return to the pan and stir over a low heat, until thick, but not boiling.

STEP 15 Remove from the heat, then stir in the gelatine to dissolve as before, then strain the blackberry mixture into a jug. Cool to room temperature, stirring frequently. When the gelée starts to thicken, pour it over the top of the custard, then chill to set.

STEP 16 To serve, carefully remove the entremet from the tin, peel away the acetate and serve decorate with blackberries and dusted with icing sugar.

BAKER'S RECIPE

PIÑA COLADA ROULADE

This is a classic cocktail combined with a classic dessert. The roasted pineapple gives the roulade a sweet and tropical tang.

SERVES 10

4 LARGE EGG WHITES

225G CASTER SUGAR

1 TSP WHITE WINE VINEGAR

50G SWEETENED DESICCATED COCONUT

GOLD SHIMMER SPRAY, TO DECORATE

ICING SUGAR, FOR DUSTING

FOR THE FILLING

3 X 435G TINS PINEAPPLE RINGS, IN SYRUP

50G CASTER SUGAR

300ML DOUBLE CREAM

150G MASCARPONE CHEESE

1 TSP VANILLA PASTE

4 TBSP COCONUT RUM

50G CREAMED COCONUT, GRATED

1 TSP COCONUT EXTRACT

YOU WILL NEED

LARGE ROASTING TIN; 22 X 33CM SWISS ROLL TIN, OILED, THEN LINED WITH BAKING PAPER; SHEET OF BAKING PAPER DUSTED WITH ICING SUGAR

STEP 1 Heat the oven to 200°C/180°C fan/400°F/Gas 6. First, start the filling. Drain the pineapple, reserving the syrup. Chop the rings into 1cm pieces and spread out in a large roasting tin. Drizzle over 2 tablespoons of the reserved syrup and roast for 20–25 minutes, until golden and sticky. Remove from the oven and set aside to cool.

STEP 2 Place the remaining pineapple syrup in a small pan with 25g of the caster sugar and bring to the boil. Reduce the heat and simmer to a thick syrup. Remove from the heat and leave to cool.

STEP 3 For the meringue, whisk the egg whites until stiff, but not dry. Add the sugar 1 teaspoon at a time, until it is all incorporated and the mixture is stiff and glossy.

STEP 4 Fold in the vinegar and coconut, then spoon the meringue into the lined Swiss roll tin and level out. Tap the tin on the worktop to remove any air pockets.

STEP 5 Bake the meringue for 8–9 minutes, until the top is lightly golden brown. Reduce the temperature to 180°C/160°C fan/350°F/Gas 4 and bake for 10 minutes more, or until the meringue is firm.

STEP 6 Remove from the oven and turn out onto baking paper dusted with icing sugar. Peel the lining paper from the base and leave the meringue to cool for 10 minutes.

STEP 7 To complete the filling, pour the double cream into a medium bowl. Add the remaining 25g of sugar, along with the mascarpone, vanilla paste, coconut rum, grated coconut and coconut extract. Whisk to stiff peaks.

STEP 8 Spread ¾ of the coconut cream evenly over the meringue and scatter ¾ of the roasted pineapple on top.

STEP 9 Using a sharp knife, score a line 1cm in from the short edge, nearest you, then fold the scored end and roll up the roulade using the baking paper to help lift and roll. Wrap the roulade in baking paper and chill for about 30 minutes.

STEP 10 Unwrap the roulade and place on a serving plate. Spoon the remaining coconut cream down the centre of the top of the roulade and arrange the remaining pineapple on top. Drizzle with pineapple syrup, spray with gold spray, then dust with icing sugar. Serve with the remaining pineapple syrup on the side.

BAKING WITH CHILDREN
BANANA TOFFEE SPONGE & CUSTARD

A warming treat for a cold winter's night, this sweet sponge is something the kids can help you make.

SERVES 6-8

75G UNSALTED BUTTER

150G DARK BROWN SOFT SUGAR

2-3 RIPE BANANAS, PEELED AND SLICED

175G SELF-RAISING FLOUR

175G UNSALTED BUTTER, SOFTENED

175G CASTER SUGAR

1 TSP MIXED GROUND SPICE

3 EGGS

VANILLA EGG CUSTARD (SEE P.306), TO SERVE

YOU WILL NEED

2-LITRE OVENPROOF DISH, GREASED; BAKING SHEET

STEP 1 Heat the oven to 180°C/160°C fan/350°F/ Gas 4 and place the ovenproof dish on a baking sheet.

STEP 2 Melt the butter and sugar together in a pan over a medium heat until bubbling, then pour into the ovenproof dish. Arrange the banana slices over the toffee.

STEP 3 Using an electric hand whisk, beat the flour, butter, sugar, spice and eggs together in a bowl until you have a smooth batter. Carefully spread the batter over the bananas.

STEP 4 Place the dish, on the baking sheet, in the oven and bake for about 30–35 minutes, or until the sponge is firm to the touch. Cut into squares and serve with custard.

DESSERTS FROM THE ARCHIVES

WHITE CHOCOLATE & YUZU ENTREMET

Zingy, citrus yuzu juice is used to good effect in this showstopper made simple.
It infuses both the rich, white chocolate bavarois and the génoise sponge base.
Impressive sugar shards complete the showstopper effect.

SERVES 12

8

FOR THE GÉNOISE SPONGE

25G UNSALTED BUTTER

4 EGGS

1 TBSP YUZU JUICE

125G CASTER SUGAR

125G PLAIN FLOUR

GOOD PINCH OF SALT

25G GOOD-QUALITY WHITE CHOCOLATE, GRATED OR IN CURLS, TO DECORATE

LARGE BOWL OF FRUIT SALAD OR BERRIES, TO SERVE (OPTIONAL)

FOR THE BAVAROIS

8G LEAF GELATINE (ABOUT 4 OR 5 LEAVES)

125G GOOD-QUALITY WHITE CHOCOLATE, FINELY CHOPPED

150ML WHOLE MILK

3 EGG YOLKS

15G CASTER SUGAR

100ML YUZU JUICE

350ML WHIPPING CREAM, WELL CHILLED

FOR THE SHARDS

80G CASTER SUGAR

¼ TSP BLACK SESAME SEEDS

YOU WILL NEED

22CM, DEEP SPRINGFORM TIN, GREASED, THEN BASE-LINED WITH BAKING PAPER; 22CM THIN CARD CAKE BASE; WIDE STRIP OF ACETATE; HEATPROOF PASTRY BRUSH; BAKING SHEET, LIGHTLY OILED; STICKY TAPE

STEP 1 Heat the oven to 180°C/160°C fan/350°F/ Gas 4.

STEP 2 To make the génoise sponge, melt the butter and set aside to cool. Break the eggs into a large heatproof bowl, add the yuzu juice and sugar, and whisk for 10 seconds using an electric hand whisk. Place the bowl over a pan of gently simmering water (don't let the base of the bowl touch the water) and whisk on full speed for 7–10 minutes, until the mixture is mousse-like and the whisk leaves a ribbon-like trail when lifted.

STEP 3 Remove the bowl from the pan. Sift the flour and salt into the bowl, and fold in until almost combined. Stir 3 tablespoons of the mixture into the cooled melted butter, then return to the rest of the batter, fold in until combined, and pour, distributing evenly, into the prepared tin.

STEP 4 Bake the sponge for 22–25 minutes, until well-risen, golden brown and springy. Loosen the sponge from the edges of the tin using a round-bladed knife, then unclip the tin and turn out onto a wire rack to cool. Wash and dry the tin.

STEP 5 Make the bavarois. Soften the gelatine in water while you make the custard. Put the chocolate into a large heatproof bowl. Heat the milk in a medium pan, until steaming hot, then remove from the heat.

STEP 6 Meanwhile, put the yolks and sugar into another heatproof bowl and whisk with an electric hand whisk for 2–3 minutes, until thick and frothy. Whisk in the yuzu juice, then the hot milk.

STEP 7 Pour the mixture back into the pan and stir over a medium–low heat, until the custard thickens to coat the back of the spoon and leave a path when you draw a finger through it – don't let it boil. Remove from the heat.

STEP 8 Lift the gelatine from the soaking water, squeeze out the excess, and stir into the custard until melted. Strain the custard onto the chopped white chocolate and allow the chocolate to melt for 2 minutes, then stir until smooth and combined. Leave to cool to room temperature and start to thicken, stirring frequently.

RECIPE CONTINUES OVERLEAF »»

STEP 9 Meanwhile, place the card cake base in the bottom of the clean springform tin. Place a wide strip of acetate around the inside of the tin to make a collar, and secure with sticky tape. Remove the baking paper, then place the sponge in the tin top downwards, pressing it in place.

STEP 10 Whip the cream for the bavarois until it forms soft peaks, then fold it into the custard until fully combined. Pour the bavarois onto the sponge and spread evenly. Chill for 3 hours, or overnight, to set.

STEP 11 To make the shards, put the sugar and 2 tablespoons of water into a small pan over a very low heat. Swirl the pan as the sugar dissolves, from time to time brushing down the sides with a heatproof pastry brush dipped in water.

STEP 12 As soon as the liquid is clear, turn up the heat so the liquid bubbles, and leave for 8–10 minutes, or until the bubbles get very large and cover the surface. Swirl, but don't stir.

STEP 13 At the first hint of a colour change, remove the pan from the heat and pour the contents in a thin layer onto the oiled baking sheet. Sprinkle with the sesame seeds. Leave until set hard, then break into shards.

STEP 14 To assemble, place the dessert on a serving plate. Scatter the grated white chocolate or chocolate curls over the top, press the sesame shards upright into the bavarois, then serve with a bowl of fruit salad or berries, if you wish.

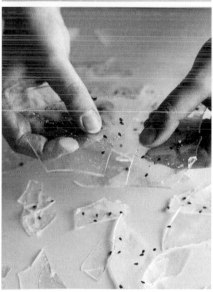  

APRICOT MERINGUE TORTE

This torte is a beauty. If you can't get hold of fresh apricots, use mangoes or summer berries instead. Fill each layer before you assemble, to avoid collapse.

SERVES 12

10 LARGE EGG WHITES

500G CASTER SUGAR

1½ TSP WHITE WINE VINEGAR

1½ TSP CORNFLOUR

6 RIPE APRICOTS, STONED AND HALVED

A SMALL BUNCH OF MINT LEAVES

50G PISTACHIO KERNELS, ROUGHLY CHOPPED, TO DECORATE

FOR THE ROASTED APRICOTS

150G GOLDEN CASTER SUGAR

6 GREEN CARDAMOM PODS

1 VANILLA POD, CUT INTO 4 PIECES

JUICE AND FINELY GRATED ZEST OF 1 UNWAXED LIME

12 RIPE APRICOTS, STONED AND HALVED

FOR THE FILLING

8 RIPE APRICOTS, STONED AND QUARTERED

1 TBSP ICING SUGAR

1 LITRE DOUBLE CREAM

YOU WILL NEED

3 LARGE BAKING SHEETS LINED WITH BAKING PAPER, EACH DRAWN WITH A CIRCLE: 1 X 27CM DIAMETER, 1 X 22CM AND 1 X 17CM

STEP 1 For the roasted apricots. Heat the oven to 220°C/200°C fan/425°F/Gas 7. Tip the sugar, cardamom and vanilla pods, and lime juice and zest into a food processor and blitz to a paste.

STEP 2 Place the 12 apricot halves in a shallow ovenproof dish, add the sugary paste and toss to coat. Roast for 20 minutes, until the apricots are soft, but not collapsed. Remove from the oven. Once the dish is cool enough to handle, drain off the syrup through a sieve into a medium pan. Set aside. Chill the roasted apricots until cold.

STEP 3 Reduce the oven temperature to 130°C/110°C fan/260°F/Gas 1. Turn the baking paper lining your baking sheets so that the drawn sides are face down.

STEP 4 Make the meringue. Put the egg whites in a stand mixer fitted with the whisk attachment and whisk to stiff peaks. Add the sugar, 1 tablespoon at a time, whisking continuously until stiff and shiny.

STEP 5 Mix the vinegar and cornflour together in a small bowl and whisk into the egg mixture. Spoon the meringue onto the baking sheets and spread out to fill the circles.

STEP 6 Bake for 1½ hours, then turn off the oven, leaving the door closed with the meringues inside for at least 4 hours, to prevent cracking.

STEP 7 Tip the 6 halved apricots into the pan of reserved syrup. Bring to the boil over a high heat, reduce the heat and simmer for 10 minutes, until soft. Take off the heat and purée with a stick blender. Pass through a sieve into a jug and leave to cool, then chill until cold.

STEP 8 Make the filling. Tip the apricot quarters into a bowl and sprinkle with icing sugar. Leave for 15 minutes. Whisk the cream until thick, then fold in ½ the roasted apricots to distribute evenly.

STEP 9 Place the largest meringue disc on a flat plate, then spread ½ the cream over the meringue. Scatter over ½ the remaining roasted apricots and drizzle with a little purée. Arrange ½ of the sugary apricots around the edge, and decorate with ½ of the mint leaves. Repeat for the other 2 meringue discs using ⅔ of the remaining ingredients, then ⅓.

STEP 10 Stack the meringues and drizzle the apricot purée over. Sprinkle the pistachios, then serve immediately.

CHOCOLATE TERRINE WITH PISTACHIO PRALINE

As smooth as silk, this dessert is a slice of heaven with a hit of nutty crunch.

SERVES 8–12

225G UNSALTED BUTTER, DICED

350G 70% DARK CHOCOLATE, BROKEN INTO PIECES

1 TSP INSTANT COFFEE

125G ICING SUGAR

40G COCOA POWDER

6 EGG YOLKS

1 TBSP COGNAC

PINCH OF SALT

3 EGG WHITES

1 TBSP CASTER SUGAR

125ML DOUBLE CREAM, CHILLED

1 TSP VANILLA EXTRACT

FOR THE PISTACHIO PRALINE

100G CASTER SUGAR

50G SHELLED PISTACHIO KERNELS

YOU WILL NEED

900G LOAF TIN, OILED AND LINED WITH OVERHANGING CLING FILM; LARGE SILICONE MAT OILED WITH SUNFLOWER OIL

STEP 1 Melt the butter, chocolate and coffee together in a heatproof bowl set over a pan of gently simmering water. Remove from the heat and, using an electric hand whisk, whisk in the icing sugar, cocoa powder, egg yolks, Cognac and salt. Remove from the heat and set aside to cool.

STEP 2 In a clean bowl whisk the egg whites and sugar together until they are firm, but not dry.

STEP 3 In a separate bowl, beat the cream and vanilla extract together until softly whipped. Fold the cream into the cooled chocolate mixture, then fold in the whisked egg white mixture.

STEP 4 Pour the mixture into the prepared loaf tin, smooth the top with a palette knife, cover with the overhanging cling film and chill for at least 4 hours, or overnight.

STEP 5 Meanwhile, make the praline. Tip the sugar into a heavy-based pan. Set over a medium heat and leave, without stirring, until the sugar dissolves and turns a deep brown colour.

STEP 6 Stir the pistachios into the melted sugar and pour the mixture onto the oiled silicone mat. Leave to harden (about 30 minutes), then break into pieces. Store in an airtight container between layers of non-stick baking paper, until you're ready to assemble the dessert.

STEP 7 To serve, turn out the terrine onto a serving plate and remove the cling film. Push pieces of pistachio praline into the top, to decorate. Serve in slices.

9

JUDGE'S RECIPE

RASPBERRY BLANCMANGE

Based on a retro classic, this blancmange is a far cry from its wobbly 1970s' reputation – it's a light and creamy raspberry and almond dessert, here served with buttery langues de chat biscuits.

SERVES 12

8 GELATINE LEAVES

750G RASPBERRIES

50ML RASPBERRY LIQUEUR

25G CORNFLOUR

300ML WHOLE MILK

150G CASTER SUGAR

40G GROUND ALMONDS

1 TSP ALMOND EXTRACT

450ML DOUBLE CREAM

CRYSTALLISED ROSE PETALS,
TO DECORATE

FOR THE LANGUES DE CHAT

40G UNSALTED BUTTER, SOFTENED

40G ICING SUGAR

¼ TSP ALMOND EXTRACT

1 LARGE EGG WHITE

40G PLAIN FLOUR

PINCH OF SALT

150G GOOD-QUALITY WHITE
CHOCOLATE, MELTED

GREEN COCOA BUTTER

YOU WILL NEED

1.4-LITRE RING OR JELLY MOULD;
MEDIUM PIPING BAG; 9MM ROUND
NOZZLE; BAKING SHEET LINED
WITH BAKING PAPER; SMALL
DISPOSABLE PIPING BAG; MEDIUM
STAR NOZZLE

STEP 1 Soak the gelatine leaves in a small bowl of chilled water for 5 minutes.

STEP 2 Tip the raspberries into the bowl of a food processor and blitz to a fine purée. Pass through a sieve into a clean bowl, discarding the pips, then stir in the raspberry liqueur.

STEP 3 Mix the cornflour with a little of the milk in a medium pan. Add the remaining milk, along with the sugar and ground almonds. Bring to the boil, then reduce the heat and simmer gently for 3–5 minutes, to thicken. Remove the pan from the heat.

STEP 4 Squeeze out any excess water from the gelatine leaves, then add them to the pan, stirring continuously until dissolved. Add the almond extract.

STEP 5 Stir in 300ml of the double cream and all the raspberry purée, combine thoroughly, then pour into the mould. Leave to set for at least 6 hours, preferably overnight.

STEP 6 To make the langues de chat, beat the butter and icing sugar until pale and smooth. Stir in the almond extract. Whisk the egg white with a fork to break it up, then gradually beat it into the mixture.

STEP 7 Sift the flour with the salt over the top of the mixture, then fold in. Place the mixture into a piping bag fitted with a 9mm round nozzle. Pipe 12 fingers, each 8cm long, onto the baking sheet, leaving a 3.5cm space between each biscuit.

STEP 8 Tap the baking sheet on the underside to release any air bubbles in the dough, then chill for 15 minutes, until the dough is firm to the touch. Heat the oven to 180°C/160°C fan/350°F/Gas 4.

STEP 9 Bake the biscuits for 8–10 minutes, or until golden brown around the edges and pale in the middle. Remove from the oven and leave to cool on the baking sheet for 2 minutes before transferring to a wire rack to cool completely.

RECIPE CONTINUES OVERLEAF »»

STEP 10 Spoon about 50g of the melted white chocolate into a small disposable piping bag and set aside.

STEP 11 Gently melt the green cocoa butter in the microwave or by placing it in a bowl stood in a jug of hot water. Add a small amount of green cocoa butter to the remaining melted chocolate to colour it mint green.

STEP 12 Dip 1 cooled langue de chat into the chocolate, lengthways on the diagonal. Allow the excess to run off, then place on a sheet of baking paper to set. Repeat with the remaining biscuits, until all 12 biscuits are half-coated in chocolate.

STEP 13 Snip the end of the piping bag and drizzle the white chocolate in lines from side to side across the langues de chat. Leave to set.

STEP 14 To serve, lightly whip the remaining 150ml of cream to soft peaks, then spoon into a medium piping bag fitted with a medium star nozzle.

STEP 15 Remove the mould from the fridge and quickly dip it into a bowl of hot water to loosen the blancmange. Invert the mould onto a serving plate to turn out the blancmange.

STEP 16 Pipe the cream around the base of the blancmange, then decorate with crystallised rose petals. Serve immediately with the langues de chat on the side.

BAKER'S RECIPE
LEMON & BLACKCURRANT DRIZZLE STEAMED PUDDING

Cut open this lemony pudding to reveal swirls of blackcurrant sauce. It's delicious served with creamy vanilla egg custard (see p.306), too.

SERVES 8

FINELY GRATED ZEST OF 5 UNWAXED LEMONS

175G SELF-RAISING FLOUR

175G UNSALTED BUTTER, SOFTENED

175G GOLDEN CASTER SUGAR

½ TSP VANILLA EXTRACT

3 EGGS, BEATEN

FOR THE BLACKCURRANT SAUCE

200G FRESH OR FROZEN BLACKCURRANTS

50G LIGHT MUSCOVADO SUGAR

FINELY GRATED ZEST OF 1 UNWAXED LEMON

4 TBSP CRÈME DE CASSIS OR BLACKCURRANT LIQUEUR

YOU WILL NEED

GREASED BAKING PAPER CUT INTO A 27CM DISC; 1-LITRE PUDDING BASIN, WELL GREASED; KITCHEN FOIL CUT INTO A 27CM DISC; KITCHEN STRING; COOKING SYRINGE OR MEAT INJECTOR

STEP 1 Place an upturned saucer on the base of a large pan and fill about ⅓ full with hot water. Cover and set over a medium heat. Fold the greased disc of baking paper, greased side down, so it has a 3cm crease in the centre. Turn by 90 degrees and fold again, to create a cross. Repeat with the 27cm foil disc.

STEP 2 Make the pudding. Put the lemon zest into a bowl, then sift in the flour and mix. Put the butter, sugar and vanilla into another bowl and beat until creamy and light. Add the eggs one at a time, beating after each addition. Add in the flour and lemon and fold to combine.

STEP 3 Spoon the batter into the basin and spread evenly. Cover the top with the baking paper (greased side down), then the foil, and secure with string around the rim. Tie a doubled length of string across the top as a handle.

STEP 4 Put the basin in the pan, on top of the saucer, and add more hot water, so that it reaches about ⅓ up the sides of the basin. Cover, and simmer gently for 2 hours. Check regularly and top up with hot water, if necessary.

STEP 5 Now, make the sauce. Put 150g of the blackcurrants into a pan with 100ml of water, the sugar and the lemon zest and set over a low heat. Stir to dissolve the sugar, then simmer for 5–7 minutes, until the blackcurrant juices have released and thickened.

STEP 6 Remove from the heat and stir in the remaining blackcurrants and the crème de cassis. Leave until cold, then strain into a jug. Tip the blackcurrants back into the pan and set aside. Pour the juice into the cooking syringe.

STEP 7 Lift the pudding from the pan. Remove the cover, loosen the sponge with a palette knife, and leave for 5 minutes to firm up, then turn out onto a warm serving plate.

STEP 8 Insert the syringe into the middle of the pudding and inject sauce while at the same time retracting the needle (to create stripes of sauce). Repeat all over the pudding.

STEP 9 Pour any remaining juice back into the pan with the fruit, warm through, then spoon a little over the pudding and serve the remainder in a warm jug. Serve with custard, too, if you like.

POACHED PEAR TORTE WITH CARDAMOM SAUCE

The deliciously subtle flavour of lemony cardamom is a perfect match for pears.

SERVES 8

FOR THE PEARS AND SAUCE

500ML DRY WHITE WINE

150G CASTER SUGAR

1 TBSP CARDAMOM PODS, CRUSHED

1 TBSP LEMON JUICE

4–5 PEARS, PEELED, CORED AND HALVED

400ML CRÈME FRAÎCHE

FOR THE PASTRY

200G PLAIN FLOUR

100G UNSALTED BUTTER, CHILLED AND DICED

20G CASTER SUGAR

ABOUT 3 TBSP CHILLED WATER

FOR THE FILLING

4 EGG YOLKS

50G CASTER SUGAR

2 TBSP CORNFLOUR

1 TSP GROUND CINNAMON

175ML WHOLE MILK, WARMED

2 TBSP GROUND ALMONDS

FOR THE TOPPING

50G PLAIN FLOUR

50G GROUND ALMONDS

50G CASTER SUGAR

50G UNSALTED BUTTER, MELTED

YOU WILL NEED

20CM LOOSE-BOTTOMED, DEEP, FLUTED TART TIN

STEP 1 Put the wine, sugar, cardamom and lemon juice in a medium pan over a high heat and bring to a simmer. Add the pears, and some water, if necessary, so that the pears are submerged (this depends on the size of your pears). Cover the pan with a lid, bring the liquid back to a simmer and cook for 30 minutes, until tender but not soft. Remove the pears with a slotted spoon and set aside.

STEP 2 Return the pan to the heat and boil the syrup until reduced to 200ml. Pass the liquid through a sieve into a bowl, leave to cool, then chill. Once the syrup is cold, whisk in the crème fraîche and pour into a serving jug. Set aside.

STEP 3 Make the pastry. Put the flour and butter into a food processor and blitz until the mixture resembles fine crumbs. Add the sugar and enough chilled water to make a dough. Wrap the dough in cling film and chill for 30 minutes.

STEP 4 Meanwhile, make the custard for the filling. Beat the egg yolks and sugar together until pale. Beat in the cornflour and cinnamon, then gradually whisk in the warmed milk.

STEP 5 Pour the mixture back into the milk pan, and heat gently, stirring, until the custard thickens. Remove from the heat and set aside.

STEP 6 For the topping, mix the flour, almonds, sugar and butter together in a bowl until fully combined. Set aside. Heat the oven to 180°C/ 160°C fan/350°F/Gas 4.

STEP 7 Remove the pastry from the fridge, unwrap it and place on a lightly floured worktop. Roll out to a 30cm circle and use this to line the tart tin. Sprinkle the 2 tablespoons of ground almonds evenly into the base, arrange the pear halves on top and pour over the custard. Sprinkle evenly with the topping mixture.

STEP 8 Bake the torte for about 1 hour, or until the pastry is cooked. Remove from the oven, leave to cool in the tin, then chill. Serve with the cardamom-flavoured crème fraîche on the side.

MELTING CHOCOLATE BALL WITH ORANGE CRAQUELIN PROFITEROLES

This showstopper may be simplified, but it still has plenty of wow factor.
What could be more impressive than deliciously filled choux buns hidden beneath
domed chocolate shells?

SERVES 4

FOR THE CHOCOLATE SPHERES

400G 70% DARK CHOCOLATE

50G GOOD-QUALITY WHITE CHOCOLATE

FOR THE ORANGE CRAQUELIN

35G UNSALTED BUTTER

35G LIGHT MUSCOVADO SUGAR

35G PLAIN FLOUR

1 TSP COCOA POWDER

FINELY GRATED ZEST OF 1 SMALL ORANGE

FOR THE CHOUX PASTRY

80G PLAIN FLOUR

40G SALTED BUTTER

2 LARGE EGGS, BEATEN

FOR THE ORANGE CRÈME DIPLOMAT

220ML WHOLE MILK

½ TSP VANILLA BEAN PASTE

4 LARGE EGG YOLKS

50G CASTER SUGAR

50G CORNFLOUR

3–4 TBSP ORANGE LIQUEUR

15 DROPS ORANGE SPICE

100ML DOUBLE CREAM

FOR THE SALTED CARAMEL SAUCE

300G CASTER SUGAR

½ TSP CRUSHED SEA SALT

300ML DOUBLE CREAM

YOU WILL NEED

LARGE PIPING BAG FITTED WITH NO.2 WRITING NOZZLE; 4 BALLOONS; 4 RAMEKINS OR TUMBLERS; LARGE PIPING BAG FITTED WITH A 1.5CM PLAIN NOZZLE; 1 BAKING SHEET LINED WITH BAKING PAPER; 3CM ROUND CUTTER; LARGE PIPING BAG FITTED WITH A DOUGHNUT FILLER NOZZLE

STEP 1 For the chocolate spheres, melt the dark and white chocolate in separate heatproof bowls set over pans of simmering water. Once melted, remove from the heat and pour the white chocolate into the large piping bag fitted with a No.2 writing nozzle.

STEP 2 Inflate the balloons, so they are all the size of large Easter eggs. One at a time, dip the balloons into the bowl of melted dark chocolate, ensuring you get enough coverage to create a dome shape, rather than a shallow bowl shape.

STEP 3 Lift each balloon out of the chocolate and hold over the bowl to allow the excess to drip off. Turn upside down and carefully place the balloons with the tied ends in the ramekins or tumblers.

STEP 4 Pipe the white chocolate in lines over the dark chocolate to create a marbled effect. Chill until ready to serve.

STEP 5 For the craquelin, cream the butter and sugar together in a bowl using an electric hand whisk, until soft and smooth, then use a wooden spoon to fold in the flour, cocoa powder and orange zest to make a dough.

STEP 6 Place the dough between 2 sheets of cling film, then roll out to a rectangle measuring about 20 x 15cm. Freeze the dough sheet while you make the choux pastry.

STEP 7 For the choux pastry, heat the oven to 190°C/170°C fan/375°F/Gas 5. Sift the flour into a bowl. Put the butter and 100ml of water into a medium pan. Set the pan over a low heat until the butter has completely melted – don't let the liquid boil.

STEP 8 Once the butter has melted, turn up the heat bring to the boil, then immediately remove the pan from the heat and quickly add the sifted flour all in one go.

STEP 9 Use a wooden spoon to beat the mixture rapidly to a smooth, glossy dough. Return the pan to a low heat and beat (less rapidly) for 1 minute, until the dough is very thick and forms a ball that leaves the sides of the pan clean.

STEP 10 Tip the dough into a stand mixer and leave until barely warm. Then, gradually add the beaten eggs, beating well after each addition, to a dropping consistency. Stop if the dough starts to become loose – you may not need all the egg.

RECIPE CONTINUES OVERLEAF »»

STEP 11 Spoon the dough into a large piping bag fitted with a 1.5cm plain nozzle and pipe 16 circles each of 4cm diameter on the lined baking sheet, setting them well apart. (You can drawn on the circles with pencil as a guide first, if you like, just make sure the drawn side is face down on the baking sheet before you pipe.)

STEP 12 Remove the craquelin from the freezer and use a 3cm round cutter to cut out 16 discs. Place one on top of each piped choux ring and bake for 20–25 minutes, until puffed, crisp and golden. Remove from the oven and transfer to a wire rack. Make a small hole in the base of each bun (find a cracked spot) with the tip of a small knife or skewer, to allow steam to escape. Leave to cool.

STEP 13 For the orange crème diplomat, pour the milk into a medium pan, add the vanilla bean paste and set over a low heat. Put the egg yolks, sugar and cornflour into a heatproof bowl and whisk for 2–3 minutes, until very smooth and light.

STEP 14 When the milk is steaming hot, pour it slowly into the bowl with the egg mixture, at the same time whisking continuously. When everything is thoroughly combined, tip the mixture back into the pan and set over a medium heat.

STEP 15 Whisk continuously over the heat, until the mixture boils and thickens to a smooth, creamy, thick custard. Remove the pan from the heat.

STEP 16 Pour the custard into a shallow container. Cover the surface with cling film to prevent a skin forming and leave to cool. Once cooled, refrigerate until set.

STEP 17 Once the custard has set, pour the orange liqueur, orange spice drops and double cream into a medium bowl and whisk to soft peaks. Gently fold into the set custard and spoon into a large piping bag fitted with a doughnut filler nozzle.

STEP 18 Pipe the crème diplomat into each choux bun through the steam hole you made in the base. Arrange the choux buns on the 4 serving plates – each plate should have 3 buns in a triangle formation, with a fourth bun crowning the top, in a stack.

STEP 19 For the salted caramel sauce, put the sugar into a medium pan. Add 100ml of water and stir with your fingers until the mixture feels like wet sand. Place over a medium heat and cook, without stirring, until the sugar has dissolved. Increase the heat and boil to a golden caramel, swirling the pan occasionally (but don't stir).

STEP 20 Remove the pan from the heat, add the salt and whisk in the cream (be very careful as it might splatter) until combined. Return the pan to a low heat and keep warm.

STEP 21 Remove the chocolate spheres from the fridge and pop the balloons. Carefully peel the balloons away from the chocolate (this can be tricky – be patient). Use a hot knife to trim the chocolate edges to neaten, if necessary. Place the chocolate domes over the choux buns and serve with a jug of hot salted caramel sauce on the side.

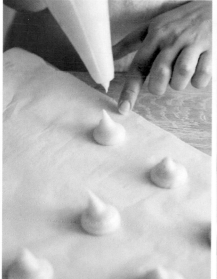

FAMILY MEALTIMES
HUNGARIAN APPLE PIE

Delicious grated apples enclosed in a soft, pillowy pastry, this is apple pie the traditional Hungarian way and perfect for a large family supper or Sunday lunch.

SERVES 16

400G PLAIN FLOUR

1 TSP BAKING POWDER

1 TSP SALT

200G UNSALTED BUTTER, CHILLED AND DICED

ABOUT 200ML SOURED CREAM

WHOLE MILK, FOR BRUSHING

CASTER SUGAR, FOR SPRINKLING

WHIPPED CREAM, TO SERVE (OPTIONAL)

FOR THE FILLING

2KG EATING APPLES, PEELED, CORED AND GRATED

250G CASTER SUGAR

JUICE OF 1 LARGE LEMON

2 TSP GROUND CINNAMON

1 TSP VANILLA EXTRACT

YOU WILL NEED

ROASTING TRAY; 26CM-SQUARE SHALLOW CAKE OR BROWNIE TIN, GREASED

STEP 1 Put the flour, baking powder, salt and butter into a food processor and blitz until the mixture resembles fine crumbs. Add enough soured cream, up to about 200ml, to make a dough.

STEP 2 Divide the dough into 2 pieces, one slightly bigger than the other. Wrap the pieces in cling film and chill for 30 minutes.

STEP 3 Meanwhile, make the filling. Squeeze any excess juice from the grated apple, then put the apple in a large pan with the sugar, lemon juice, cinnamon and vanilla. Place over a medium heat and simmer for 5 minutes, or until the apple is tender. Remove from the heat, spread out on a roasting tray and leave to cool completely.

STEP 4 Heat the oven to 180°C/160°C fan/350°F/Gas 4. Roll out the larger piece of pastry to about a 30cm square and about 3mm thick. Line the prepared tin with the pastry sheet and cover with the cooled apple.

STEP 5 Roll out the remaining pastry to a 26cm square and use this to cover the apples. Crimp the edges to seal, and then use a fork to prick holes all over the top of the pie to allow steam to escape.

STEP 6 Brush the pie with the milk and sprinkle generously with sugar. Bake for 40–45 minutes, or until the pastry is crisp and golden. Cut into 16 squares and serve warm, with whipped cream, if you wish.

AFTER-DINNER MINT SURPRISE ALASKA TARTLETS

These rich tartlets are a sophisticated take on a Baked Alaska. The cocoa-rich pastry needs careful handling, but it's worth the effort.

MAKES 6

FOR THE ICE CREAM

300ML DOUBLE CREAM, WELL CHILLED

150ML CONDENSED MILK

PEPPERMINT EXTRACT, TO TASTE

GREEN FOOD-COLOURING GEL

75G 70% DARK CHOCOLATE, BROKEN UP

FOR THE CHOCOLATE PASTRY

150G PLAIN FLOUR

1/4 TSP SALT

70G COCOA POWDER

90G ICING SUGAR

150G UNSALTED BUTTER, CHILLED AND DICED

2 EGG YOLKS

FOR THE CHOCOLATE FILLING

75G 70% DARK CHOCOLATE, BROKEN INTO PIECES

50G MILK CHOCOLATE, BROKEN INTO PIECES

100ML DOUBLE CREAM

50ML WHOLE MILK

1 EGG

1/2–1 TBSP CRÈME DE MENTHE

FOR THE ITALIAN MERINGUE

3 EGG WHITES

PINCH OF CREAM OF TARTAR

170G CASTER SUGAR

YOU WILL NEED

ICE-CREAM MACHINE; ICE-CREAM SCOOP; FREEZER-PROOF TRAY LINED WITH CLING FILM; DEEP (8 X 2.5CM), LOOSE-BOTTOMED TARTLET TINS X6; BAKING SHEET; BAKING BEANS; HEATPROOF PASTRY BRUSH; SUGAR THERMOMETER; LARGE PIPING BAG FITTED WITH LARGE STAR NOZZLE; KITCHEN BLOWTORCH

STEP 1 To make the ice cream, whisk the cream and condensed milk together in a chilled mixing bowl. Add the peppermint extract to taste, then enough green food colouring to give a 'minty' colour. Whisk until thick and floppy, then pour into the ice-cream machine and churn until semi-frozen.

STEP 2 Blitz the chocolate in a food processor until gravel-like. Add to the semi-frozen ice cream and continue churning until firm. Place in the freezer, checking it every 20 minutes, until firm enough to scoop. Then, scoop 6 balls of ice cream and place them on a cling-film-lined tray. Return the scoops and remaining ice cream to the freezer.

STEP 3 Make the pastry cases. Put the flour, salt, cocoa and icing sugar into a food processor and pulse to combine. Add the butter and blitz until the mixture resembles fine crumbs. Add the egg yolks and 1 tablespoon of water and process to a heavy, slightly sticky dough.

RECIPE CONTINUES OVERLEAF »»

STEP 4 Divide the dough into 6 equal portions. Shape each into a thick disc, then wrap each in cling film and chill for 15–20 minutes, until firm.

STEP 5 Unwrap 1 portion of dough, place it between 2 sheets of baking paper, and roll out to a 15cm disc. Use the disc to line the base and sides of a tartlet tin. Cut off the excess dough and gently ease the pastry above the rim of the tin, then prick the base with a fork. Repeat with the remaining dough portions. Place the tartlet cases on a baking sheet and chill for 15 minutes.

STEP 6 Heat the oven to 180°C/160°C fan/350°F/ Gas 4. Line each chilled pastry case with baking paper. Fill with baking beans and bake blind for 10 minutes, or until the pastry is just set. Remove the paper and beans and return the pastry cases to the oven for a further 7–10 minutes, until firm. Remove from the oven and leave to cool. Reduce the oven temperature to 110°C/ 90°C fan/225°F/Gas ½.

STEP 7 While the tartlets cool, make the filling. Melt both chocolates together in a heatproof bowl set over a pan of simmering water. Remove the bowl from the pan and stir to combine until glossy.

STEP 8 Heat the cream and milk until steaming hot. Whisk the egg in a heatproof bowl until frothy, then whisk in the hot cream mixture. Pour the mixture through a sieve onto the melted chocolate and whisk until smooth. Whisk in the Crème de Menthe to taste, then pour the filling mixture into a jug.

STEP 9 Fill each tartlet with filling, then place in the oven and bake for about 25 minutes, or until the filling has set without a wobble. Remove and cool to room temperature.

STEP 10 When you're ready to assemble, make the meringue. Put the egg whites and cream of tartar into the bowl of a stand mixer. Put the sugar into a small pan with 85ml of water over a low heat. Melt gently, stirring occasionally, until clear (brush down the sides with the heatproof pastry brush as necessary).

STEP 11 Boil the syrup rapidly for 5 minutes, or until it reaches 116°C/241°F on the sugar thermometer. While the syrup is boiling, whisk the egg whites to soft peaks. Pour the hot syrup over the egg whites in a thin stream, whisking at full speed. Continue whisking until the meringue is thick and glossy and cooled to room temperature.

STEP 12 Transfer the meringue to the large piping bag fitted with the large star nozzle. Place the tartlets on a serving platter. Place a scoop of ice cream in the middle of each tartlet, then pipe meringue over the top to encase. Use a kitchen blowtorch to give the meringue a golden-brown finish. Decorate with mint leaves and serve immediately.

MERINGUE FROM THE ARCHIVES

RAINBOW MERINGUE CENTREPIECE

A simplified version of our meringue sculpture challenge, this golden meringue nest is filled with mango and passionfruit cream, puddles of blueberry jam and an abundance of colourful fresh fruit.

SERVES 10-12

FOR THE MERINGUE

4 EGG WHITES

½ TSP CREAM OF TARTAR

LARGE PINCH OF SALT

250G GOLDEN CASTER SUGAR

¾ TSP VANILLA EXTRACT

2 TSP CORNFLOUR

FOR THE BLUEBERRY PUDDLES

200G BLUEBERRIES

200G CASTER SUGAR

1 TSP LEMON JUICE

FOR THE FRESH FRUIT SALAD

2 LARGE RIPE MANGOES,
PEELED STONED, AND FLESH
CUT INTO 5MM SLICES

2 KIWI FRUIT, PEELED, CORED AND
CUT INTO CHUNKS OR SLICES

125G CHERRIES OR RED SEEDLESS
GRAPES, HALVED IF LARGE

400G RED BERRIES, SUCH AS
STRAWBERRIES (HALVED AND
HULLED IF LARGE), RASPBERRIES,
TAYBERRIES AND BLACKBERRIES

FOR THE MANGO &
PASSIONFRUIT CREAM

300ML DOUBLE CREAM,
WELL CHILLED

2 TBSP ICING SUGAR, SIFTED

125G MANGO TRIMMINGS
(FROM FRUIT SALAD, ABOVE),
FINELY DICED

3 PASSIONFRUIT, SEEDS
AND PULP SCOOPED

YOU WILL NEED

LARGE BAKING SHEET LINED
WITH A 23CM CIRCLE
OF BAKING PAPER; 2.5CM
HEART-SHAPED CUTTER

STEP 1 Heat the oven to 140°C/120°C fan/275°F/ Gas 1. To make the meringue, put the egg whites into a large bowl or the bowl of a stand mixer and whisk at medium speed for about 20 seconds, or until frothy.

STEP 2 Add the cream of tartar and the salt and whisk on full speed until the whites form soft peaks. Whisk in half the sugar 1 tablespoon at a time, plus the vanilla, and keep whisking just until the whites form firm peaks. Sift in the rest of the sugar and the cornflour and fold in by hand.

STEP 3 Spoon the mixture onto the prepared baking sheet and gently spread to make a nest-like disc 23cm in diameter, with a deep bowl of about 12cm diameter in the middle and about 4cm high at the sides.

STEP 4 Bake for about 1½ hours, or until very crisp on the outside and soft in the centre of the thick edges. If the meringue starts to turn brown, turn down the oven for the remaining baking time. Allow the meringue to cool in the oven, with the door closed, to help prevent cracking.

STEP 5 Meanwhile, make the blueberry puddles. Put the blueberries, sugar, lemon juice and 2 tablespoons of water into a medium pan over a low heat. Stir occasionally until the sugar dissolves.

STEP 6 Bring to the boil and cook rapidly, stirring frequently, for about 5 minutes, until the mixture is thick like soft-set jam with some visible berries. Transfer to a heatproof bowl, leave to cool, then cover and chill.

STEP 7 Meanwhile, prepare the fruit salad. Cut the mango slices into hearts using the shaped cutter, then combine all the fruit together in a large bowl. Chill until needed.

STEP 8 To make the mango and passionfruit cream, pour the cream into a large bowl or the bowl of a stand mixer and whip until it forms very soft peaks. Add the icing sugar and whip again to bring back to soft peaks. Combine the diced mango trimmings and passionfruit seeds and pulp in a small bowl, then fold into the cream.

STEP 9 To assemble the dessert, peel the meringue nest away from the lining paper and place it on a very large serving platter. Gently stir the mango cream, then spoon it into the hollow of the meringue nest. Pile all the prepared fruits and berries on top, letting them spill over the edges of the nest.

STEP 10 Finally, stir the blueberry jam and spoon or drizzle it in small puddles over the filled meringue nest and down the sides. Serve as soon as possible.

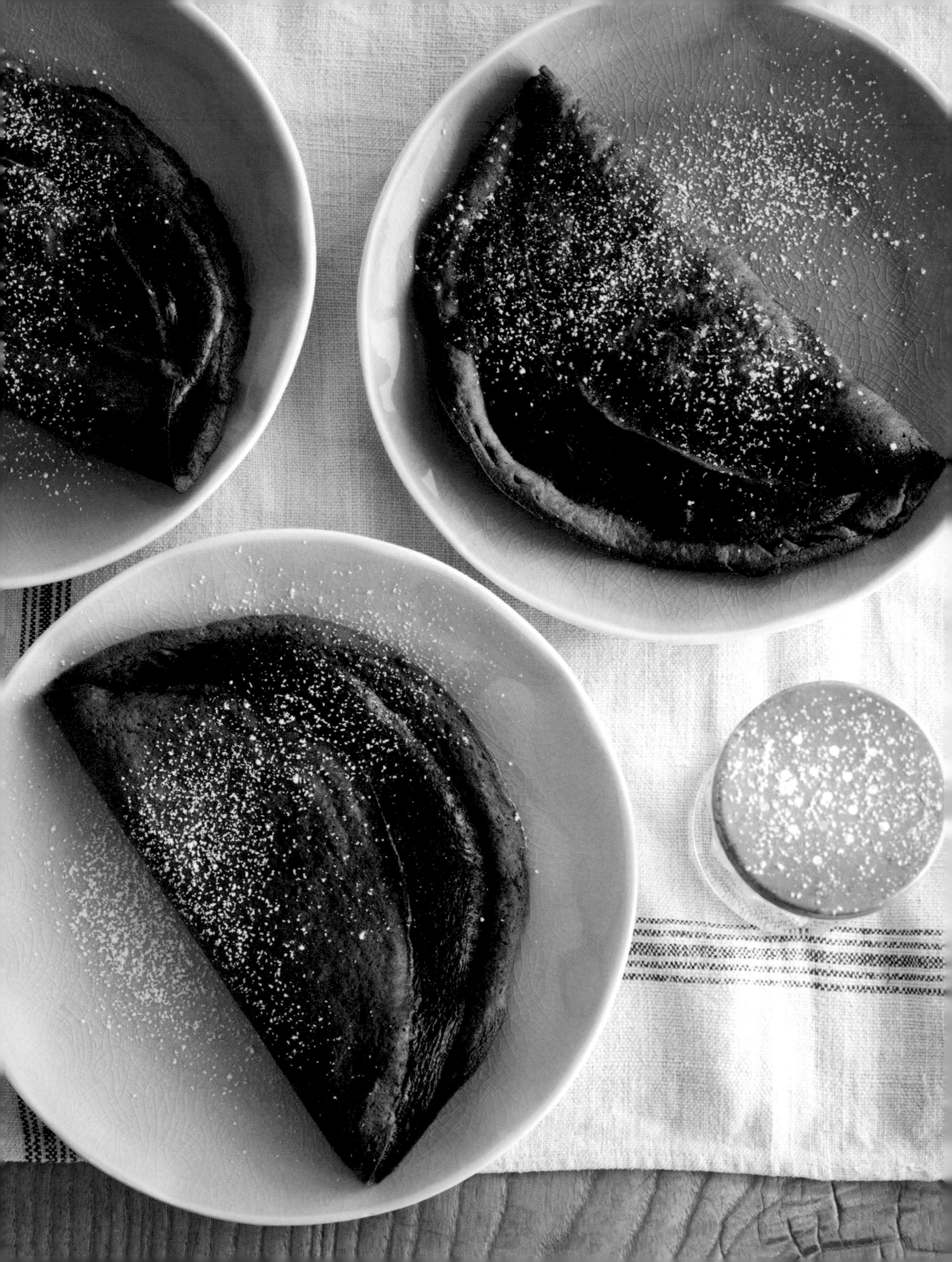

CHOCOLATE SOUFFLÉ CRÊPES

These look so swish when you serve them up, but they're super-easy to make.

MAKES 4

100G PLAIN FLOUR

15G COCOA POWDER

85G CASTER SUGAR

2 EGGS

1 TBSP VEGETABLE OIL

100ML WHOLE MILK

UNSALTED BUTTER, FOR GREASING

FOR THE FILLING

50G 70% DARK CHOCOLATE, MELTED AND COOLED SLIGHTLY

1 EGG YOLK

3 EGG WHITES

ICING SUGAR, FOR DUSTING

YOU WILL NEED

18CM CRÊPE PAN; 2 BAKING SHEETS

STEP 1 Whisk the flour, cocoa powder, sugar, eggs, oil and milk together in a bowl to make a smooth batter. Set aside to rest for 20 minutes, until all the bubbles have subsided.

STEP 2 Heat the crêpe pan, then lightly grease with a little butter. Add ¼ of the batter, swirl it around the pan and cook over a medium heat for about 2 minutes on each side, until cooked through.

STEP 3 Remove the cooked crêpe to a plate lined with baking paper and place another sheet of baking paper on top. Set aside while you repeat to make 4 crêpes altogether, each time stacking the cooked crêpe between sheets of baking paper.

STEP 4 Heat the oven to 220°C/200°C fan/425°F/Gas 7. For the filling, beat the melted chocolate and egg yolk together in a bowl, then set aside. Whisk the egg whites until stiff but not dry, then carefully fold them into the chocolate mixture, taking care to retain as much air in the mixture as possible without any pockets of egg white.

STEP 5 Arrange 2 crêpes on each baking sheet. Fill ½ of each crêpe with the chocolate soufflé mixture, then fold over the other ½ of each crêpe to enclose.

STEP 6 Bake the filled crêpes for 5 minutes, until the soufflé mixture has puffed up and cooked through. Remove from the oven and dust with icing sugar before serving.

RHUBARB CRUMBLE CHEESECAKE

What could be better? Rhubarb crumble and cheesecake all in one bite.

SERVES 8–10

FOR THE PASTRY

50G CHOPPED HAZELNUTS

185G PLAIN FLOUR

125G CASTER SUGAR

60G UNSALTED BUTTER, CHILLED AND DICED

1 EGG YOLK

1–2 TBSP CHILLED WATER

FOR THE FILLING

600G RHUBARB, ROUGHLY CHOPPED

JUICE OF 1 LEMON

2 TBSP CASTER SUGAR

900G FULL-FAT CREAM CHEESE

125G CASTER SUGAR

1 TSP VANILLA EXTRACT

150ML SOURED CREAM

1 TSP GROUND GINGER

4 EGGS

FOR THE CRUMBLE TOPPING

100G PLAIN FLOUR

100G CASTER SUGAR

1 TSP GROUND GINGER

50G UNSALTED BUTTER, CHILLED AND DICED

YOU WILL NEED

23CM SPRINGFORM TIN; BAKING SHEET

STEP 1 To make the pastry, put the chopped hazelnuts in a food processor and grind to a fine crumb. Add the flour, sugar and butter and blitz to a crumb. Add the egg yolk and enough chilled water, a little at a time, to make a dough. Wrap in cling film and chill for 30 minutes.

STEP 2 Roll out the dough on a lightly floured worktop to 3mm thick. Use to line the base and sides of the cake tin, leaving the pastry overhanging. Chill for 20 minutes, then trim the pastry in line with the top of the tin.

STEP 3 Heat the oven to 180°C/160°C fan/350°F/ Gas 4 and put a baking sheet on the middle shelf. To make the filling, put the rhubarb, lemon juice and 2 tablespoons of sugar in an ovenproof dish. Cover with foil and bake for 40 minutes, until tender. Pass through a sieve and leave the rhubarb to go cold, reserving the syrup.

STEP 4 Using a hand-held electric whisk, beat the cream cheese, sugar, vanilla, soured cream, ginger and eggs together until smooth. Whisk in the rhubarb, then pour the filling into the chilled pastry case. Place the tart on the hot baking sheet in the oven and bake for 40 minutes, until set.

STEP 5 Make the crumble topping. Put the flour, sugar and ginger into a bowl and rub in the butter until the mixture resembles fine crumbs.

STEP 6 Remove the cheesecake from the oven and sprinkle over the crumble topping. Bake for a further 30 minutes, until golden and crumbly.

STEP 7 Turn off the oven and leave the cheesecake in the oven for 2 hours to cool, then transfer to the fridge to chill until completely cold. Release the tin and transfer the cheesecake onto a serving plate. Serve with the rhubarb syrup.

MOCHA & CHOCOLATE-LAYERED REFRIGERATOR CAKE

This dessert doesn't actually need baking so it is beautifully easy to make. Simply layer, then chill.

SERVES 12

FOR THE MOCHA LAYER

750G MILK OR DARK CHOCOLATE DIGESTIVE BISCUITS, VERY ROUGHLY CRUSHED

150ML HOT ESPRESSO OR STRONG RICH COFFEE

FOR THE CHOCOLATE GANACHE LAYER

300ML DOUBLE CREAM

300G 70% DARK CHOCOLATE, BROKEN INTO SMALL PIECES

FOR THE CREAM-CHEESE LAYER

600G FULL-FAT CREAM CHEESE

600ML DOUBLE CREAM

250G ICING SUGAR

1 TSP VANILLA PASTE

50G 70% DARK CHOCOLATE, MELTED, TO DECORATE

YOU WILL NEED

23 X 33CM RECTANGULAR BAKING TIN (ABOUT 5CM DEEP)

STEP 1 Make the mocha layer. Tip the crushed biscuits into a large bowl and sprinkle over the hot coffee. Stir until the biscuits have absorbed the coffee, then set aside.

STEP 2 Make the chocolate ganache layer. Put the cream in a medium pan over a medium heat, and bring to the boil. Remove from the heat, add the chocolate and stir until the chocolate has melted and the mixture is smooth. Leave for 5 minutes, until thickened, but still spreadable. Set aside.

STEP 3 Make the cream-cheese layer. Put the cream cheese in a bowl and using an electric hand whisk, gradually whisk in the cream, then the icing sugar and vanilla paste until the mixture has thickened to form soft peaks.

STEP 4 To assemble, spread ⅓ of the crushed biscuits into the base of the baking tin, creating an even layer. Spoon over ⅓ of the chocolate ganache and level with a palette knife, then spread with ⅓ of the cream-cheese mixture and level again.

STEP 5 Repeat the layers, ending with a cream-cheese layer. Cover with cling film and refrigerate overnight, until the cake is firm enough to cut without falling apart.

STEP 6 To decorate the final cream-cheese layer, drizzle spoonfuls of melted chocolate over the top of the refrigerator cake. Serve chilled.

STRAWBERRY RICOTTA TORTE

Make this easy family dessert when English strawberries are at their best and you can pick your own.

SERVES 8–12

FOR THE BASE

75G SELF-RAISING FLOUR

75G CASTER SUGAR

75G GROUND ALMONDS

50G UNSALTED BUTTER, DICED

1 EGG, BEATEN

FOR THE FILLING

250G RICOTTA CHEESE

2 EGGS

150ML DOUBLE CREAM

50G CASTER SUGAR

1 TSP VANILLA EXTRACT

400G STRAWBERRIES, HULLED AND HALVED

ICING SUGAR, FOR DUSTING

YOU WILL NEED

20CM SPRINGFORM TIN, GREASED, THEN BASE-LINED WITH BAKING PAPER

STEP 1 Make the base. Tip the flour, sugar, almonds and butter into the bowl of a food processor and blitz until the mixture resembles fine crumbs. Add ½ the egg and pulse to a wet dough.

STEP 2 Using a spatula, scrape the dough into the base of the lined springform tin. Spread it out to fill the tin, level off with the back of a spoon and chill for 15 minutes. Heat the oven to 190°C/170°C fan/375°F/ Gas 5.

STEP 3 Once chilled, bake the base for 25 minutes, or until risen and a skewer inserted into the centre comes out clean. Remove from the oven and set aside while you make the filling.

STEP 4 Lower the oven temperature to 160°C/ 140°C fan/315°F/Gas 2. Put the ricotta into the bowl of a stand mixer fitted with the beater attachment. Add the eggs and the remaining beaten egg (from the pastry), along with the double cream, sugar and vanilla, and beat together until smooth.

STEP 5 Pour the filling mixture into the cooked torte base and bake for 50 minutes, or until the filling has set.Remove the torte from the oven and leave to cool completely in the tin.

STEP 6 Once cool, release the sides of the tin and transfer the torte to a serving plate. Fill with the strawberries, then dust with icing sugar to serve.

BAKER'S RECIPE

MANGO, PASSIONFRUIT & APRICOT ROULADE

This roulade is topped with culinary science in the form of mango spheres. If you're short of time, though, you can replace them with tinned apricot halves.

SERVES 8

- 4 LARGE EGG WHITES
- 225G CASTER SUGAR
- ICING SUGAR, FOR DUSTING

FOR THE MANGO SPHERES

- 6G CALCIUM LACTATE
- ½ RIPE MANGO, PEELED, STONED AND ROUGHLY CHOPPED
- 2 TBSP VEGETABLE OIL
- 1 LITRE SODIUM ALGINATE

FOR THE CURD

- 4 PASSIONFRUITS, HALVED
- 30ML LIME JUICE
- 80G CASTER SUGAR
- 40G UNSALTED BUTTER
- 1 LARGE EGG, BEATEN
- 1 LARGE EGG YOLK, BEATEN

FOR THE FILLING

- 150G GOOD-QUALITY WHITE CHOCOLATE, CHOPPED
- 300ML DOUBLE CREAM
- ½ LARGE, RIPE MANGO, PEELED AND STONED

YOU WILL NEED

- 6-HOLE ROUND ICE-CUBE TRAY; 20 X 30CM SWISS ROLL TIN, GREASED, THEN LINED WITH BAKING PAPER; SMALL DISPOSABLE PIPING BAG; SMALL PIPING BAG FITTED WITH A MEDIUM STAR NOZZLE

STEP 1 Start the mango spheres. Mix the calcium lactate in a bowl with 50ml of water. Place the mango in a blender and add the calcium lactate mixture. Blend to a purée. Pour the purée into the round ice cube tray and freeze for at least 1½ hours.

STEP 2 To make the roulade meringue, heat the oven to 180°C/160°C fan/350°F/ Gas 4. Whisk the egg whites until stiff, but not dry. Add the sugar, 1 teaspoon at a time, until it is all incorporated and the mixture is stiff, smooth and glossy. Spoon into the lined tin and level with a palette knife. Bake for 25–30 minutes, until the top is lightly golden brown.

STEP 3 For the curd, scrape out the passionfruit seeds into a food processor and gently pulse to separate the seeds from the juicy bits. Put the passionfruit, lime juice, sugar and butter into a heatproof bowl over a pan of simmering water. Stir occasionally until the butter has melted.

STEP 4 Using a small whisk or fork, stir in the beaten egg and egg yolk. Gently whisk the mixture over the heat for about 10 minutes, until thickened like custard.

STEP 5 Remove the bowl from the heat and pass the custard through a sieve into a clean bowl, then leave to cool.

STEP 6 For the filling, melt the white chocolate in a bowl over a pan of simmering water. Spoon 2 tablespoons of the melted chocolate into a small disposable piping bag and set aside. In a separate bowl, whisk the cream to soft peaks, then fold the cream into the remaining melted chocolate. Chop the mango into ½cm cubes.

STEP 7 Remove the meringue from the oven and turn it out onto a clean tea towel lined with a sheet of baking paper dusted with icing sugar. Peel the lining paper from the base and leave the meringue to cool for 5–10 minutes.

RECIPE CONTINUES OVERLEAF »

STEP 8 Spread ¾ of the white chocolate cream over the meringue, then spread the curd over the cream and scatter with mango cubes. Spoon the remaining cream into a small piping bag fitted with a medium star nozzle.

STEP 9 Using the tea towel, carefully roll up the meringue from the short edge, then transfer to a serving plate.

STEP 10 To finish the mango spheres, fill 2 small bowls with water and put the vegetable oil in a third. Put the sodium alginate in a large bowl.

STEP 11 Turn out 3 of the mango ice spheres and place them in the sodium alginate. Swirl them around with a spoon for 3 minutes.

STEP 12 Carefully lift the spheres out of the sodium alginate and place into one of the bowls of water for 1 minute. Lift out and place in the second bowl of water for 1 minute. Then, place in the vegetable oil and leave until needed. Repeat steps 11 and 12 with the remaining mango ice spheres.

STEP 13 To serve, pipe 6 rings of white chocolate cream in a line along the centre of the top of the roulade. Sit a mango sphere on top of each ring. Snip the end of the small disposable piping bag and pipe fine lines of white chocolate over the mango spheres. Dust with icing sugar before serving.

CHAPTER FIVE

SWEET PASTRY
AND
PATISSERIE

Few things are as irresistible as exquisitely decorated sweet pastries and patisserie.

In this chapter you can travel all around the world from the comfort of your own kitchen. Head to Scandinavia via Danish Dreams and Danish Kleiner, or to Hungary with an Esterhazy Torte. The best recipes from some of the Series 8 bakers will transport you to Italy with scrumptious Gianduja Cannoli and the intricate shell-like *sfogliatelle*, which are flavoured with ginger and chocolate.

Paul and Prue also have two recipes for you to try at home – nutty, fragrant Middle Eastern Ma'amoul pastries, and historical Puits d'Amour, a combination of puff and choux pastry guaranteed to intrigue your loved ones.

We know that patisserie can be daunting, but we've laid out the methods in an easy-to-follow and digestible form. Work your way through and by the end you will have a huge array of delicious and impressive recipes in your baking repertoire.

BAKER'S RECIPE

GIANDUJA CANNOLI

These crisp cinnamon cannoli shells are filled with a combination of roasted hazelnuts, milk chocolate, mascarpone and ricotta.

MAKES ABOUT 24

280G PLAIN FLOUR

50G CASTER SUGAR

¼ TSP GROUND CINNAMON

25G SOLID 100% VEGETABLE BAKING FAT, DICED

2 EGGS, 1 SEPARATED

4 TBSP MARSALA WINE

1 TSP DISTILLED WHITE VINEGAR

ABOUT 2 LITRES SUNFLOWER OIL, FOR DEEP FRYING

150G MILK CHOCOLATE, FINELY CHOPPED, TO DECORATE

100G ROASTED CHOPPED HAZELNUTS, TO DECORATE

ICING SUGAR, FOR DUSTING

FOR THE GIANDUJA FILLING

125G ROASTED HAZELNUT BUTTER

100G MILK CHOCOLATE, FINELY CHOPPED

250G MASCARPONE CHEESE

250G RICOTTA CHEESE

YOU WILL NEED

PASTA-ROLLING MACHINE; 10CM ROUND CUTTER; DEEP-FAT FRYER; COOKING THERMOMETER; AT LEAST 3 CANNOLO TUBES (ABOUT 10 X 2.6CM), LIGHTLY GREASED WITH SUNFLOWER OIL; HEATPROOF TONGS; BAKING PAPER; LARGE DISPOSABLE PIPING BAG

STEP 1 Sift the flour, sugar and cinnamon into the bowl of a stand mixer fitted with the paddle attachment. Add the baking fat and work in on slow speed until combined, then make a well. Combine 1 whole egg plus 1 yolk, the Marsala and the vinegar in a small bowl, then pour into the well. Mix to a firm dough.

STEP 2 Turn out the dough onto a lightly floured worktop and knead for 8–10 minutes, until smooth and pliable. Wrap in cling film and leave to rest for 30 minutes.

STEP 3 Meanwhile, make the filling. Blitz the hazelnut butter and the chopped chocolate in a food processor to a smooth paste. Spoon the mascarpone and ricotta into a mixing bowl and stir well. Add the hazelnut mixture and mix thoroughly. Cover and chill.

STEP 4 Divide the dough into 6. Take 1 portion, flatten it, and run it through the widest setting on a pasta machine. Fold it in 3 and re-roll, then fold and roll again. Reduce the setting to the next widest and run the dough through. Repeat until the dough is as thin as it can be, then lay the strip of dough out along a lightly floured worktop. Repeat for all the dough portions.

STEP 5 Use a floured cutter to stamp out discs from the dough until you have at least 24 discs (allow for breakages).

STEP 6 Heat the oil in a deep-fat fryer to 180°C/350°F. Roll 1 disc around a cannolo tube and fix the join with a dab of beaten egg white. Use tongs to lower the tube into the oil and fry for 1 minute, or until crisp and golden. Remove, cool on a wire rack lined with kitchen paper, then, when cool enough to handle, ease the tube out of the shell.

STEP 7 Cook the cannoli in batches of 3, making sure the oil comes back up to temperature each time.

STEP 8 To decorate, melt the chopped chocolate in a bowl over a pan of simmering water. Remove from the heat and stir until the chocolate is smooth. Put the chopped nuts in a dish. One at a time, dip both ends of each cannolo in the melted chocolate and then in the nuts. Put aside to set.

STEP 9 Fill the cannoli just before serving. Transfer the filling to a piping bag, snipping a 1.5cm opening at the end. Pipe the filling into both ends of each cannolo, filling all the way through. Dust with icing sugar and serve.

PRUE'S MINCE PIES

The lattice on these mince pies is really impressive, but you can top with a simple pastry lid if you prefer.

MAKES 12

170G PLAIN FLOUR

100G UNSALTED BUTTER, DICED

2 TBSP ICING SUGAR

1 EGG YOLK

2 TBSP CHILLED WATER

1 EGG, BEATEN

FOR THE MINCEMEAT

25G RAISINS

25G SULTANAS

25G DRIED FIGS, CHOPPED

15G CHOPPED MIXED PEEL

1 PIECE OF STEM GINGER, FINELY CHOPPED

20G PECANS, CHOPPED

¼ TSP MIXED SPICE

1 TBSP WHISKY

25G SOFT LIGHT BROWN SUGAR

20G UNSALTED BUTTER, MELTED

1 SMALL FIRM PEAR, GRATED

FOR THE BRANDY BUTTER

125G UNSALTED BUTTER

125G ICING SUGAR, PLUS EXTRA FOR DUSTING (OPTIONAL)

GRATED RIND OF ½ AN UNWAXED ORANGE

3 TBSP BRANDY

YOU WILL NEED

12-HOLE ROUND-BOTTOMED MINCE PIE TIN; 10CM ROUND CUTTER

STEP 1 Make the pastry. Sift the flour into a mixing bowl. Then, using your fingertips, rub in the butter until the mixture resembles fine crumbs. Stir in the icing sugar.

STEP 2 Mix the egg yolk and chilled water together and stir into the flour mixture first with a table knife, then with one hand. Add a little more water, if necessary, but the pastry should not be damp.

STEP 3 Divide the pastry into 2 balls, wrap them in cling film and chill for 30 minutes.

STEP 4 Make the mincemeat. Mix the raisins, sultanas, figs, mixed peel, ginger, pecans, mixed spice, whisky, sugar and butter together in a bowl, then fold in the grated pear.

STEP 5 To make the brandy butter, cream the butter and sugar together, until very light. Mix in the orange rind and brandy. Chill until needed.

STEP 6 Heat the oven to 200°C/180°C fan/400°F/ Gas 6. Unwrap 1 ball of pastry and roll out on a lightly floured worktop until 3mm thick.

STEP 7 Cut the pastry into 10cm rounds and use them to line a 12-hole mince pie tin, re-rolling the trimmings as necessary.

STEP 8 Fill each pie case ¾ full with mincemeat. Roll out the other half of the pastry, along with any remaining trimmings, and cut into 108 small strips, ½cm wide and a little longer than the diameter of the holes in your mince pie tin.

STEP 9 Weave 9 strips to create a 5 x 4 lattice the same size as the top of the mince pie. Repeat until you have 12 completed lattices.

STEP 10 Dampen the edges of the pastry cases with a little water and top each with a lattice. Press down lightly on the edges to seal, then trim to neaten. Brush the tops with beaten egg and bake for 15–20 minutes, until golden.

STEP 11 Remove from the oven and leave to cool in the tin for 5 minutes. Transfer the mince pies to a wire rack and leave to cool completely. Dust with icing sugar, if you like, and serve with brandy butter.

MINI NEAPOLITAN RUM BABAS

These delicate, light and airy little yeast cakes are soaked in rum. Enjoy them like the Neapolitans – with friends and an espresso.

MAKES 8

200G STRONG WHITE BREAD FLOUR

100G UNSALTED BUTTER, SOFTENED

2 TSP FAST-ACTION DRIED YEAST

½ TSP FINE SEA SALT

3 TBSP CASTER SUGAR, PLUS EXTRA FOR LINING THE MOULDS

85ML WHOLE MILK, WARMED

1 LARGE EGG

1 TSP VANILLA PASTE

FOR THE RUM SYRUP

250G CASTER SUGAR

100ML DARK RUM

TO SERVE

150ML DOUBLE CREAM

75G ICING SUGAR, SIFTED

½ TSP VANILLA PASTE

8 RASPBERRIES

YOU WILL NEED

8 SMALL (5 X 5.5CM) DARIOLE MOULDS, GREASED; MEDIUM PIPING BAG FITTED WITH SMALL STAR NOZZLE

STEP 1 Place the flour, butter, yeast, salt and sugar in the bowl of a stand mixer fitted with a dough hook. Begin to mix on a slow speed. Add the warm milk, egg and vanilla paste and continue mixing until all the ingredients are incorporated.

STEP 2 Increase the speed to medium and mix for 5 minutes, until the dough is very soft and sticky. Remove the bowl from the mixer, cover with cling film and leave to prove for at least 2 hours, until doubled in size (the longer you leave the dough, the lighter your babas will be).

STEP 3 Divide the dough equally between the prepared moulds so that each hollow is ¾ full. Prove for 2–4 hours, until the dough rises just above the mould edge.

STEP 4 Meanwhile, make the syrup. Put the sugar in a pan with 250ml of water and heat gently, until the sugar has dissolved, taking care not to let the sugar boil. Turn off the heat, add the rum and stir to combine. Transfer the syrup to a shallow dish.

STEP 5 Heat your oven to 200°C/180°C fan/400°F/Gas 6. Once the baba doughs have risen above the edges of the mould, place them in the oven and bake for 10–12 minutes, or until risen and light golden brown. Remove from the oven, then leave to cool for 5 minutes in the mould before removing and cooling completely.

STEP 6 One at a time, place the babas in the syrup. Turn them that so they are soaked all the way through. Set aside until ready to serve.

STEP 7 To serve, whip the cream with the icing sugar and vanilla paste until it is firm enough to pipe. Transfer the flavoured cream to a piping bag fitted with a star nozzle. Slice each baba vertically from the top to open up, but don't cut all the way through. Pipe cream into the centre, decorate with a raspberry and serve immediately.

PATISSERIE FROM THE ARCHIVES

CHOCOLATE & GINGER SFOGLIATELLE

These seashell-shaped pastries from southern Italy are regarded as a challenge for every good pastry chef. A multi-layered roll of pastry is sliced, then opened out to make a clam shell and baked with a rich, sweet ricotta filling.

MAKES ABOUT 24

FOR THE PASTRY

500G VERY STRONG WHITE
BREAD FLOUR

1 TSP SALT

ABOUT 125G LARD, SOFTENED,
FOR BRUSHING

ABOUT 50G UNSALTED BUTTER
OR VEGETABLE FAT, SOFTENED,
FOR SHAPING

ICING SUGAR, FOR DUSTING

FOR THE FILLING

250G RICOTTA CHEESE

250ML WHOLE MILK

100G CASTER SUGAR

2 GOOD PINCHES OF SALT

¼ TSP GROUND CINNAMON

40G FINE SEMOLINA

2 EGG YOLKS

FINELY GRATED ZEST OF
1 SMALL UNWAXED ORANGE

100G 70% DARK CHOCOLATE
CHIPS

4 PIECES OF STEM GINGER,
DRAINED AND FINELY CHOPPED

YOU WILL NEED

PASTA-ROLLING MACHINE; SMALL
PIECE OF CHEESECLOTH OR
MUSLIN; 2 LARGE BAKING SHEETS
LINED WITH BAKING PAPER

STEP 1 Sift the flour and salt into the bowl of a stand mixer fitted with the paddle attachment. Make a well in the centre and, with the mixer on its slowest setting, pour in 165ml of water. As the dough starts to come together, gradually add more water, up to about 60ml, to make a firm dough.

STEP 2 Turn out the dough onto a lightly floured worktop and knead for 3 minutes, then cover with an upturned bowl and leave to rest for 5 minutes. Repeat the kneading and resting twice more, until the dough is smooth and pliable. Divide the dough into 8, wrap each piece in cling film and refrigerate for 2 hours.

STEP 3 Take 1 portion of dough and knead it to a flat disc. Run it through the widest setting on the pasta roller then fold in 3, turn it 90 degrees and run through the roller again. Repeat 3 more times, until the dough is very smooth and pliable. Adjust the rollers to the next widest setting and run the dough through again. Keep rolling out the dough, decreasing the width setting each time, until on the narrowest setting.

STEP 4 Place the dough strip on the worktop and gently pull it out – first from one end, then at the centre portion to double the width, then at the other end. The dough will be an odd shape and may have a tear, but that's fine. Brush very lightly with softened lard.

STEP 5 Tightly roll up the dough like a Swiss roll, starting at one end, and slightly stretching the dough by pulling towards you as go. It will have a thick middle and 2 straggly ends. Gently pull on the ends to make the roll a bit longer and thinner.

STEP 6 Roll out a second portion of dough, exactly as before. Place the previously rolled dough at one end of the new strip. Use the new strip to extend the roll, pulling and stretching as you roll, as in Step 5.

STEP 7 Repeat until you have rolled out, stretched, brushed with lard and rolled together all 8 dough portions to make one big roll. Then, gently pull, squeeze and stretch the roll to about 36 x 6cm, with straggly ends. Brush the whole roll with lard, then wrap in cling film and chill for at least 2 hours, preferably overnight.

RECIPE CONTINUES OVERLEAF »»

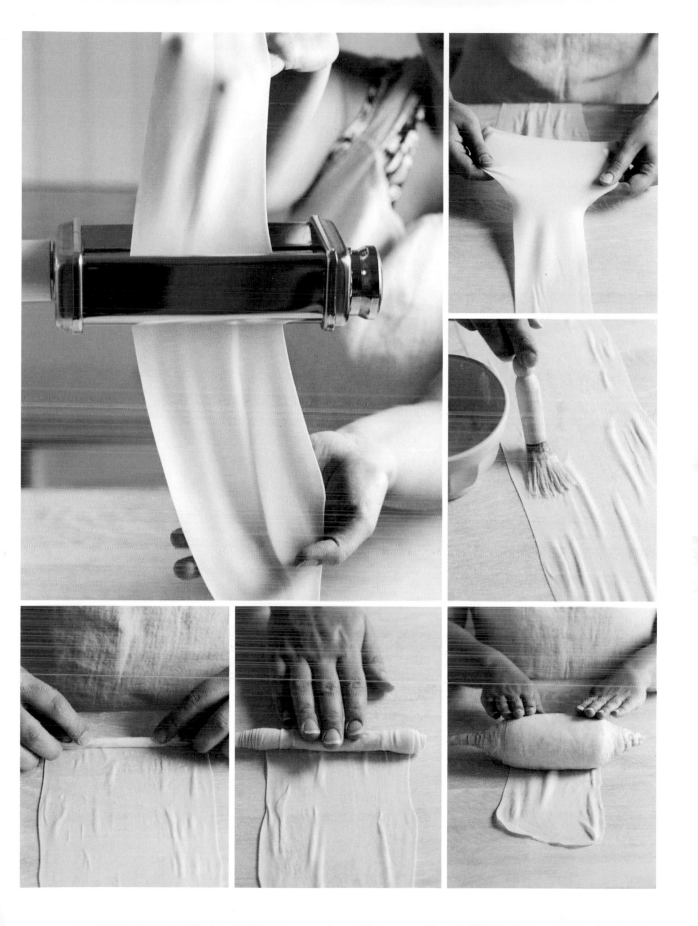

STEP 8 To make the filling, line a sieve with cheesecloth or muslin and set it over a bowl. Put the ricotta into the sieve, cover with the excess cheesecloth, set a small saucer, then a heavy weight on top. Chill for at least 1–2 hours to drain the cheese.

STEP 9 Pour the milk into a medium pan, add the sugar, salt and cinnamon and bring to the boil. Sprinkle in the semolina, stirring continuously over a medium–low heat for about 5 minutes, until the mixture is very thick. Tip into a heatproof bowl, press a piece of cling film onto the surface to prevent a skin forming and leave until cold.

STEP 10 Tip the cooled semolina mixture into the bowl of a stand mixer fitted with the paddle attachment. Mix on a medium–high speed until very smooth. Add the egg yolks and the drained ricotta and combine thoroughly, then mix in the orange zest, chocolate and ginger. Transfer to a clean bowl, cover and chill until ready to assemble.

STEP 11 To assemble, unwrap the dough and cut off the straggly ends. Cut the roll into discs about 1cm thick. Grease your fingers, hold a disc between your thumbs and forefingers, and gently start to separate the layers – starting from the centre and working out to the edges – to form a cone shape, with the centre of the disc making the point, and creating an opening of about 7cm in diameter.

STEP 12 Spoon in a heaped teaspoon of filling, making sure the filling reaches down into the tip. Gently pinch the opening to seal it. Repeat with the remaining discs, then arrange them on the lined baking sheets and chill for 20 minutes, or until firm. Heat the oven to 230°C/ 210°C fan/450°F/Gas 8.

STEP 13 Bake for 10 minutes, then rotate the sheets and reduce the temperature to 220°C/200°C fan/425°F/ Gas 7. Bake for a further 5–8 minutes, until golden and crisp. Transfer to a wire rack, dust with icing sugar and leave to cool. Serve just warm.

CHOCOLATE PALMIERS

The name 'palmiers' – from the French for palm tree – refers to the shape of these crunchy, buttery pastries, also known as elephants' ears! Deeply indulgent with chocolate on the inside, they are irresistible.

MAKES 20

....

50G ICING SUGAR

....

25G COCOA POWDER

....

3 TBSP GRANULATED SUGAR

....

500G HOMEMADE PUFF PASTRY (SEE P.309) OR GOOD-QUALITY SHOP-BOUGHT PUFF PASTRY

....

1 EGG, BEATEN

....

YOU WILL NEED

....

2 BAKING SHEETS LINED WITH BAKING PAPER; WATER SPRAY; BAKING PAPER FOR WRAPPING

....

STEP 1 Mix the icing sugar and cocoa together in a small bowl. Set aside.

STEP 2 Scatter half the granulated sugar on your worktop, place the pastry over the top and roll it out into a rectangle, approximately 25 x 30cm.

STEP 3 Brush the pastry with a little of the beaten egg. Then, hold a fine sieve over the pastry and tip in the icing sugar and cocoa mixture. Using the sieve, sprinkle it over the pastry, then spray with water, to help the sugar stick.

STEP 4 With the short end of the pastry facing you, take one long edge in each hand and gently roll the long edges inwards until they meet in the middle. Seal the join with a little beaten egg. Wrap the rolled pastry in baking paper and then place in the fridge for at least 30 minutes.

STEP 5 Heat your oven to 200°C/180°C fan/400°F/ Gas 6. Remove the pastry roll from the fridge. Cut 1.5cm-thick slices all along the length and place the slices, cut sides up, on the prepared sheets, leaving space for expansion between each slice. Brush the slices with the remaining egg and sprinkle with the remaining granulated sugar.

STEP 6 Bake the slices for 10–15 minutes, then remove from the oven and turn them over, and cook the other side for about 5–7 minutes, until crisp and golden. Remove from the oven and transfer to a wire rack to cool.

EASY ESPRESSO TART

With no actual baking required, this decadent tart is super-easy to make and tastes as good as it looks.

SERVES 12

75G AMARETTI BISCUITS

125G DIGESTIVE BISCUITS

100G UNSALTED BUTTER, MELTED

A LITTLE COCOA POWDER, FOR DUSTING

RASPBERRIES OR OTHER BERRIES, TO SERVE (OPTIONAL)

FOR THE FILLING

100G 70% DARK CHOCOLATE, BROKEN INTO SMALL PIECES

100G MILK CHOCOLATE, CHOPPED

250ML DOUBLE CREAM

1 TSP ESPRESSO POWDER

3 TBSP LIQUID GLUCOSE

YOU WILL NEED

36 X 12CM RECTANGULAR LOOSE-BOTTOMED TIN, OR 23CM ROUND LOOSE-BOTTOMED TIN

STEP 1 First, make the base. Place the biscuits in the bowl of a food processor and blitz until you have fine crumbs. Add the melted butter and pulse until the mixture begins to form clumps.(Alternatively, place the biscuits in a food bag and bash with a rolling pin until they resemble fine crumbs, then stir through the melted butter.)

STEP 2 Press the crumb mixture into your prepared tin, evenly coating the base and sides. Place in the fridge to set for at least 1 hour.

STEP 3 Meanwhile, to make the filling, place all the chopped chocolate in a large bowl. Pour the cream into a small pan, add the espresso powder and glucose and heat over a medium heat, until the liquid just comes to the boil, about 2 minutes. Pour the hot cream mixture over the chocolate and stir to melt the chocolate.

STEP 4 Remove the chilled biscuit base from the fridge and pour in the chocolate mixture. Place the tart in the fridge for 4 hours to set, then dust with a little cocoa powder just before serving. Serve in slices with a few raspberries or other berries, if you wish.

DANISH DREAMS

Making rich, buttery Danish pastry dough takes time, but it's worth the effort. The sharpness of the lemon filling in these Danish Dreams beautifully cuts through the richness.

MAKES 18

- 450G STRONG WHITE BREAD FLOUR
- 4 TBSP CASTER SUGAR
- 1½ TSP SALT
- ½ TSP FAST-ACTION DRIED YEAST
- 1 LARGE EGG
- 80ML CHILLED WATER
- 100ML WHOLE MILK
- 225G UNSALTED BUTTER, CHILLED
- 1 EGG, BEATEN
- 2 TBSP APRICOT JAM, LOOSENED WITH A SPLASH OF WATER AND WARMED
- 100G ICING SUGAR, SIFTED, MIXED WITH 3–4 TSP LEMON JUICE

FOR THE LEMON CRÈME PÂTISSIÈRE

- 125ML WHOLE MILK
- 1 LARGE EGG YOLK
- 2 TBSP CASTER SUGAR
- ½ TSP VANILLA PASTE
- 1½ TBSP CORNFLOUR
- 2 TBSP LEMON CURD

YOU WILL NEED

- 2 BAKING SHEETS LINED WITH BAKING PAPER

STEP 1 Place the flour, sugar, salt and yeast into the bowl of a stand mixer fitted with a dough hook. Add the egg, water and milk. Mix on a slow speed until combined, then increase the speed and mix for 5 minutes to form a dough.

STEP 2 Tip the dough onto a lightly floured worktop and shape into a disc. Wrap in cling film and chill for 1 hour, then unwrap and roll it out into a 1cm-thick rectangle, measuring 45 x 20cm.

STEP 3 Flatten the butter into a 30 x 18cm rectangle, then lay it on the dough so it covers the bottom ⅔.

STEP 4 Fold down the dough to cover ⅓ of the butter. Cut off the exposed butter, without cutting into the dough. Place this butter on top of the folded dough and fold the bottom ½ of the dough up. Squeeze the dough edges to seal. Wrap in cling film and chill for at least 1 hour to firm up.

STEP 5 Place the dough, short side facing you, on a lightly floured worktop. Roll into a 45 x 20cm rectangle. Fold ⅓ of the dough up and the top ⅓ down. Chill for 1 hour. Repeat twice more, chilling between folds. After the final fold, chill overnight.

STEP 6 Make the crème pâtissière. Heat the milk until it just boils. In a bowl, beat the yolks with the sugar, vanilla paste and cornflour, then pour in the hot milk, and whisk. Transfer to the milk pan and place over a low heat. Whisk until the mixture just begins to boil and thicken. Transfer to a bowl, fold in the lemon curd, then cover the surface with cling film.

STEP 7 Roll out the pastry to 7mm thick and cut it into 18 squares of 8cm. Make diagonal cuts 2.5cm from the corners of each square. Place the squares onto the baking sheets. Gather every second point of dough to the centre of each square, and press down to make a hollow. Cover the sheets loosely with cling film and leave to prove for 2 hours, or until doubled in size.

STEP 8 Heat the oven to 200°C/180°C fan/400°F/ Gas 6. Put 1 teaspoon of lemon crème pât into the hollow of each pastry. Brush the dough with beaten egg, then bake for 15–20 minutes, until golden.

STEP 9 While still warm, brush the pastries with the warmed apricot jam. Transfer to a wire rack to cool. Drizzle the cooled pastries with lemony icing sugar to finish.

INSPIRED BY THE SHOW

DANISH KLEINER

Sweet, crisp deep-fried twists of dough, these are a Christmas snack from Denmark, but delicious at any time of year.

MAKES 50–60

125G CASTER SUGAR, PLUS EXTRA FOR DUSTING (OPTIONAL)

125G UNSALTED BUTTER, SOFTENED

2 LARGE EGGS, BEATEN

400G PLAIN FLOUR, PLUS EXTRA FOR DUSTING

1/2 TSP BAKING POWDER

1/2 TSP GROUND CARDAMOM

1/4 TSP GROUND CINNAMON

2 TBSP DOUBLE CREAM

SUNFLOWER OR VEGETABLE OIL, FOR DEEP FRYING

YOU WILL NEED

COOKING THERMOMETER (OPTIONAL); KITCHEN PAPER

STEP 1 Put the sugar and butter into a large bowl and cream together until light and fluffy. Add half of the beaten egg and mix thoroughly to combine.

STEP 2 In a separate bowl, mix together the flour, baking powder, cardamom and cinnamon.

STEP 3 A little at a time, add the flour mixture into the butter, sugar and egg mixture, using an electric hand mixer to combine the ingredients between each addition. As the mixture gets dry, add more egg. Continue to add the flour and eggs until everything is incorporated. Then, beat in just enough of the cream to form a soft pastry.

STEP 4 Tip out the pastry onto a lightly floured worktop and gently knead until smooth. Shape the pastry into a ball, wrap it in cling film, and chill for 30 minutes, or until firm.

STEP 5 Lightly dust your worktop with flour again and remove the pastry from the fridge. Roll it out until it is 3mm thick and measures about 25 x 30cm.

STEP 6 Cut the dough into 5cm-wide strips, then cut the strips on an angle to make diamond shapes that measure about 5 x 5cm. Cut a 2cm slit lengthways in the centre of each strip.

STEP 7 Pull one corner of each pastry diamond through the slit to the other side to form a knot shape. Repeat until all the strips are knotted.

STEP 8 Half fill a large saucepan with oil, or use a deep-fat fryer, and heat the oil to about 180°C/350°F, or until a cube of day-old bread dropped into the hot oil turns golden within 30 seconds.

STEP 9 Deep fry the knots in batches for 2–3 minutes each, turning them with a long-handled spoon as they fry, until golden brown on all sides. As each batch cooks, remove the knots using a slotted spoon and set aside to drain on kitchen paper. Serve warm, dusted with caster sugar, if you like.

ESTERHAZY TORTE

This Austrian torte has layers of nutty dacquoise sandwiched together with a walnut cream. You can substitute the walnuts for almonds or hazelnuts, and add a splash of liqueur in the filling, if you like.

SERVES 12

FOR THE DACQUOISE

10 LARGE EGG WHITES

210G CASTER SUGAR

70G PLAIN FLOUR

210G WALNUTS, BLITZED TO A POWDER

FOR THE FILLING

10 LARGE EGG YOLKS, LIGHTLY BEATEN

210G CASTER SUGAR

260G UNSALTED BUTTER, SOFTENED AND DICED

130G FINELY CHOPPED WALNUTS

TO DECORATE

50G APRICOT JAM, MIXED WITH 1 TSP WATER AND WARMED

50G MILK CHOCOLATE, MELTED (SEE P.311) AND MIXED WITH 2 TSP SUNFLOWER OIL

300G ICING SUGAR, SIFTED

100G TOASTED CHOPPED WALNUTS

YOU WILL NEED

20CM SANDWICH TINS X 5, BASE-LINED WITH BAKING PAPER; SMALL DISPOSABLE PIPING BAG; COCKTAIL STICK

STEP 1 Heat your oven to 160°C/140°C fan/ 325°F/ Gas 3. To make the dacquoise discs, whisk the egg whites in a stand mixer until they form soft peaks, then add the sugar, 1 tablespoon at a time, mixing well between each addition.

STEP 2 Whisk until the meringue is thick and glossy and forms stiff peaks. Fold in the flour and blitzed walnuts.

STEP 3 Put $\frac{1}{5}$ of the mixture in a thin layer in the base of each of the prepared tins. Bake for 20 minutes, until the discs are cooked and feel firm to the touch, but not crisp. Remove from the tins and leave to cool. (If you don't have 5 tins, do this in batches.)

STEP 4 To make the filling, place the egg yolks and sugar in a large bowl over a pan of simmering water. Using an electric hand whisk, carefully beat the yolks and sugar until the mixture is pale, voluminous and thick, and leaves a distinct trail when you lift the whisk.

STEP 5 Remove the bowl from the pan and leave to cool for 3–5 minutes. Slowly whisk in the butter a few cubes at a time, beating to incorporate between each addition.

STEP 6 Fold through the chopped walnuts and place in the fridge to firm up.

STEP 7 To assemble, use a blob of filling to stick 1 meringue disc onto a serving plate, bottom-side down. Spread a thin layer of filling over the disc, then place the next meringue disc on top and spread over another thin layer. Repeat until you place the last disc bottom-side up at the top (don't cover this one).

STEP 8 Brush the top and sides with the apricot jam. Use the remaining filling to cover the sides of the cake.

STEP 9 Put the melted chocolate in a small piping bag. Put the icing sugar in a bowl and add water 1 teaspoon at a time to create a thick icing (aim for spreadable, but not runny). Spread over the top of the cake and smooth to level.

STEP 10 Snip a small hole in the piping bag and pipe 4 concentric circles into the icing. Use a cocktail stick to drag a line from the centre of the cake to the edge, then from the edge inward. Repeat all around the cake. Press the toasted walnuts around the edge of the cake to finish.

JUDGE'S RECIPE

PAUL'S MA'AMOUL

Stuffed with date paste, or chopped walnuts, and dusted with powdered sugar, these short, buttery pastries originate from the Levantine region of the Middle East.

MAKES 12

PINCH OF MASTIC

20G CASTER SUGAR

175G FINE SEMOLINA

20G PLAIN FLOUR

½ TSP GROUND MAHLEB

90G CHILLED GHEE

2 TSP ORANGE BLOSSOM WATER

2 TSP ROSE WATER

ICING SUGAR, TO DUST

FOR THE DATE FILLING

75G MEDJOOL DATES, STONED

1 TBSP ROSE WATER

¼ TSP GROUND CINNAMON

¼ TSP GROUND MAHLEB

FOR THE WALNUT FILLING

25G WALNUTS

25G GOLDEN RAISINS

1 TBSP ORANGE BLOSSOM HONEY

¼ TSP GROUND CARDAMOM

YOU WILL NEED

MA'AMOUL MOULD; BAKING SHEET LINED WITH BAKING PAPER; MA'AMOUL TONGS

STEP 1 Put the mastic in a mortar with 1 teaspoon of the sugar and grind to a powder. Tip into a bowl and add the remaining sugar, along with the semolina, flour and mahleb. Mix together.

STEP 2 Add the ghee and rub in with your fingertips until the mixture resembles fine crumbs. Add the orange blossom and rose waters and bring the dough together with your hands. Tip out onto a floured worktop. Knead for 5 minutes, until smooth, then wrap in cling film and chill for 30 minutes, to rest.

STEP 3 For the date filling, place the dates in the bowl of a mini food processor with the rose water, cinnamon and mahleb and blitz to a paste. Divide the mixture into 6 and roll into balls (wet hands will prevent the paste sticking).

STEP 4 For the walnut filling, place the walnuts in the bowl of a mini food processor with the raisins, honey and cardamom and blitz to a paste. Divide the mixture into 6 and roll into balls.

STEP 5 Heat the oven to 200°C/180°C fan/400°F/ Gas 6. Divide the dough into 12 pieces, each of about 25g. Roll each piece into a ball and cover with a damp tea towel.

STEP 6 With damp hands, flatten each ball of dough in the palm of one hand, turning it around as you go and lifting the edges to form a little cup. The cups should be about 3mm thick and the sides about 3cm high.

STEP 7 Fill 6 of the pastry cups with a ball of date filling and the remaining 6 pastry cups with a ball of walnut filling. Pinch the dough over the filling to seal and roll each into a ball.

STEP 8 Lightly flour the ma'amoul mould and press one of the walnut-filled balls into the mould. Turn it out onto the lined baking sheet. Repeat with the remaining 5 walnut-filled balls.

STEP 9 With the 6 date-filled balls, use the ma'amoul tongs and pinch the pastry to create a decorative design. Place on the lined baking sheet.

STEP 10 Bake all the ma'amoul for 12–14 minutes, until golden on the bottom, but pale or very lightly golden around the edges. Remove from the oven, leave to cool on the sheet for 5 minutes, then transfer to a wire rack to cool completely. Dust the walnut ma'amoul with icing sugar before serving.

CHERRY FRANGIPANE PIES

Compared to puff and flaky pastry, rough puff is straightforward to make. It works well for these sweet cherry pies with an almond filling.

MAKES 6

225G PLAIN FLOUR

¼ TSP SALT

85G UNSALTED BUTTER, CHILLED AND CUT INTO SMALL DICE

85G LARD, CHILLED AND DICED

110ML CHILLED WATER

1 TSP LEMON JUICE

1 EGG, BEATEN

3 TBSP CHERRY CONSERVE OR JAM

6–8 CHERRIES, HALVED

2 TBSP FLAKED ALMONDS

ICING SUGAR, TO SERVE

FOR THE FILLING

50G UNSALTED BUTTER, SOFTENED

100G CASTER SUGAR

1 LARGE EGG

2 TBSP PLAIN FLOUR

2 TBSP GROUND ALMONDS

1 DROP OF ALMOND EXTRACT

YOU WILL NEED

BAKING SHEET LINED WITH BAKING PAPER; 8.5CM ROUND CUTTER

STEP 1 To make the rough puff pastry, in a bowl mix the flour and salt together§. Toss the butter and lard in the flour, but don't rub it in. Add the water and lemon juice, then stir to form a stiff dough.

STEP 2 Tip out the dough onto a lightly floured worktop. Roll it out into a rectangle about 30 x 12cm. Turn the dough so that one of the short ends is facing you. Fold the top ⅓ of dough down and the bottom ⅓ up, as if you were folding an A4 business letter.

STEP 3 Wrap the dough in cling film and chill for 15 minutes, then remove from the fridge and repeat the rolling and folding 3 more times, leaving the dough to rest for 15 minutes between each rolling and folding.

STEP 4 Meanwhile, make the filling. Use a wooden spoon to beat together the butter and sugar in a bowl until light and fluffy. Add the large egg and beat until combined. Stir in the flour, ground almonds and almond extract and mix well. Set aside.

STEP 5 Tip out the dough onto a lightly floured worktop and roll to a circle 4mm thick. Use the 8.5cm cutter to stamp out 12 rounds, re-rolling the trimmings as necessary.

STEP 6 Place 6 cut rounds on the baking sheet. These are your pie bases. Roll the remaining rounds so that they are slightly bigger than the bases. These will be the lids.

STEP 7 Brush the edges of the pastry bases with the beaten egg. Spread a little jam in the middle of the bases, but do not spread right to the edge. Top with 1 teaspoon of the filling mixture and add 2 or 3 cherry halves. Top with the remaining pastry circles, pressing to seal the edges. Chill for 30 minutes.

STEP 8 Heat your oven to 200°C/180°C fan/400°F/ Gas 6. Brush the pies with egg and scatter with the flaked almonds. Bake for 25–30 minutes, until risen and golden brown. Remove from the oven and leave to cool for 5 minutes, then dust with icing sugar before serving.

STRAWBERRY SHORTCAKE PETITS FOURS

Bite-sized mouthfuls of crisp shortbread filled with strawberries and cream, these are a delicious and tasty treat that brings a little summer sparkle to any gathering – at any time of the year.

MAKES 17

200G PLAIN FLOUR

2 TBSP DRIED STRAWBERRIES

65G ICING SUGAR, PLUS EXTRA TO SERVE

110G UNSALTED BUTTER, SOFTENED

1 EGG

FOR THE FILLING

155ML DOUBLE CREAM

60G ICING SUGAR, SIFTED

100G STRAWBERRIES, HULLED AND CHOPPED INTO SMALL PIECES, PLUS 4-5 STRAWBERRIES, QUARTERED, TO DECORATE

YOU WILL NEED

4.5CM ROUND CUTTER; 2 BAKING SHEETS LINED WITH BAKING PAPER; SMALL PIPING BAG FITTED WITH A SMALL STAR NOZZLE

STEP 1 Put the flour, dried strawberries and icing sugar in a bowl and mix together. Add the butter and egg, then work the ingredients with your fingers to form a smooth dough. Shape the dough into a ball, wrap in cling film and refrigerate for at least 30 minutes.

STEP 2 Tip out the dough onto a lightly floured worktop and roll out to 5mm thick. Stamp out 34 rounds of 4.5cm each, re-rolling the trimmings as necessary, and place the rounds on the prepared baking sheets, leaving plenty of space between each round. Chill the rounds for 20 minutes. Heat the oven to 170°C/150°C fan/325°F/Gas 3.

STEP 3 Remove the rounds from the fridge and bake them for 10–12 minutes, until the biscuits are lightly coloured. Remove from the oven, then leave to cool and firm up on the tray, before transferring to a wire rack to cool completely.

STEP 4 To make the filling, whisk the cream with the icing sugar until thick enough to pipe. Fill a small piping bag fitted with a small star nozzle with cream. Turn 17 of the shortbread biscuits underside up and pipe them with small rosettes of cream.

STEP 5 Arrange pieces of the chopped strawberry around the piped cream, then gently place the remaining biscuits, underside downwards, on top, to create strawberry-and-cream-filled shortbread sandwiches.

STEP 6 Top each biscuit with a strawberry quarter, and finish off with a good dusting of icing sugar.

BAKING WITH CHILDREN

APPLE PLATE PIE

The cooking apples give this pie a sharpness and softness, while the eating apples give sweetness and bite. As the pie crust is not baked blind, dusting the pastry base with semolina prevents a soggy bottom.

SERVES 6

275G PLAIN FLOUR

2 TBSP ICING SUGAR

140G UNSALTED BUTTER, CHILLED AND DICED

3-4 TBSP CHILLED WATER

1 EGG, BEATEN

2 TSP CASTER SUGAR, FOR SPRINKLING

FOR THE FILLING

2 LARGE COOKING APPLES (ABOUT 700G), PEELED, CORED AND SLICED

4 TBSP CASTER SUGAR

1 CINNAMON STICK

2 EATING APPLES, PEELED, CORED AND THINLY SLICED

2 TBSP SEMOLINA

YOU WILL NEED

24CM PIE PLATE

STEP 1 First, make the pastry. Put the flour and icing sugar in a large bowl and mix to combine. Add the butter and use your fingertips to rub it in until the mixture resembles fine crumbs. Add the water, a couple of teaspoons at a time, mixing between each addition, until you've added just enough to bring the pastry together. Gently knead the pastry into a ball, then wrap it in cling film and chill for 30 minutes to rest.

STEP 2 Meanwhile, make the filling. Place the cooking apple slices in a pan along with the caster sugar, cinnamon stick and 3 tablespoons of water. Cook, stirring occasionally, over a medium heat, until the apples begin to fall, but still hold their shape. Transfer the apples to a clean bowl, discarding the cinnamon stick, and allow to cool.

STEP 3 Heat the oven to 200°C/180°C fan/400°F/Gas 6. Remove the pastry from the fridge and divide into 2 pieces, roughly ⅔ and ⅓. Place the larger piece on a lightly floured worktop and roll out to 2–3mm thick. Use this pastry sheet to line the base of the pie plate, then roll out the smaller pastry to 2–3mm thick to form the pie lid.

STEP 4 Sprinkle the semolina over the pastry base. Mix the sliced eating apples with the cooled apple filling and tip the apple mixture onto the pie base, spreading it out evenly but leaving a ring of pastry around the edge.

STEP 5 Brush the edges of the pie with beaten egg, then cover with the lid. Crimp the edges using the tines of a fork to press down on the pastry rim, then trim away any excess. Use any pastry trimmings to make decorations for the top, if you wish.

STEP 6 Brush the top of the pie with more beaten egg, then sprinkle with the 2 teaspoons of caster sugar. Make 3 small slits in the top of the pie to let the steam out.

STEP 7 Bake the pie for 30–35 minutes, until golden brown. Remove from the oven and leave to rest for 15 minutes before serving. Enjoy with ice cream, cream or custard.

VEGAN PISTACHIO PRALINE MERINGUES

The liquid you drain from tinned chickpeas is known as aquafaba. With a structure similar to egg white, it is perfect for making vegan meringues. As with all meringue-making, though, the key to success is to ensure the liquid is whipped to stiff peaks, before gradually adding the sugar. Don't worry if these meringues flatten a bit during baking.

MAKES 8

DRAINED LIQUID FROM A 400G CAN OF CHICKPEAS

¼ TSP CREAM OF TARTAR

150G CASTER SUGAR

FRESH FRUIT, TO SERVE

FOR THE PRALINE

50G GRANULATED SUGAR

50G PISTACHIO KERNELS

¼ TSP GROUND CINNAMON

½ TSP GROUND CARDAMOM

YOU WILL NEED

3 BAKING SHEETS LINED WITH BAKING PAPER

STEP 1 First, make the praline. Place the granulated sugar in a clean pan with 1½ teaspoons of water. Dissolve the sugar, over a medium–high heat, without stirring, until it turns golden amber (tip and swirl the pan from time to time to help the sugar dissolve evenly).

STEP 2 When the sugar has dissolved, add the pistachios and gently shake the pan to coat the nuts. Pour the mixture onto a prepared tray, spread it out to an even layer and leave to cool and set, about 5–10 minutes.

STEP 3 Break the praline into small pieces and place the pieces in the bowl of a food processor, then blitz to a rough powder. Add the ground cinnamon and cardamom and pulse a few times to combine. Set aside.

STEP 4 Heat the oven to 170°C/150°C fan/325°F/Gas 3. To make the meringue, place the chickpea liquid in the bowl of a stand mixer fitted with a whisk. Add the cream of tartar and whisk using a medium speed, until the liquid has tripled in volume and holds stiff peaks.

STEP 5 With the mixer still running, slowly add the caster sugar, 1 tablespoon at a time. Wait for each addition to be incorporated before adding the next. Once you have added all the sugar, keep whisking until you have a smooth, glossy meringue. Turn off the mixer and very gently fold ½ the pistachio praline through the meringue.

STEP 6 Using a large metal spoon, place big dollops of meringue onto the remaining baking sheets. Sprinkle the remaining praline over the top, then place the sheets in the oven. Lower the temperature to 120°C/100°C fan/200°F/Gas ½ and bake the meringues for 2 hours. (During this time don't open your oven door.)

STEP 7 After 2 hours, turn off the oven and still without opening the oven door – leave the meringues to go cold (about 1 hour). Remove from the oven and serve with fresh fruit. (These meringues are best eaten on the same day; they won't keep in the way that egg meringues will.)

MINI CHOUX WREATHS WITH CRAQUELIN

Craquelin is super-easy, and yet an impressive way to lift your bakes to the next level.

MAKES 16

FOR THE CRAQUELIN
60G UNSALTED BUTTER, SOFTENED

75G LIGHT SOFT BROWN SUGAR

75G PLAIN FLOUR

FOR THE CHOCOLATE CRÈME PÂTISSIÈRE
250ML MILK

2 LARGE EGG YOLKS

50G CASTER SUGAR

½ TSP VANILLA PASTE

2 TBSP CORNFLOUR

2 TSP COCOA POWDER

15G 54% DARK CHOCOLATE, GRATED

15G UNSALTED BUTTER

FOR THE CHOUX WREATHS
100ML WHOLE MILK

75G UNSALTED BUTTER

1 TSP CASTER SUGAR

100G PLAIN FLOUR

2 OR 3 EGGS

50G WHITE CHOCOLATE, MELTED, TO DECORATE

YOU WILL NEED
2 BAKING TRAYS LINED WITH BAKING PAPER DRAWN WITH 16 6.5CM-DIAMETER CIRCLES, DRAWN-SIDE DOWNWARDS; 6.5CM AND 3.5CM CUTTERS; MEDIUM PIPING BAG FITTED WITH A MEDIUM STAR NOZZLE

STEP 1 First, make the craquelin. Beat the butter and sugar together with an electric hand mixer, then add the flour and, with a wooden spoon, mix to a soft dough. Place the dough between 2 sheets of baking paper and roll to 3mm thick. Place in the freezer for 30 minutes.

STEP 2 Take the craquelin from the freezer and remove the top sheet of baking paper. Stamp out 6.5cm rounds, then stamp out the middle of each round using a 3.5cm cutter, to create a ring. Continue until you have 16 rings, re-rolling the trimmings as necessary. Set aside in the fridge.

STEP 3 Make the crème pâtissière. Heat the milk until it just boils. Beat the yolks in a bowl with the sugar, vanilla paste, cornflour and cocoa powder, then whisk in the hot milk. Return to the milk pan over a low heat, and whisk until the mixture just begins to boil, and thickens. Turn off the heat and mix in the chocolate and butter, until melted, smooth and glossy. Transfer to a bowl and cover the surface with cling film.

STEP 4 Heat the oven to 180°C/160°C fan/350°F/Gas 4.

STEP 5 Take the 3.5cm cutter and draw around it inside each of the circles you've drawn on the baking paper, to create doughnut shapes.

STEP 6 Make the choux wreaths. Place the milk, butter, sugar and 100ml of water in a pan. Heat until the mixture begins to boil. Beat in the flour to a stiff dough.

STEP 7 Transfer the dough to a bowl, add 1 egg and, using an electric hand whisk, beat to incorporate. Add another egg and beat until glossy, smooth and pipeable. If the mixture is too thick, add a third egg and mix again.

STEP 8 Transfer the choux to a medium piping bag fitted with a medium star nozzle. Pipe 16 circles of pastry using the lines on your baking paper to guide you. Put the craquelin rings on top and bake for 15–20 minutes, until risen, golden and cooked. Turn off the oven and leave to cool.

STEP 9 To assemble, halve each choux ring, then spoon the chocolate crème pâtissière into a medium piping bag fitted with a medium star nozzle. Pipe the filling into each choux base, top with a lid and decorate with melted chocolate.

PRUE'S PUITS D'AMOUR

The French puits d'amour means 'wells of love' – which says it all.

MAKES 9

1 QUANTITY OF ROUGH PUFF PASTRY (SEE P.310)

4½ TSP DEMERARA SUGAR

FOR THE COMPOTE

250G STRAWBERRIES, HULLED

25G CASTER SUGAR

1 TBSP LEMON JUICE

50G RASPBERRIES

FOR THE CRÈME PÂTISSIÈRE

500ML WHOLE MILK

½ VANILLA POD, SPLIT, SEEDS SCRAPED, POD RESERVED

100G CASTER SUGAR

4 EGG YOLKS

40G CORNFLOUR

40G UNSALTED BUTTER

FOR THE CHOUX PASTRY

55G UNSALTED BUTTER, DICED

PINCH SALT

70G PLAIN FLOUR

2 EGGS, BEATEN

BEATEN EGG, FOR BRUSHING

NIBBED SUGAR, FOR SPRINKLING

YOU WILL NEED

10CM ROUND CUTTER; 2 BAKING SHEETS LINED WITH BAKING PAPER; LARGE PIPING BAG; 1CM PLAIN NOZZLE; 1.5CM PLAIN NOZZLE; KITCHEN BLOWTORCH

STEP 1 For the compote, tip the strawberries into a pan with the sugar and lemon juice and cook over a medium heat for 10 minutes. Add the raspberries and cook for a further 5–10 minutes, until reduced to a thick compote (but not a jam). Remove from the heat, cool, then chill.

STEP 2 For the crème pâtissière, put the milk in a pan with the vanilla pod and seeds. Bring to the boil, then remove from the heat. Whisk the sugar, yolks and cornflour together in a large bowl. Whisk a little hot milk into the sugar and egg mixture, then whisk in the rest of the hot milk until well combined. Return to the pan. Cook over a gentle heat, stirring, until the mixture thickens.

STEP 3 Remove from the heat and pass through a sieve into a clean bowl. Add the butter and stir until melted. Leave to cool, cover with cling film and chill until cold.

STEP 4 Heat the oven to 220°C/200°C fan/425°F/Gas 7. Lightly dust your worktop and roll out the rough puff to a 35cm square. Using the 10cm cutter, cut out 9 discs. Place on the baking sheets and prick each disc all over with a fork. Chill for 30 minutes.

STEP 5 For the choux pastry, place the butter, salt and 150ml of water in a medium pan. Heat gently to melt the butter, then bring to the boil. Immediately remove from the heat and tip in the flour. Beat with a wooden spoon to form a smooth ball of dough that leaves the sides of the pan.

STEP 6 Vigorously beat the egg into the hot dough, a little at a time, until the dough is stiff and glossy. You may not need all the egg – stop if the dough becomes loose. Spoon the mixture into a piping bag fitted with a 1cm plain nozzle.

STEP 7 Pipe the choux in a circle ½cm in from the edge of each disc. Brush each choux ring with beaten egg and sprinkle with nibbed sugar. Bake for 20–25 minutes, until puffed, crisp and golden. Remove from the oven and transfer to a wire rack to cool completely.

STEP 8 To assemble, spoon the crème pâtissière into a piping bag fitted with a 1.5cm plain nozzle. Spoon the strawberry compote into the pastry shells and pipe the crème pâtissière over the top. Sprinkle ½ teaspoon of demerara sugar on top and, using a blowtorch, brûlée the sugar. Serve immediately.

HONEY CREAM APPLE FLAN

This flan is a crisp, buttery pastry filled with a smooth apple bavarois and finished with a layer of apple jelly.

SERVES 10

200G PLAIN FLOUR

2 TSBP ICING SUGAR, SIEVED

100G UNSALTED BUTTER, CHILLED AND DICED

1 EGG, BEATEN

3–4 TSP CHILLED WATER

RASPBERRIES, TO SERVE

FOR THE BAVAROIS FILLING

1 LARGE COOKING APPLE (ABOUT 375G), PEELED, CORED AND CHOPPED

1 TBSP CASTER SUGAR

JUICE OF ½ LEMON

100ML WHOLE MILK

200ML DOUBLE CREAM

3 LARGE EGG YOLKS

3 TBSP RUNNY HONEY

3 GELATINE LEAVES, SOAKED

FOR THE FRUIT JELLY

150ML APPLE JUICE

2 TBSP CASTER SUGAR

4 GELATINE LEAVES, SOAKED

1 DROP OF GREEN FOOD COLOURING

YOU WILL NEED

36 X 12CM RECTANGULAR LOOSE-BOTTOMED TART TIN, OR 23CM ROUND LOOSE-BOTTOMED TART TIN, BASE-LINED WITH BAKING PAPER; BAKING BEANS

STEP 1 First, make the pastry. Mix together the flour and icing sugar in a bowl. Rub in the butter with your fingertips until the mixture resembles fine crumbs. Add the egg and stir to combine. Add enough chilled water to form a soft dough. Tip out onto a lightly floured worktop and knead to a smooth ball. Flatten into a disc, wrap in cling film and chill for 30 minutes.

STEP 2 Heat the oven to 200°C/180°C fan/400°F/Gas 6. Roll out the pastry on a lightly floured worktop to 3mm thick, then line the tart tin, overhanging the sides. Prick the base, line with baking paper and fill with baking beans. Bake blind for 15 minutes, then remove the paper and beans and return to the oven for 5 minutes, until golden. Trim away the excess.

STEP 3 To make the filling, place the apple, sugar and lemon juice in a small pan with 2 tablespoons of water. Heat, stirring occasionally, until the apples fall and create an apple purée. Pass through a sieve into a bowl, and cool.

STEP 4 Heat the milk and 100ml of cream until it just boils. Whisk the yolks and honey together until light and increased in volume.

STEP 5 Pour the hot milk onto the egg mixture, whisking all the time, then return the mixture to the pan and heat gently until it thickens. Turn off the heat.

STEP 6 Squeeze any excess water from the soaked gelatine and stir the sheets into the custard to dissolve. Transfer the custard to a bowl, cover the surface with cling film and leave to one side to cool to room temperature.

STEP 7 Whip the remaining double cream to soft peaks. Fold into the cooled custard along with the apple purée. Pour into the pastry case and chill for at least 2 hours to set.

STEP 8 For the jelly, heat the apple juice with the sugar in a small pan until the sugar has dissolved. Squeeze out any excess water from the gelatine and add the leaves to the pan. Stir to dissolve, but do not boil. Stir in the green food colouring to create an even colour. Allow to cool a little.

STEP 9 Pour the apple jelly onto the set tart (you may not need it all). Return the tart to the fridge for at least 1 hour. Remove from the fridge 30 minutes before serving. Slice into fingers and serve with a few raspberries.

CELEBRATIONS

VACHERIN

This French dessert, not to be confused with the cheese of the same name, has layers of crisp meringue discs sandwiched between ice cream and sorbet.

SERVES 8

3 LARGE EGG WHITES

¼ TSP CREAM OF TARTAR

175G CASTER SUGAR

1KG VANILLA ICE CREAM

500G RASPBERRY SORBET

250ML DOUBLE CREAM, WHIPPED

1 TSP VANILLA PASTE

ABOUT 80G RASPBERRIES, TO DECORATE

YOU WILL NEED

2 BAKING SHEETS LINED WITH BAKING PAPER DRAWN WITH 20CM CIRCLES X 2; 20CM SPRINGFORM TIN

STEP 1 Heat the oven to 160°C/140°C fan/315°F/ Gas 3.

STEP 2 First, make the meringue. Whisk the egg whites in a stand mixer with the cream of tartar until they form soft peaks. Add the caster sugar 1 tablespoon at a time, making sure the sugar is fully incorporated before adding the next spoonful. Once you have used up all the sugar, whisk until the meringue is thick, glossy and forms stiff peaks.

STEP 3 Using the 20cm circles on the baking paper as a guide, spread ½ the meringue on each sheet of baking paper, to form 2 circles. Smooth each surface with a palette knife and place the trays in the oven to bake the meringues for 1 hour, until crisp. Turn off the oven, and without opening the oven door, leave the meringues to cool in the oven for 1 hour.

STEP 4 Once cooled, remove the meringues from the oven and trim them to fit into the 20cm tin. Place 1 meringue disc in the base of the tin.

STEP 5 Cover the meringue base with ½ the vanilla ice cream, then cover the vanilla ice cream with all the raspberry sorbet, in an even layer. Use the remaining vanilla ice cream to cover the raspberry sorbet forming a third layer. Top this with the other meringue disc. Place the vacherin in the freezer for at least 1 hour

STEP 6 Remove the vacherin from the freezer 20 minutes before serving. (To help free the vacherin from the tin, wrap a hot cloth around the sides for a few minutes.) Transfer to a serving plate.

STEP 7 To finish, mix the whipped cream with the vanilla paste, then spread or pipe the flavoured cream over the uppermost meringue. Decorate with raspberries and serve straightaway.

CHAPTER SIX

SAVOURY
BAKES

If you have a craving for savoury, you've arrived at just the right chapter.

There is arguably nothing more homely or satisfying than encasing a tasty savoury filling inside a pastry crust – whether that's shortcrust, hot-water crust, filo or puff, and they all feature here.

Bakers of all ages and abilities can get the knack for making a homemade pie or quiche. There are delicious recipes for Potato Crust Quiche, Individual Courgette & Kale Tarts and Spicy Salmon Quiche. For pie-lovers on the move, there are Individual Picnic Pies (great for lunch boxes as well as picnics) and from Series 8 two wonderful recipes – Nan's Sunday Dinner Pie and Old-fashioned Minced Beef Pies. You can round off an elegant supper with your own homemade cracker selection – incredibly impressive served with cheese and chutney, and brilliantly easy to make.

From the Mushroom Bourguignon Pithivier made with puff to the Duck B'steeya made with filo, and the Savoury Veggie Samosas made with authentic ghee pastry, whatever the occasion – small and humble or large and glamorous – there is the perfect savoury recipe here for you to share with anyone who comes to visit.

BAKER'S RECIPE

SAVOURY VEGGIE SAMOSAS

**A classic vegetarian samosa
in a crisp ghee crust.**

MAKES 10

125G '00' FLOUR

PINCH OF SALT

25G GHEE

1 TBSP PLAIN FLOUR

PINK FOOD-COLOURING PASTE

FOR THE FILLING

300G MARIS PIPER POTATOES,
PEELED AND CUT INTO 1CM DICE

1½ TBSP VEGETABLE OIL

1¼ TSP CUMIN SEEDS

½ WHITE ONION, SLICED

50G FROZEN PEAS

20G UNSALTED BUTTER

1 TSP SALT

3 GREEN FINGER CHILLIES,
FINELY CHOPPED

1 TSP GARAM MASALA

17G CORIANDER, CHOPPED

15G ROOT GINGER, FINELY CHOPPED

½ WHITE ONION, CHOPPED

FOR THE CHUTNEY

1 LARGE TOMATO

5G CORIANDER

½ WHITE ONION

1 GREEN FINGER CHILLI

1 TSP MINT SAUCE

½ TSP GARAM MASALA

¾ TBSP TOMATO KETCHUP

¼ TSP SALT

YOU WILL NEED

DEEP-FAT FRYER; KITCHEN PAPER;
BAKING SHEET; STAR CUTTER

STEP 1 Sift the flour and salt into a bowl. Rub in the ghee until the mixture resembles fine crumbs. Little by little, add 3–4 tablespoons of water to form a dough. Knead until smooth, then wrap in cling film and chill for 30 minutes.

STEP 2 Make the filling. Boil the potatoes in salted water for 5 minutes, until just tender. Drain and set aside.

STEP 3 Heat the oil in a pan, over a high heat. Add the cumin and cook, stirring, for 30 seconds. Add the sliced onions, reduce the heat, and cook for a further 5 minutes, until soft. Stir in the cooked potatoes and cook for 5 more minutes, then stir in the peas and butter. Tip out into a shallow tray and leave to cool.

STEP 4 Once cool, add the salt, chillies, garam masala, coriander, ginger and chopped onion. Mash lightly with a potato masher, leaving some pieces whole. Mix well together, then set aside.

STEP 5 For the chutney, place the tomatoes, coriander, onion and chilli in a food processor and pulse until finely chopped. Add the mint sauce, garam masala, ketchup and salt and pulse again to combine. Set aside.

STEP 6 Mix the plain flour with 1½ tablespoons of water to make a pastry glue. Set aside.

STEP 7 Heat the oil in a deep-fat fryer to 180°C/350°F. Divide the dough into 5 equal balls, then cover with damp kitchen paper.

STEP 8 Roll out 1 of the balls on a lightly floured worktop, to 1mm thick – so that you can see your hand through it. Cut out a 20cm circle from the dough and set aside, covered with damp kitchen paper. Repeat for all the dough balls, reserving the trimmings.

STEP 9 Cut the dough circles in ½ to give 10 semi-circles. Fold over ⅓ of 1 semi-circle, to create a triangle. Use the pastry glue to stick together the 2 straight edges, creating a cone. Spoon ⅒ of the filling into the cone. Glue the top and press to seal the edges. Place on a baking sheet, then repeat for the remaining circles.

STEP 10 Make a small ball of pastry trimmings, colour it pink and roll it out to 1mm thick. Cut out 30 stars and stick 3 on each samosa.

STEP 11 Fry the samosas in batches of 3, for 3–5 minutes until crisp and golden. Drain on kitchen paper, then serve with the chutney.

SPICY SALMON QUICHE

The key to achieving the silky smooth texture of a quiche is beating the cream and eggs until they foam. Don't over-bake, though – the quiche is ready when it's risen and has a tiny wobble in the centre.

SERVES 6

FOR THE CREAM-CHEESE PASTRY

100G FULL-FAT CREAM CHEESE

70G UNSALTED BUTTER, SOFTENED

200G PLAIN FLOUR, PLUS EXTRA FOR DUSTING

½ TSP SALT

2 TBSP WHOLE MILK

FOR THE FILLING

180G HOT SMOKED SALMON, PLAIN OR SWEET CHILLI

½ RED PEPPER, DICED FINELY

4 SPRING ONIONS, SLICED

200ML DOUBLE CREAM

4 EGGS, PLUS 2 EGG YOLKS

PINCH OF CHILLI FLAKES

1 TSP CREAMED HORSERADISH

½ TSP SALT

1 TBSP CHOPPED PARSLEY

YOU WILL NEED

36 X 12CM LOOSE-BOTTOMED RECTANGULAR TART TIN OR 23CM LOOSE-BOTTOMED ROUND OR FLUTED TART TIN; BAKING PAPER; BAKING BEANS

STEP 1 First, make the pastry. In a bowl, use a wooden spoon to beat together the cream cheese with the butter. Add the flour and salt and beat until incorporated. Add the milk and use your hands to bring the pastry together. Gently knead to form a ball. Wrap the pastry in cling film and leave to rest in the fridge for 30 minutes.

STEP 2 Heat your oven to 200°C/180°C fan/400°F/ Gas 6. On a lightly floured worktop, roll out the pastry until it is 3mm thick and use it to line the tart tin. Leave the excess pastry overhanging the edge.

STEP 3 Line the pastry case with baking paper and fill with baking beans. Bake the pastry case blind for 15 minutes, until the pastry is dry to the touch. Remove the beans and baking paper and return the pastry case to the oven for 5 more minutes, until golden. Remove from the oven and trim away any excess pastry from the rim to neaten.

STEP 4 Lower the oven temperature to 190°C/170°C fan/375°F/Gas 5. Now, make the filling. Flake the salmon into a bowl and mix in the diced peppers and sliced spring onions. Scatter the mixture over the pastry case.

STEP 5 In a clean bowl, whisk the cream with the eggs and egg yolks until light and foamy. Add the chilli flakes, horseradish, salt and parsley, and stir to combine.

STEP 6 Carefully pour the mixture over the salmon and spring onions. Bake the quiche for 25–30 minutes, until risen and golden, with a slight wobble in the middle. Leave in the tin for 15 minutes, then serve warm.

PIES FROM THE ARCHIVES

DOWN-THE-RABBIT-HOLE BANQUET PIE

This delicious banquet pie is fit for any family celebration. Rich venison filling in a hot-water crust and decorated with trinkets from the tales of Alice's adventures, this is a magical showstopper indeed.

SERVES 12

FOR THE FILLING

2 LARGE SWEET POTATOES, PEELED, CUT INTO 5MM ROUNDS

4 TBSP LIGHT OLIVE OIL

2 TSP HERBES DE PROVENCE

300G MIXED MUSHROOMS, SLICED

2 RED ONIONS, DICED

1 TSP CHOPPED GARLIC

500G MINCED PORK

500G VENISON SAUSAGES, SKINS REMOVED

200G SMOKED BACK BACON, DICED

1 BEEF STOCK CUBE

2 TSP MIXED SPICE

250ML RED WINE

100G BLACKBERRIES

SALT AND PEPPER, TO SEASON

FOR THE HOT-WATER CRUST

100G LARD

½ TSP SALT

450G PLAIN FLOUR

100G STRONG WHITE BREAD FLOUR

75G UNSALTED BUTTER, DICED

2 EGGS, BEATEN

FOR THE DECORATION

½ QUANTITY OF SAVOURY SHORTCRUST PASTRY (SEE P.310)

PURPLE, RED AND BLACK FOOD-COLOURING GEL

125G ROYAL ICING SUGAR, MIXED WITH 1 TSP WATER

EDIBLE GOLD PAINT

YOU WILL NEED

2 BAKING TRAYS LINED WITH BAKING PAPER; 20CM LOOSE-BOTTOMED CAKE TIN, OILED; CAKE-DECORATING PAINTBRUSH; TEAPOT, RABBIT AND 3CM-ROUND CUTTERS; PIPING BAG WITH A NO.1 WRITING NOZZLE; RICE PAPER CIRCLE FOR THE WATCH FACE AND RECTANGLES FOR THE CARDS

STEP 1 Heat your oven to 200°C/180°F/400°F/Gas 6. Place the sweet potato slices onto the prepared tray. Brush with half the olive oil and sprinkle with the herbs. Bake for 25 minutes, until tender.

STEP 2 Heat 1 tablespoon of the remaining olive oil in a large frying pan. In batches fry the mushrooms until golden brown. Set aside in a bowl.

STEP 3 Mix the onion, garlic, pork, sausagemeat and bacon in a large bowl until fully combined. Heat the frying pan to a medium–high heat. Add the remaining oil and cook the meat mixture, stirring, until browned. Crumble over the stock cube, add the mixed spice, then season, and stir to combine. Add the wine, stir, and simmer for 20–25 minutes, until the liquid has evaporated. Transfer to the bowl with the mushrooms. Add the blackberries, stir, and leave to cool completely.

STEP 4 To make the hot water crust, heat the lard, salt and 200ml of water in a small pan until the lard has melted. Place the flours in a large bowl and rub in the butter. Pour in the hot lard liquid and mix to combine. Tip out the dough onto a lightly floured worktop and knead until smooth.

STEP 5 Roll ¼ of the pastry to an oval about 30 x 20cm. Place on a prepared tray. Put ½ the beaten egg in a bowl and colour it purple. Brush the coloured wash over the pastry.

STEP 6 Roll another ¼ of the pastry into a 20cm circle. Set aside. Roll the remaining pastry into a large circle and use it to line the cake tin, overhanging the excess.

STEP 7 Place a layer of sweet potato over the pastry base in the tin. Top with a ⅓ of the meat filling. Layer to use up the ingredients, then top with the 20cm pastry circle. Trim the excess and pinch to seal.

STEP 8 Carefully invert the tin and place it onto the purple base. Remove the tin and mould the pastry to make the bottom of the 'hat' narrower than the top. Colour red the remaining beaten egg and brush it over the hat.

STEP 9 Heat the oven to 200°C/180°C fan/400°F/Gas 6. Tie a baking paper 'collar' around the pie with string, for support. Bake for 45 minutes.

STEP 10 Roll the shortcrust out and cut out 3 teapots, 2 playing cards, 2 rabbits and 1 'watch' and chain. Use more pastry and red wash to make roses. Remove the pie from the oven and stick on the decorations with egg wash. Bake for 40 minutes more, then cool for 30 minutes.

STEP 11 Use the royal icing to pipe details on the teapots and rabbits. Use the black food colouring to add rabbit eyes, and to paint a watch face and playing cards on the pieces of rice paper. Paint the watch pastry gold. Use egg wash to stick on the rice paper details.

CRACKER SELECTION

Homemade crackers are simple to make. Here are a few recipes to get you started – feel free to create your own versions by adding different spices, herbs and toppings.

CELERY SALT CRACKERS

MAKES ABOUT 15

125G PLAIN FLOUR

1 TSP CELERY SALT

60G UNSALTED BUTTER, DICED

2 TSP RUNNY HONEY

A LITTLE SEA SALT, FOR TOPPING

YOU WILL NEED

BAKING SHEET LINED WITH BAKING PAPER; 2 SHEETS OF BAKING PAPER

STEP 1 Mix the flour and celery salt together. Rub in the butter until the mixture resembles fine crumbs. Add the honey and just enough water to bring the dough together. Wrap in cling film and chill for 30 minutes.

STEP 2 Heat the oven to 200°C/180°C fan/400°F/Gas 6. Roll out the dough between 2 sheets of baking paper until it is 2mm thick. Remove the top sheet. Trim the ends and sides of the dough, then cut into 5cm squares.

STEP 3 Put the squares on the baking tray. Sprinkle with salt and bake for 8–10 minutes until golden and crisp. Leave to cool on the baking tray for 5 minutes, then transfer to a wire rack to cool completely.

OATCAKES

MAKES ABOUT 30

100G UNSALTED BUTTER, SOFTENED

65G CASTER SUGAR

1 LARGE EGG, BEATEN

200G WHOLEMEAL PLAIN FLOUR

100G PORRIDGE OATS

1 TSP SALT

¼ TSP BAKING POWDER

YOU WILL NEED

2 BAKING SHEETS LINED WITH BAKING PAPER; 6.5CM ROUND CUTTER

STEP 1 Heat the oven to 200°C/180°C fan/400°F/Gas 6. Cream the butter and sugar together in a mixing bowl, until pale. Add the egg, then stir in the flour, oats, salt and baking powder to form a dough.

STEP 2 Tip out the dough onto a lightly floured worktop and knead until smooth. Roll out to 5mm thick, then stamp out 6.5cm rounds, re-rolling the offcuts, as necessary.

STEP 3 Transfer the oatcakes to the lined trays. Bake for 10 minutes, or until firm to the touch and light golden brown. Leave to cool on the trays for 5 minutes, then transfer to a wire rack to cool completely.

SEEDED CRACKERS

MAKES ABOUT 14

75G PLAIN FLOUR

40G FINE SEMOLINA

½ TSP SALT

1 TSP SMOKED PAPRIKA

55G MIXED SEEDS

2 TSP RUNNY HONEY

1 TBSP SUNFLOWER OIL

YOU WILL NEED

BAKING SHEET LINED WITH BAKING PAPER

STEP 1 Mix the all the dry ingredients in a bowl, and in a jug mix the honey and oil with 5 tablespoons of water. Slowly pour the wet mixture into the dry. Stir to combine, until the sides of the bowl are clean and you have a firm dough.

STEP 2 Tip out the dough onto a lightly floured worktop and knead for a few minutes until smooth. Wrap in cling film and chill for 30 minutes.

STEP 3 Heat the oven to 200°C/180°C fan/400°F/Gas 6. Roll out the dough to 2–3mm thick. Cut into triangles, then place on the baking tray. Bake for 15 minutes, until golden. Leave to cool on the baking tray for 5 minutes, then transfer to a wire rack to cool completely.

INDIVIDUAL COURGETTE & KALE TARTS

These pretty tarts will be
a crowd pleaser – whether
your guests are vegetarian
or not. They are light and
fresh, with tarragon and just
a hint of tangy goat's cheese.

MAKES 5

75G UNSALTED BUTTER,
SOFTENED

150G PLAIN FLOUR

1 EGG YOLK

1 TBSP CHILLED WATER

FOR THE FILLING

100G SOFT GOAT'S CHEESE

1 COURGETTE, SLICED
INTO RIBBONS USING
A VEGETABLE PEELER

HANDFUL OF KALE, TORN INTO
SMALL PIECES

100ML DOUBLE CREAM

150ML WHOLE MILK

2 LARGE EGGS, PLUS 2 LARGE EGG
YOLKS

1 TBSP CHOPPED TARRAGON

SALT AND WHITE PEPPER

YOU WILL NEED

INDIVIDUAL 10CM LOOSE-
BOTTOMED TART TINS (3CM DEEP)
X 5; BAKING TRAY; 10CM CIRCLES
OF BAKING PAPER X 4; BAKING
BEANS

STEP 1 First, make the
pastry. Put the butter and
flour in a mixing bowl, and
rub with your fingertips until
it resembles fine crumbs.
Add the egg yolk and stir to
combine. Sprinkle over the
water and mix to form a soft
pastry. If you need more water
add it 1 teaspoon at a time.

STEP 2 Tip out the dough
onto a lightly floured worktop
and gently knead (don't
overwork it) until smooth.
Use your hands to shape the
dough into a flat disc, then
wrap it in cling film and
chill for 30 minutes.

STEP 3 Heat the oven to
200°C/180°C fan/400°F/Gas
6. Tip out the pastry onto a
lightly dusted worktop. Divide
it into 5 equal pieces. Roll
each piece to a circle 3–4mm
thick and large enough to fill a
tart tin with a little overhang.

STEP 4 Line each tin with
a pastry circle, leaving the
excess to overhang. Place the
tart tins on a baking sheet and
line each case with baking
paper, then fill with baking
beans. Blind bake the cases
for 10 minutes, until the
pastry is dry to touch. Remove
the paper and beans and
return the cases to the oven
for 5 minutes, until golden.
Trim away any excess.

STEP 5 Lower the oven
temperature to 190°C/
170°C fan/375°F/Gas 5. Using
½ the goat's cheese, place
½-teaspoon-sized dots on the
base of each tart case. Roll the
courgette ribbons into loose
coils and place them in and
around the cheese dots.
Wedge kale pieces between
the courgette coils.

STEP 6 Whisk the cream,
milk, eggs and egg yolks until
light and foamy. Season with
salt and pepper and add the
tarragon. Carefully pour the
mixture into the pastry cases,
filling them ¾ full. Chop up
the remaining goat's cheese
and dot it over the courgettes.

STEP 7 Bake the tarts for
15–20 minutes, until the
filling is golden and just set.
Remove from the oven, leave
to cool in the tins a little,
then remove from the tins
and serve warm.

DUCK B'STEEYA

This Moroccan pie is an aromatic mix of spices encased in filo pastry. Traditionally a dish made with pigeon, this version uses duck. None of the steps to make the dish is difficult, but you do need patience. Serve with a salad.

SERVES 6

4 DUCK LEGS, CHILLED

2 LARGE ONIONS, SLICED

3 GARLIC CLOVES, CHOPPED

3CM PIECE OF GINGER, PEELED AND FINELY DICED

1 CINNAMON STICK

PINCH OF SAFFRON

500ML CHICKEN STOCK

½ TSP GROUND NUTMEG

1 TBSP RUNNY HONEY

4 DRIED FIGS, CHOPPED INTO SMALL PIECES

1 TBSP CHOPPED PARSLEY

1 TBSP CHOPPED CORIANDER

3 TBSP PINE NUTS

3 EGGS, BEATEN

6 SHEETS OF FILO PASTRY

60G UNSALTED BUTTER, MELTED

1 TBSP ICING SUGAR MIXED WITH 1 TSP GROUND CINNAMON, FOR DUSTING (OPTIONAL)

SALT AND GROUND BLACK PEPPER

YOU WILL NEED

20CM SPRINGFORM TIN; BAKING SHEET; 20CM ROUND CUTTER (OR USE THE SPRINGFORM TIN RING)

STEP 1 Place the chilled duck legs in a large casserole dish, skin-side down. Slowly cook the duck over a medium heat for about 10–15 minutes, until the fat melts and the skin turns golden. (Cooking the duck from cold allows the fat to melt.) Remove from the pan and set aside. Discard half the duck fat in the pan.

STEP 2 Add the onions to the casserole and cook slowly in the remaining duck fat for 10–15 minutes, until soft and turning golden. Add the garlic, ginger, cinnamon and saffron, season with salt and pepper, then stir. Cook for 2 minutes, until you can smell the ginger and garlic. Return the duck legs to the pan, add the stock, cover and cook for 45 minutes to 1 hour, until the meat is coming away from the bone.

STEP 3 Remove the pan from the heat, scoop out the duck and leave until cool enough to handle. Strip the meat from the bone, discarding the skin and bones.

STEP 4 Strain the cooking liquid through a sieve into a clean pan, reserving the contents of the sieve. Heat the liquid until it boils, then continue to boil for about 5–10 minutes, until reduced by half. Set aside.

STEP 5 Discard the cinnamon stick from the sieve contents, then transfer the remaining contents to a bowl. Add the duck, nutmeg, honey, figs, parsley, coriander and pine nuts. Mix well.

STEP 6 Stir the beaten eggs into the reduced stock. Cook over a low heat until the egg scrambles, about 5 minutes. Add to the duck mixture with the pine nuts, season to taste, stir, then leave to cool completely.

STEP 7 Heat the oven to 190°C/170°C fan/375°F/ Gas 5. Lay 1 sheet of filo on your worktop, brush with butter and place on the base of the springform tin with the edges overhanging the sides. Repeat with 3 further sheets of filo, so that the base and sides of the tin are completely covered.

STEP 8 Tip the duck filling into the filo case. Use a cutter to cut the remaining filo into 20cm circles, brush with butter and place on top of the filling. Fold the overhanging filo over the circles and brush with more butter. Bake for 20–25 minutes, until crisp. Cool in the tin for 10 minutes.

STEP 9 While the pie is still warm, dust with the icing sugar and cinnamon mixture, if using. Serve warm.

PIES FROM THE ARCHIVES

NAN'S SUNDAY DINNER PIE

This turmeric-infused pastry case contains a spicy and colourful filling of meat, peppers, potatoes and plantains, richly seasoned with curry powder, ginger and garlic, and topped with salsa just before serving.

SERVES 12

FOR THE CURRY FILLING

1KG DICED GOAT, MUTTON
OR LAMB LEG

1 LEMON (OPTIONAL)

2 GARLIC CLOVES, FINELY
CHOPPED

40G ROOT GINGER, PEELED
AND FINELY CHOPPED

1 LARGE RED ONION,
FINELY CHOPPED

1 RED PEPPER, DESEEDED
AND CUT INTO 1CM CHUNKS

1 YELLOW PEPPER, DESEEDED
AND CUT INTO 1CM CHUNKS

1 TBSP SMOKED SWEET PAPRIKA

1 TBSP MILD CURRY POWDER

1 LARGE POTATO, PEELED AND
CHOPPED INTO 1CM CHUNKS

2 TBSP RAPESEED OR
SUNFLOWER OIL

1½ LARGE PLANTAINS,
PEELED AND CHOPPED
INTO 0.5CM CHUNKS

SALT AND GROUND
BLACK PEPPER

FOR THE HOT-WATER CRUST

500G PLAIN FLOUR

150G STRONG WHITE BREAD
FLOUR

125G UNSALTED BUTTER,
CHILLED AND DICED

½ TSP FINE SEA SALT

2 TSP GROUND TURMERIC

150G LARD, DICED

1 EGG, BEATEN

FOR THE SALSA TOPPING

1 VERY LARGE MANGO
(ABOUT 550G), PEELED,
STONED AND DICED

2 RIPE AVOCADOS, PEELED,
STONED AND DICED

125G POMEGRANATE SEEDS

1 SMALL RED ONION, FINELY
CHOPPED

FINELY GRATED ZEST AND JUICE
OF 1 LARGE UNWAXED LIME

1 TBSP OLIVE OIL

SMALL BUNCH OF CORIANDER,
FINELY CHOPPED

YOU WILL NEED

17CM ROUND CAKE TIN;
HEATPROOF PASTRY BRUSH;
BAKING TRAY LINED WITH
BAKING PAPER

STEP 1 Put all the curry filling ingredients, except the potato, oil and plantain, into a large bowl, season to taste and use your hands to thoroughly combine. Cover and chill for at least 1 hour, or overnight.

STEP 2 To make the crust, put both flours into a large heatproof bowl. Rub in the butter until the mixture resembles fine crumbs. Make a well in the centre.

STEP 3 Pour 250ml of water into a saucepan, then add the salt, turmeric and lard, and heat until the lard melts and the mixture comes to the boil. Pour the lard mixture into the well in the dry mixture and mix using a wooden spoon.

STEP 4 Turn out the dough onto a lightly floured worktop and knead for 3–4 minutes, until very smooth and glossy. Cut off ¼ of the dough, wrap it in cling film and set aside.

STEP 5 Cover the outer base and sides of the cake tin with cling film and place it upside down on the worktop. Roll out the large piece of pastry to a disc about 1cm thick, and lift it over the cake tin. Press it onto the base then firmly mould it down the sides so the pastry covers the tin with no creases or pleats and is at least 10cm high all round.

RECIPE CONTINUES OVERLEAF »»

 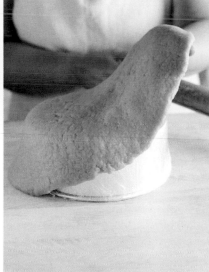 

STEP 6 Roll out the remaining pastry to a neat disc to make the pie lid. Set on a plate or baking sheet lined with cling film and cover. Refrigerate the pie case and lid for about 1 hour, until very firm.

STEP 7 Meanwhile finish the filling. Stir the potato chunks into the chilled meat mixture. Heat ⅓ of the oil in a large non-stick frying pan and add about ⅓ of the filling. Stir-fry so it just starts to colour, then transfer to a heatproof bowl. Repeat twice more.

STEP 8 Heat the oven to 200°C/180°C fan/400°F/ Gas 6. Remove the pastry case from the fridge and place it upright on the lined baking sheet. Trim the pastry sides with a sharp knife so they are even. Remove the cake tin, then peel away the cling film, leaving a neat pastry shell.

STEP 9 Spoon in ⅓ of the cooled filling into the pastry shell. Scatter with ⅓ of the plantain. Repeat the filling and plantain layers twice more. Brush the pastry rim with beaten egg, then gently set the pastry lid on top and pinch the edges together to seal. Crimp the pastry rim, then brush the whole pie with beaten egg.

STEP 10 Bake the pie for 30 minutes, until just starting to colour, then reduce the temperature to 170°C/150°C fan/325°F/Gas 3 and bake for a further 90 minutes, until the pastry is golden and crisp. Leave to cool and firm up for 20 minutes, then transfer to a wire rack to cool completely.

STEP 11 Meanwhile, make the salsa by combining all the ingredients in a bowl. To serve, spoon a little salsa around and over the pie and serve the remainder on the side.

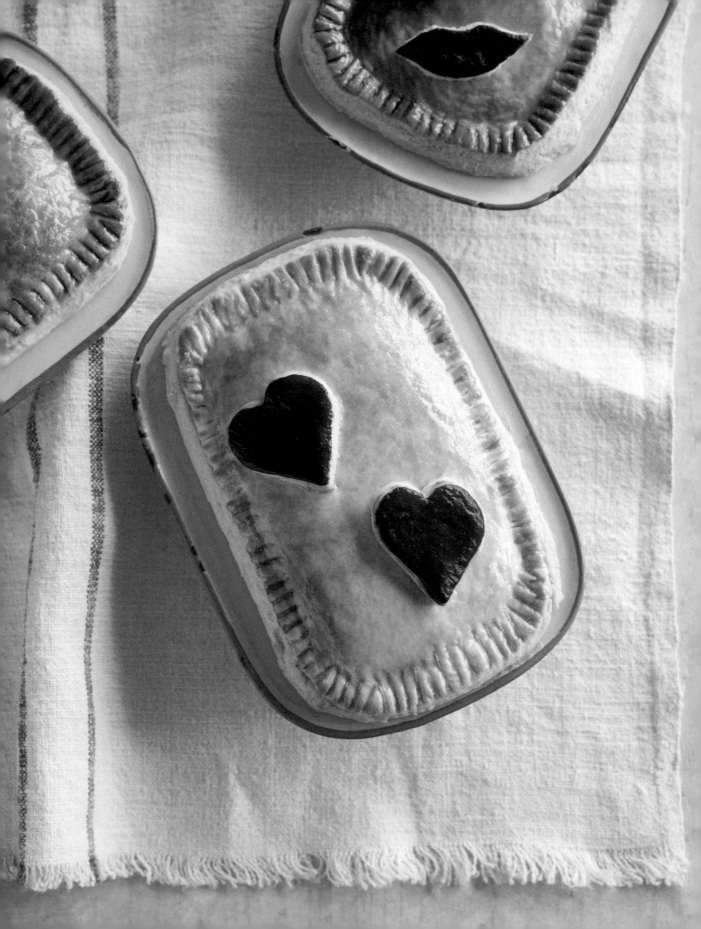

BAKER'S RECIPE

OLD-FASHIONED MINCED BEEF PIES

Made with a traditional butter-rich shortcrust pastry, these classic pies are filled with lean minced beef and flavoured with warm, aromatic spices. Shaped cutters and coloured egg wash make for creative and fun pie lids.

MAKES 4 INDIVIDUAL PIES

50G PINE NUTS

2 TBSP SUNFLOWER OIL

1 ONION, FINELY CHOPPED

500G VERY LEAN MINCED BEEF

¼ TSP GROUND CINNAMON

½ TSP GROUND ALLSPICE

2 PINCHES OF DRIED RED CHILLI FLAKES

1½ TBSP TOMATO PURÉE

100ML HOT BEEF STOCK

SALT AND GROUND BLACK PEPPER

FOR THE SHORTCRUST PASTRY

600G PLAIN FLOUR

¼ TSP SALT

300G UNSALTED BUTTER, CHILLED AND DICED

ABOUT 125ML CHILLED WATER

1 EGG, BEATEN

EDIBLE FOOD COLOURING (OPTIONAL)

YOU WILL NEED

4 INDIVIDUAL PIE TINS (13.5 X 10CM), GREASED; LARGE BAKING SHEET; SHAPED PASTRY CUTTERS (SUCH AS HEARTS); CAKE-DECORATING PAINTBRUSH (OPTIONAL)

STEP 1 Toast the pine nuts in a dry frying pan over a low heat, until just coloured. Set aside. Heat half the oil in a medium pan, add the chopped onion, cover and cook over a low heat for about 10 minutes, until very soft and golden. Transfer to a heatproof plate.

STEP 2 Add the remaining oil to the pan and set over a medium–high heat. When hot, add the minced beef and stir until lightly browned. Stir in the cinnamon, allspice and chilli, season with salt and pepper, then add the purée and cooked onions. Stir in the stock and bring to the boil.

STEP 3 Reduce the heat to low, then cover and simmer for about 15 minutes, or until the meat is soft. Uncover and cook until the liquid has almost evaporated. Stir in the pine nuts and leave to cool.

STEP 4 To make the pastry, tip the flour and salt into a food processor. Add the butter and blitz to fine crumbs. With the machine running, add enough of the chilled water to bring together to a soft dough.

STEP 5 Divide the dough into 8 equal portions. Shape each into a thick disc, then wrap in cling film and chill for about 15 minutes.

STEP 6 Unwrap half the dough discs and place on a lightly floured worktop. Roll out each portion to an oval 2.5mm thick and use it to line the base and sides of the pie tins. Trim off the excess, reserving the scraps. Chill the pastry cases for 15 minutes.

STEP 7 Divide the filling equally between the pie dishes. Roll out the remaining pastry pieces to 2.5mm thick, and, using a sharp knife, cut oval discs to cover each pie. Brush the pie rims with egg, then press each pastry lid in place, sealing all around the rim with the tines of a fork. Re-roll all the trimmings, and cut or mould them to decorate the pie lids, securing with beaten egg. Return the pies to the fridge.

STEP 8 Heat the oven to 220°C/200°C fan/425°F/Gas 7 and put a large baking sheet inside to heat up. Brush each chilled pie with beaten egg. If you wish to colour the decorations, portion out the remaining beaten egg and stir a few drops of a different edible food colouring into each portion – 'paint' your pies with the glazes. Bake the pies on the heated baking sheet for 25 minutes, until the pastry is a rich golden brown. Serve hot.

POTATO CRUST QUICHE

This spring-inspired tart is a perfect lunch or supper dish. Serve it up warm with new potatoes and a salad on the side.

SERVES 6

180G POTATOES, SUCH AS MARIS PIPER OR DESIRÉE, LEFT WHOLE

200G GLUTEN-FREE PLAIN FLOUR

PINCH OF SALT

½ TSP XANTHAN GUM

100G UNSALTED BUTTER, DICED

1 EGG, BEATEN

FOR THE FILLING

25G UNSALTED BUTTER

2 SHALLOTS, FINELY DICED

1 COURGETTE, COARSELY GRATED

1 TSP SALT, PLUS EXTRA TO SEASON

PINCH OF WHITE PEPPER, PLUS EXTRA TO SEASON

3 LARGE EGGS, PLUS 1 LARGE EGG YOLK

175ML DOUBLE CREAM

GRATED ZEST OF 1 UNWAXED LEMON

2 TBSP FINELY CHOPPED CHIVES

30G FROZEN PEAS

50G FROZEN SOYA BEANS

4 SPRING ONIONS, FINELY SLICED

75G RICOTTA CHEESE

YOU WILL NEED

20CM LOOSE-BOTTOMED TART TIN (3.5CM DEEP); BAKING PAPER; BAKING BEANS; BAKING SHEET

STEP 1 First, make the crust. Cook the potatoes in boiling salted water in their skins, until tender (how long they take will depend on the size of the potatoes). Once cooked, drain and leave until cool enough to handle, then remove the skins and mash using a potato ricer. Set aside to cool completely.

STEP 2 Place the flour in a bowl with the salt and xanthan gum and stir to combine. Rub in the butter, until the mixture resembles fine crumbs. Add the cold mashed potato and mix to a soft dough. Wrap in cling film and chill for 30 minutes to firm up.

STEP 3 Make the filling. Melt the butter in a medium frying pan over a low–medium heat. Add the shallots and cook until soft and golden, about 5–8 minutes. Add the courgette and cook for 2–3 minutes, until soft. Increase the heat to high, keep stirring and cook until any liquid has evaporated. Mix in the salt and pepper, then transfer to a bowl to cool.

STEP 4 Heat the oven to 200°C/180°C fan/400°F/Gas 6. Remove the potato crust dough from the fridge.

STEP 5 Unwrap the dough onto a lightly floured worktop. Roll it out to a circle 3mm thick and use this to line the tart tin, leaving the excess hanging over the edge. Don't worry if the pastry breaks, just push and mould it in the tin to repair. Prick the base, then line with baking paper and fill with baking beans.

STEP 6 Place the pastry case on a baking tray, bake blind for 20 minutes, then remove the paper and beans. Brush the base with beaten egg. Return the pastry case to the oven and cook for 10 minutes, until the base is dry. Trim away the excess pastry from the rim.

STEP 7 Reduce the oven temperature to 190°C/170°C fan/375°F/Gas 5. Whisk the eggs, egg yolk, cream, and lemon zest together in a bowl. Add the chives and season with salt and pepper.

STEP 8 Spoon the cooled shallot and courgette mixture into the pastry base and spread it out evenly. Scatter over the peas, soya beans and spring onions. Dot over the ricotta cheese, then pour the egg mixture over. Bake for 30–35 minutes, until the filling is just set and golden on top. Leave in the tin for 5 minutes before serving.

MUSHROOM BOURGUIGNON PITHIVIER

Impress your guests with this stunning but easy-to-make vegetarian pie. It uses different varieties of fresh mushroom, which, along with dried porcini, gives the filling texture and depth of flavour.

SERVES 4

1 TBSP DRIED PORCINI MUSHROOMS

90ML BOILING WATER

25G BUTTER

2 TBSP OLIVE OIL

2 LARGE FLAT MUSHROOMS, SUCH AS PORTOBELLO, SLICED

100G BABY BUTTON MUSHROOMS

1 ONION, THINLY SLICED

1 GARLIC CLOVE, CRUSHED

2 TSP TOMATO PURÉE

4 THYME SPRIGS

1 BAY LEAF

1 TSP RUNNY HONEY

300ML RED WINE

500G PUFF PASTRY (SEE P.309)

1 EGG, BEATEN, TO GLAZE

SALT AND GROUND BLACK PEPPER

YOU WILL NEED

BAKING TRAY LINED WITH BAKING PAPER; RULER

STEP 1 Soak the dried porcini mushrooms in the boiling water, until softened and plumped up.

STEP 2 Heat the butter and half the oil in a large frying pan over a medium–high heat for 2–3 minutes, until melted and combined. In batches, fry the sliced flat and baby mushrooms for about 3–4 minutes per batch, until they are golden brown. Remove each batch from the pan and set aside.

STEP 3 In the same pan, add the remaining oil and gently fry the onion over a medium heat for 5–6 minutes, until soft and light golden brown.

STEP 4 Add the garlic and cook for 1 minute. Add the tomato purée, stir and cook for 1–2 minutes. Then, add the thyme, bay leaf, honey and wine, along with the soaked mushrooms and their soaking liquid. Bring the liquid to a simmer and cook for 25 minutes, until the liquid has reduced and thickened.

STEP 5 Transfer the mixture to a bowl, leave to cool, then refrigerate to cool completely. (This is important to make sure the mixture isn't sloppy.)

STEP 6 Divide the puff pastry in two, roughly ⅔ and ⅓. On a lightly dusted worktop, roll out the smaller piece of pastry to 4mm thick, then cut out a circle 23cm in diameter. Place the pastry circle on the lined baking tray. This is the pithivier base. Roll the remaining pastry to a circle larger than the base – this will form the lid.

STEP 7 Spoon the cold filling onto the pastry base, leaving a 2cm border around the edge. Brush the edge with a little beaten egg.

STEP 8 Place the lid over the filling and press the edges together to seal. Brush the top with beaten egg, then use a small, sharp knife to score curved lines from the centre out to the edge of the pastry. Make a small hole in the centre. Refrigerate the pie for at least 30 minutes to rest.

STEP 9 Heat the oven to 200°C/180°C fan/400°F/ Gas 6. Bake the pithivier for 35–40 minutes, until the pastry is risen and golden. Serve hot with seasonal vegetables.

INDIVIDUAL PICNIC PIES

Crisp, hot-water pastry cases filled with chicken, apricots and pistachio nuts, these little pies are perfect for a family picnic. You need to work quickly with this pastry, as when it cools it begins to crack.

MAKES 6

....

70G LARD

....

175G PLAIN FLOUR

....

75G STRONG WHITE BREAD FLOUR

....

1 TSP SALT

....

50G UNSALTED BUTTER, CHILLED AND DICED

....

FOR THE FILLING

2 SHALLOTS, FINELY CHOPPED

....

200G TURKEY THIGH MINCE

....

200G CHICKEN BREAST, DICED

....

75G DRIED APRICOTS, CHOPPED

....

2 TBSP PISTACHIO KERNELS

....

1 TSP SALT

....

½ TSP GROUND WHITE PEPPER

....

½ TSP GROUND MACE

....

3 TBSP CHOPPED PARSLEY

....

1 EGG, BEATEN

....

1 CHICKEN STOCK CUBE

....

100ML BOILING WATER

....

1 GELATINE LEAF

....

YOU WILL NEED

6-HOLE MUFFIN TRAY;
7CM ROUND CUTTER

....

STEP 1 Heat the oven to 190°C/170°C fan/375°F/ Gas 5. First, make the pastry. Melt the lard in a small pan with 100ml of water over a medium heat. Stir, then heat until the water just begins to boil, about 5–8 minutes. Remove from the heat.

STEP 2 Working quickly, in a bowl mix the flours and salt together. Rub in the butter until the mixture resembles fine crumbs. Make a well in the centre and pour in the hot lard liquid (don't wash the pan). Use a wooden spoon to mix to a soft pastry.

STEP 3 Tip out the dough onto a lightly dusted worktop and knead gently until the pastry is smooth and glossy. Cut off a ⅓ of the pastry, pop it into the hot pan you used for the lard and cover with cling film. (This helps to keep it warm while you roll out the bases.)

STEP 4 Divide the remaining pastry into 6 equal pieces and roll each into a 9cm circle. Use these to line the muffin tray. Remove the warm pastry from the pan. Roll it out to a rough circle 4mm thick, and stamp out lids using the 7cm cutter. Re-roll the trimmings as necessary.

STEP 5 To make the filling, mix together the shallots, turkey, chicken, apricots, pistachios, salt, pepper, mace and parsley in a bowl. Divide the filling equally between the pastry cases in the muffin tray, piling it up to a well-filled mound, and brush the edge of each case with beaten egg. Top each with a pastry lid and press the edges to seal. Trim away any excess.

STEP 6 Make a small slit in the top of each pie and brush with beaten egg. Bake for 35–40 minutes, until the pastry is crisp and golden.

STEP 7 Dissolve the stock cube in the boiling water. Soak the gelatine sheet in a little water. Once the gelatine is soft, squeeze out any excess, then add to the hot stock. Pour a little stock into the hole in the top of each pie. Leave to cool, then place in the fridge for at least 2 hours to set.

CONVERSION TABLES

WEIGHT

METRIC	IMPERIAL	METRIC	IMPERIAL	METRIC	IMPERIAL	METRIC	IMPERIAL
25g	1oz	200g	7oz	425g	15oz	800g	1lb 12oz
50g	2oz	225g	8oz	450g	1lb	850g	1lb 14oz
75g	2½oz	250g	9oz	500g	1lb 2oz	900g	2lb
85g	3oz	280g	10oz	550g	1lb 4oz	950g	2lb 2oz
100g	4oz	300g	11oz	600g	1lb 5oz	1kg	2lb 4oz
125g	4½oz	350g	12oz	650g	1lb 7oz		
140g	5oz	375g	13oz	700g	1lb 9oz		
175g	6oz	400g	14oz	750g	1lb 10oz		

VOLUME

METRIC	IMPERIAL	METRIC	IMPERIAL	METRIC	IMPERIAL	METRIC	IMPERIAL
30ml	1fl oz	150ml	½ pint	300ml	½ pint	500ml	18fl oz
50ml	2fl oz	175ml	6fl oz	350ml	12fl oz	600ml	1 pint
75ml	2½fl oz	200ml	7fl oz	400ml	14fl oz	700ml	1¼ pints
100ml	3½fl oz	225ml	8fl oz	425ml	¾ pint	850ml	1½ pints
125ml	4fl oz	250ml	9fl oz	450ml	16fl oz	1 litre	1¾ pints

LINEAR

METRIC	IMPERIAL	METRIC	IMPERIAL	METRIC	IMPERIAL	METRIC	IMPERIAL
2.5cm	1 in	7.5cm	3 in	13cm	5 in	20cm	8 in
3cm	1¼ in	8cm	3¼ in	14cm	5½ in	22cm	8½ in
4cm	1½ in	9cm	3½ in	15cm	6 in	23cm	9 in
5cm	2 in	9.5cm	3¾ in	16cm	6¼ in	24cm	9½ in
5.5cm	2¼ in	10cm	4 in	17cm	6½ in	25cm	10 in
6cm	2½ in	11cm	4¼ in	18cm	7in		
7cm	2¾ in	12cm	4½ in	19cm	7½ in		

SPOON MEASURES

METRIC	IMPERIAL
5ml	1 tsp
10ml	2 tsp
15ml	1 tbsp
30ml	2 tbsp
45ml	3 tbsp
60ml	4 tbsp
75ml	5 tbsp

COOK'S NOTES

Oven temperatures: Ovens vary – not only from brand to brand, but from the front to the back of the oven, as well as between the top and bottom shelves. Get to know your oven, and where its hotspots are, and invest in a cooking thermometer if you can. Always preheat the oven, and use dry oven gloves.

Eggs: Some recipes may contain raw or partially cooked eggs. Pregnant women, the elderly, babies and toddlers, and people who are unwell should be aware of these recipes.

Fresh herbs and fruit: Use fresh herbs and fruit unless the recipe specifies otherwise.

Salt: If a recipe calls for a small, or hard-to-weigh amount, a ½ teaspoon fine salt weighs 2.5g, and a ¼ teaspoon weighs 1.25g. If you're using sea salt it is best to crush the flakes into a fine powder before measuring and adding to your recipe (unless specified).

Spoon measures: All teaspoons and tablespoons are level unless otherwise stated.

BASIC RECIPES

ICING

BUTTERCREAM

Richer, lighter and creamier than butter icing, buttercream is also slightly trickier. Use a sugar thermometer for the best results.

Makes: enough to decorate 24 fairy cakes, 12 larger cupcakes, or to fill and top a 20cm sponge cake

85g caster sugar
2 large egg yolks
150g unsalted butter, well
    softened, but not runny
For vanilla buttercream
1 tsp vanilla extract
For chocolate buttercream
75g 70% dark chocolate, melted
    and cooled
For coffee buttercream
1–2 tbsp very strong liquid
    coffee, cooled

STEP 1 Put the sugar and 4 tablespoons of water into a small pan and heat gently, without boiling, until the sugar dissolves. Swirl the pan from time to time as the sugar melts. Then, bring to the boil and boil for 5 minutes, or until the temperature reaches 110°C/225°F on a sugar thermometer, but the syrup hasn't caramelised.

STEP 2 While the sugar is dissolving, beat the egg yolks briefly in a heatproof bowl. Pour the hot syrup into the bowl in a thin, steady stream, whisking continuously with an electric whisk as you pour. Once you've added all the syrup, keep whisking until the mixture becomes pale and very thick, and cold.

STEP 3 Gradually whisk in the softened butter, followed by the vanilla, chocolate or coffee, as required. Spoon or pipe the buttercream onto the cakes.

BUTTER ICING

Use to fill and top cupcakes and sponges. Add edible food colouring to colour.

Makes enough to decorate 24 fairy cakes, 12 larger cupcakes, or to fill and top a 20cm sponge cake

125g unsalted butter, softened
400g icing sugar
3–4 tbsp milk
For vanilla butter icing
1 tsp vanilla extract
For chocolate butter icing
3 tbsp cocoa powder

STEP 1 Put the butter into a mixing bowl and beat until pale and creamy.

STEP 2 Sift in the icing sugar, then add the milk and the vanilla or cocoa and beat slowly until smooth and thick. Pipe the icing onto your cakes, or spoon and smooth with a palette knife.

POURING FONDANT

Use to cover fondant fancies, or other cakes for a smart finish.

Makes enough to cover a 23cm sponge cake

250g fondant icing sugar
½ tsp flavouring, such as vanilla
    or pistachio essence (optional)

STEP 1 Sift the fondant icing sugar into a mixing bowl, then add water, a little at a time, to make a thick, pourable fondant. You'll need 3–4 tablespoons of water.

STEP 2 Add the flavouring, if using, and mix thoroughly until completely smooth.

ROLLING FONDANT

Use for sugarcraft or to cover celebration cakes to give a smooth finish.

Makes about 1.2kg

20g powdered gelatine
2 tbsp glycerine
275g liquid glucose
About 900g icing sugar, sifted
Food colouring gel of choice,
    from a 28g tub (optional)

STEP 1 Put 30ml of water into a heatproof bowl and sprinkle over the gelatine. Leave to soak for 5 minutes, or until the mixture looks spongy, then set the bowl onto a pan of very hot water and leave for a few minutes, until the gelatine is smooth and melted. Remove the bowl before the mixture gets hot, and stir in the glycerine and glucose.

STEP 2 Sift the icing sugar into a large bowl and make a well in the centre. Pour the gelatine mixture into the well and start to mix in the icing sugar. As soon as the mixture feels less 'damp', turn it out onto a worktop liberally dusted with icing sugar.

STEP 3 Gradually knead in enough of the remaining icing sugar to make a firm but easy-to-roll fondant icing (you may not need all the icing sugar).

STEP 4 To colour the fondant, if needed, using the tip of a small knife dot the food colouring on the icing and knead it in thoroughly to create an even colour. Add more colouring, little by little, kneading well between each addition, until you reach the desired colour.

CREAMY FILLINGS, CUSTARDS & SAUCES

CRÈME CHANTILLY

Whipped, sweetened cream flavoured with vanilla, crème Chantilly is for spooning and piping. Chill the bowl and whisk, as well as the cream, before you begin, for maximum volume.

Makes about 400g

....

300ml double cream
50g icing sugar
1 tsp vanilla bean paste
You will need
A chilled mixing bowl; a chilled balloon whisk

....

STEP 1 Pour the cream into the bowl and add the icing sugar and vanilla bean paste.

STEP 2 Whisk then whip the cream until it holds a soft peak. Use immediately, or cover and chill for up to 1 hour.

CRÈME PÂTISSIÈRE

Often shortened to 'crème pât', this is a custard-like filling. The cornflour gives a characteristic glossy finish, while whipped cream adds lightness.

Makes about 500ml

....

250ml whole milk
3 large egg yolks
50g caster sugar
1½ tbsp cornflour
150ml double or whipping cream, well chilled
For vanilla crème pâtissière
1 vanilla pod, split lengthways
For citrus crème pâtissière
finely grated zest of 1 unwaxed orange or lemon
For liqueur crème pâtissière
1–2 tbsp liqueur of choice, to taste

....

STEP 1 Put the milk in a medium pan and add the split vanilla pod or the citrus zest (as relevant). Place over a medium heat and warm until the liquid just comes to the boil. Remove the pan from the heat and leave the milk to infuse for 10 minutes. (If you're making vanilla crème pâtissière, remove the vanilla pod and scrape out a few seeds into the milk.)

STEP 2 In a heatproof bowl, whisk the egg yolks with the sugar and cornflour for about 1–2 minutes, until smooth, thick and light. Whisk in the hot milk until combined, then tip the mixture back into the pan and set over medium heat. Whisk until the mixture boils and thickens to a smooth custard.

STEP 3 Pour the custard into a clean bowl and press a piece of cling film on to the surface to prevent a skin forming. Cool, then chill thoroughly.

STEP 4 Whip the cream until it holds a soft peak. Stir the custard until smooth, then add the liqueur, if using, a little at a time, to taste, and stir again. Fold in the whipped cream to combine. You can use the crème pâtissière immediately, or cover it tightly and chill for up to 4 hours.

VANILLA EGG CUSTARD

The best flavour vanilla custard comes from using whole milk and a vanilla pod (not essence).

Serves 4–6

....

425ml creamy milk, such as Jersey or Guernsey
1 vanilla pod, split
4 egg yolks
2½ tbsp caster sugar

....

STEP 1 Put the milk into a medium pan. Scrape some of the tiny seeds from the vanilla pod into the milk, then add the whole pod.

STEP 2 Bring the milk mixture to the boil, stirring frequently with a wooden spoon, then turn off the heat, cover the pan and leave to infuse for about 20 minutes.

STEP 3 Meanwhile, put the yolks and sugar into a heatproof mixing bowl and beat thoroughly with a wooden spoon until very smooth and pale, about 1 minute.

STEP 4 Remove the vanilla pod from the milk (see tip, below). Slowly pour the warm milk on to the yolk and sugar mixture in a thin, steady stream, stirring continuously with the wooden spoon. Tip the mixture back into the pan and stir continuously over medium heat, until the custard thickens enough to coat the back of the spoon – don't let the mixture boil.

STEP 5 As soon as the custard has thickened, pour it into a serving jug and serve immediately. Or, to serve the custard cold or chilled, sprinkle the surface with a thin layer of caster sugar to prevent a skin forming, then cover the top of the jug with cling film. Stir gently before serving. You can keep the custard, tightly covered, in the fridge for up to 2 days.

TIP

Rather than discarding the vanilla pod, rinse it thoroughly, dry it, then use it to make vanilla sugar: simply place the pod in a large screw-top jar and fill with caster sugar. You can use the flavoured sugar for baking cakes in place of regular caster sugar, or for sprinkling.

BITTER CHOCOLATE SAUCE

This sauce will reheat the next day, if you have any leftovers.

Serves 4–6

....

100g 70% dark chocolate, broken into pieces
25g unsalted butter
2 tbsp icing sugar

....

STEP 1 Put all the ingredients in a small pan with 100ml of water. Heat gently over a low heat, stirring frequently, until the chocolate has melted and is smooth. Serve warm.

TIP

To make a chocolate-coffee sauce, substitute the water in the method with 100ml of strong coffee.

FRUIT & NUT FILLINGS & SAUCES

FRESH RASPBERRY SAUCE

This zingy sauce is just as delicious made with defrosted frozen fruit as with fresh. Serve chilled or warm.

Makes about 300ml

....

250g fresh or frozen (and defrosted) raspberries
1 tsp lemon juice, raspberry liqueur or kirsch
4 tbsp icing sugar, or to taste

....

STEP 1 Put all the ingredients in a food processor and blitz to a thick and smooth purée. Taste and add a little more icing sugar, if needed.

STEP 2 To remove the seeds, if required, pass the mixture through a fine sieve. Cover and chill until needed. The sauce will keep in the fridge for up to 4 days.

QUICK & EASY RASPBERRY JAM

This tangy, fruit-packed jam is perfect for sandwiching biscuits and sponges, and topping scones.

Makes about 425g

....

250g raspberries
250g jam sugar
You will need
1 sterilised, warmed jam jar with wax disc (optional) and lid; sugar thermometer (or, see tip)

....

STEP 1 Tip the berries into a large heavy-based pan. Add the sugar and gently squash the fruit with a potato masher, or the back of a wooden spoon, making sure you keep a bit of texture in the mash.

STEP 2 Set the pan over low heat and stir gently with a wooden spoon as the juice starts to run. Keep the heat low, and keep stirring until the sugar has dissolved (it won't take long).

STEP 3 Turn up the heat and boil the liquid rapidly, stirring to prevent the jam 'catching' around the base of the pan, until the jam reaches 102°C/216°F on a sugar thermometer (this is setting point). (See also tip, below.)

STEP 4 Carefully pour the jam into the warm jar. Put a wax disc on the surface (waxed-side down), if using, then leave until cold. Cover tightly with a lid. Store in a cool spot and use within a month.

TIP

If you don't have a sugar thermometer, test the jam using a saucer that has been left in the freezer for at least 30 minutes. After the jam has been boiling for 4 minutes (see step 3), take the pan off the heat, put a ½ teaspoon of jam onto the saucer, leave it for a few seconds, then draw your finger though it. If the jam forms a skin that wrinkles, it has reached setting point. If not, boil it up for another 1 minute and test again.

VALENCIAN ORANGE MARMALADE

Makes about 1kg

....

2 Valencian oranges, halved
1kg preserving sugar
You will need
Muslin bag ; rubber gloves; jam thermometer; 2 x 500g sterilised jam jars with lids

....

STEP 1 Line a small sieve with a muslin bag and place over a deep-sided non-aluminium pan. Squeeze the juice from the oranges into the bag, catching any pips and pith in the muslin. Tie the bag and add to the pan with the juice.

STEP 2 Cut the orange peel into ¼cm strips and add to the pan. Cover with 600ml of water and bring to the boil. Turn off the heat, cover and leave to stand overnight.

STEP 3 Bring back to the boil, reduce the heat and simmer gently, uncovered, for 1 hour, until the peel is very soft. Remove from the heat.

STEP 4 Remove the muslin bag and, wearing rubber gloves, squeeze out as much liquid as possible into the pan. Set the muslin bag aside.

STEP 5 Return the pan to a low heat and add the sugar. Warm over a low heat, stirring until the sugar dissolves. Bring to the boil, then boil rapidly for 15–25 minutes, until the marmalade reaches setting point. Leave to cool for 15 minutes, then pour into sterilised jam jars.

LEMON CURD
Makes about 400g

....

70g unsalted butter, diced
125g caster sugar
finely grated zest of 3 unwaxed
lemons
100ml lemon juice
2 eggs plus 2 yolks, beaten
You will need
2 x 200g sterilised jars or
containers with lids, and
wax discs (optional)

....

STEP 1 Put the butter, sugar,
and lemon zest and juice into a
heatproof bowl. Set the bowl over
a pan of simmering water (don't
let the bowl touch the water) and
stir with a wooden spoon until
the sugar has dissolved.

STEP 2 Remove the bowl from
the pan. Strain the egg into the
lemon mixture and combine.
Set the bowl over the pan of
simmering water again (leave the
heat low) and stir until it becomes
very thick and opaque. To test
when the curd is ready, take a
spoonful of the mixture and draw
your finger through it – if it leaves
a distinct path, it's ready.

STEP 3 Lift the bowl from the pan
and spoon the lemon curd into the
sterilised jars or containers. Cover
with wax discs, if using, then leave
until cold before securing the lids.
Store the curd in the fridge and
use within 2 weeks.

SWEET CURED LEMONS
Makes 5 or 6 lemons

....

300g granulated sugar
30g salt
4 tbsp brandy
5 or 6 good-sized unwaxed lemons
You will need
1-litre sterilized preserving jar

....

STEP 1 Pour 900ml of water
into a large pan and add the sugar.
Bring to the boil, then simmer
gently for about 5 minutes, until
the sugar has dissolved. Remove
from the heat and set aside.

STEP 2 Trim the base off each
lemon so that you can stand each
lemon up. Cut a cross in the top
of each, cutting almost all the way
to the bottom, so that the lemon
quarters open up like a flower.
Sprinkle the salt into the middle
of each lemon, then close up and
pack them into the preserving jar.

STEP 3 Stir the brandy into the
hot sugar syrup, then pour the
syrup over the lemons until the
jar is full. Close the lid and set
aside for 30 minutes. Reserve
any remaining syrup.

STEP 4 After 30 minutes, check
that the syrup is covering all the
lemons; if not top up with the
reserved syrup, then seal the jar.
Leave the lemons to cure for
3–6 months before using. Once
opened use within 6–8 weeks.

HOMEMADE MARZIPAN
Makes about 500g

....

90g golden caster sugar
140g icing sugar
225g ground almonds
½ tsp lemon juice
1 egg
½ tsp almond essence
Food-colouring paste of choice
    (optional)

....

STEP 1 Mix together the caster
sugar, icing sugar and ground
almonds. Add the lemon juice,
egg, and almond essence and
combine to a dough.

STEP 2 Turn out the dough onto a
worktop lightly dusted with icing
sugar and knead until smooth.

STEP 3 To colour the marzipan,
use food-colouring paste of your
chosen colour, adding a little at a
time until you reach the desired
hue. Store the marzipan in an
airtight container in the fridge
for up to 3 weeks.

HOMEMADE LOW-SUGAR GRANOLA

Granola is more than just for
breakfast. You can add it to give
crunch to cookies (see p.88) and
muffins, or even for a nutty bite
in an Irish soda bread.

Makes about 525g

....

150g porridge oats
100g pecans, roughly chopped
85g flaked almonds
35g coconut flakes (unsweetened)
40g pumpkin seeds
40g sunflower seeds
¼ tsp fine sea salt
3 tbsp maple syrup
3 tbsp light olive oil
You will need
Large roasting tin, lightly oiled
with vegetable oil

....

STEP 1 Heat the oven to
170°C/150°C fan/325°F/
Gas 3. Place the oats, pecans,
almonds, coconut flakes, and
pumpkin and sunflower seeds
in a mixing bowl and add the
salt. Use your hands to combine.

STEP 2 Put the syrup in a small
bowl, then stir in the oil. Drizzle
the mixture over the dry
ingredients, then mix well with
a wooden spoon, making sure the
dry ingredients are thoroughly
coated in the oil and syrup.

STEP 3 Tip the mixture into the
prepared roasting tin and spread
evenly, without pressing down and
compressing. Bake for 15 minutes,
stir well, and return the tin to the
oven. Bake for another 15 minutes,

stir again, and then bake for a final 15 minutes, until the mixture has turned golden and crisp.

STEP 4 Remove from the oven, stir gently, then set aside to cool. Once cold, transfer to an airtight container and store in a cool place. Use within 10 days.

PASTRY

PUFF

This is the lightest, richest, flakiest and trickiest of all pastries. What makes it so delicious is its butteriness – the pastry is made with as much butter as flour. Its flakiness comes from the way the butter is rolled into the dough to make hundreds of fragile layers. The lightness is the result of the water in the dough turning to steam in the oven and puffing up those layers.

Makes about 750g

300g plain flour
¼ tsp salt
300g block of unsalted butter, lightly chilled
1 tsp lemon juice
about 140ml chilled water

STEP 1 Put the flour and salt into the bowl of a food processor and pulse a few times to combine. Cut 50g of the cold butter into small pieces and add to the bowl, then process until the mixture looks like fine crumbs.

STEP 2 Mix the lemon juice with the water and pour through the feed tube in your processor, with the motor running, until you have a ball of slightly moist dough.

STEP 3 Turn out the dough onto a lightly floured worktop and cut a deep cross in the top. Wrap in cling film and place in the fridge to chill for 15 minutes.

STEP 4 Sprinkle a little flour on the remaining piece of butter, then set it between two sheets of cling film. Pound it with a rolling pin until it is about 1.75cm deep once pounded. Remove the cling film, fold in two, then cover with film and pound again. Keep doing this until the butter is pliable, but still very cold. Beat it into a square with sides about 13cm long.

STEP 5 Put the ball of dough onto a floured worktop, then roll the edges out in 4 directions, thinning out each side of the dough as you roll. You are aiming to create 4 slightly thinned-out dough flaps, top and bottom and to each side, with a thick square of dough in the centre.

STEP 6 Lightly dust the butter with flour and place it in the centre of the pastry. Fold the flaps of dough over to enclose the butter. Gently press the seams with a rolling pin to seal in the butter, then turn over the dough, so that the seams are face down, and lightly press the dough parcel with the rolling pin to flatten it. Take care not to squeeze out the butter.

STEP 7 Gently roll out the dough to a rectangle measuring about 54 x 18cm. Turn it, if necessary, so that the short end is closest to your body. Fold the dough in 3 as if you were folding an A4 business letter: fold the bottom ⅓ up to cover the centre ⅓, then fold the top ⅓ down to cover the other two layers, to make a neat square. Lightly press the edges with the rolling pin to seal. This is your first 'turn'.

STEP 8 Lift up the dough and give it a ¼ turn anticlockwise, so that the folded edge is by your left hand. Roll out the dough to a rectangle, as before, and fold it in 3 again. This is your second turn. Wrap and chill the dough for 15 minutes, then give it 2 more turns.

STEP 9 Wrap and chill the dough as before – at this point you can chill or freeze the dough (see tips, below). Before using, give the dough 2 more turns to make 6 turns in total.

TIP

⟫ It is important not to develop the gluten in the flour, as you don't want overworked, over-stretched pastry that shrinks in the oven. Don't handle the dough (like you have to do with bread) any more than absolutely necessary, and stick to the chilling times, particularly before baking.

⟫ Don't let the butter get warm – make sure it's well chilled before you begin. If it starts to ooze out of the dough, wrap and chill the dough or it will be hard to handle and end up greasy and heavy.

⟫ Keep a dry pastry brush next to the rolling pin and brush off the excess flour before folding the dough – this will stop the pastry becoming dry and heavy.

⟫ It's difficult to make puff pastry in really small quantities. However, after the dough has had 4 turns (see above), you can wrap it in cling film and chill it for up to 4 days, or freeze it. Defrost the dough in the fridge, if necessary, before using, otherwise the edges will go squishy before the centre is thawed. You will need to make the last 2 turns when you want to use the dough.

ROUGH PUFF

When you really want puff pastry, but time is short, use this quick, shortcut method. It might be called rough puff, but it's a worthy alternative to the real thing.

Makes about 300g

....

165g plain flour
good pinch of salt
115g salted butter, frozen
6–7 tbsp chilled water

....

STEP 1 Mix the flour and salt together in a large bowl. Using the coarse side of a cheese grater, grate long lengths of the frozen butter onto the flour. Mix with a palette or butter knife.

STEP 2 Sprinkle 6 tablespoons of chilled water into the bowl, and using the knife, mix until the dough begins to hold together. Quickly bring the pastry together with a floured hand, avoiding over-handling. (Add the remaining water, if necessary, to bring it into a soft single lump.)

STEP 3 Shape the dough into a flat rectangle measuring about 15 x 10cm. Wrap in cling film and chill for 30 minutes.

STEP 4 Unwrap the pastry and place on a lightly floured work surface. Roll into a narrow rectangle measuring about 36 x 12cm.

STEP 5 With a short end of the pastry closest to you, fold the bottom 1/3 of the pastry up onto the middle 1/3, then the top 1/3 down, as if you were folding an A4 business letter. This is called a roll and fold. Wrap the pastry in cling film and place in the fridge to chill for 30 minutes.

STEP 6 Take the pastry out of the fridge and, with the seam on the left, repeat the roll and fold as before. Wrap the pastry in cling film and return to the fridge to chill for 30 minutes before using.

SAVOURY SHORTCRUST

This buttery shortcrust is rich, crisp and flaky. Use as little water as possible and try not to handle the dough too much. If you want a slightly less rich flavour, you can use half-butter, half-lard.

Makes about 1kg

....

500g plain flour
1 tsp salt
200g unsalted butter, chilled and diced
150–200ml chilled water

....

STEP 1 Place the flour and salt in a large mixing bowl. Rub in the butter, a little at a time, until the mixture resembles fine crumbs.

STEP 2 Gradually add the chilled water, little by little, until you've added just enough to bring the pastry together into a ball (you may not need all the water).

STEP 3 Wrap the pastry in cling film and place it in the fridge for at least 30 minutes to rest before using.

BAKING TIPS & TECHNIQUES

Baking can be one of life's great pleasures and anything that helps make it go better is all for the good. The baking tips over the following pages are intended to help decode some of the terms used in the book. However, the most valuable tips of all are to relax (it's just food), have patience (some things take a bit of time), and practice (yes, that way does lie perfection).

FOLDING IN

This is a way to combine 2 (or more) ingredients as delicately as possible so you don't knock out all the air. A large metal spoon or a plastic spatula is best for folding.

Turn the spoon so that one side cuts down through the mixture. When you touch the bottom of the bowl, turn the spoon upwards and draw it up through the mixture to the top, then flip the spoon over so the mixture flops on to the surface. Give the bowl a ¼ turn and repeat, until you can't see any streaks of unmixed ingredients.

RUBBING IN

One of the most basic, and most useful baking techniques you can learn, this is a way to combine butter and flour and add air when making pastry and simple cake mixtures. Use only your fingertips and thumbs (which are cooler than your palms) – try to keep your palms clean.

Pick up a little of the butter and flour mixture, lift your hands and gently rub your fingers and thumbs together to combine the mixture as it falls. Keep doing this until the mixture has a crumb-like consistency. This is also the way to make pastry by hand if you don't have a processor. Then, use a round-bladed knife to stir in just enough water for the r ight consistency.

SIFTING

This means shaking flour, a raising agent, cocoa powder, icing sugar, ground spices or other dry ingredients through a sieve into a bowl. Sifting remove lumps, adds air, and helps to combine ingredients.

WORKING

This is a way of saying to mix, stir, blend or combine ingredients using a spoon, plastic spatula or your hands until they come together (or look smooth, soft or thickened), depending on the recipe instructions.

PREPARING A TIN

To grease and base-line a cake tin, lightly and thoroughly brush the base and sides of the tin (including the rim) with melted butter. Set the tin on a sheet of baking paper and draw around it, then cut out the base shape. Turn the baking paper over, to be sure any pencil or pen marks are underneath, and press it on to the base of the tin.

To grease and line a cake tin, brush the base and sides with melted butter, then cut out 2 rounds of baking paper very slightly smaller than the base of the tin. Also cut out a double-thickness strip of baking paper long enough to go around the tin and stand about 5cm above it. Make a 2.5cm fold along one edge of this strip, then snip diagonally up to the fold at 1cm intervals (it will look like a thick fringe). Press one paper round on to the base of the tin, then place the strip around the inside of the tin, so the snipped edge lies flat on the base and the paper is pressed smoothly to the sides of the tin. Brush the paper on the base and the snipped

edge of the side strip with a little more melted butter, then press the second round of paper on top. Lightly brush the paper on the base and sides with melted butter to hold it all in place.

To grease and line a loaf tin, lightly brush the base, sides and rim of the tin with melted butter. Cut a strip of baking paper the width of the tin and long enough to cover the base and 2 short sides. Press the paper into the greased tin to line it. The long ends of the paper will help you lift out the loaf after baking.

MELTING CHOCOLATE

Chop or break up the chocolate into even-sized pieces. Put it into a heatproof bowl and set this over a pan of steaming hot, but not boiling water – don't let the base of the bowl touch the water. As the chocolate softens, stir it gently. It is ready to use as melted chocolate as soon as it is liquid and smooth, around 30°C/86°F. Take care not to leave it over the heat any longer. You can also melt chocolate in the microwave. For best results, microwave in 10 second bursts, checking and stirring each time.

TEMPERING CHOCOLATE

This is the way of melting and cooling chocolate to give it a shiny and very smooth look. You'll need a cooking thermometer. First, melt the chocolate (see above), then slightly increase the heat under the pan and keep stirring until the temperature of the chocolate rises to 45°C/113°F (no higher). Immediately remove the bowl from the pan and set it in a larger bowl of cold, but not icy water to quickly cool the chocolate. Gently stir until the temperature falls to 27°C/81°F.

Set the bowl over the pan of steaming hot water again and reheat the chocolate, stirring, until it reaches 29–30°C/84–86°F. Then, remove the bowl from the pan. The tempered chocolate is now ready to use.

WHISKING EGG WHITES
Eggs whisk up to maximum volume when they are at room temperature (see p.21). Separate your eggs carefully, ensuring there is no trace of yolk or shell. Put the whites into a large, clean and grease-free bowl. Whisk, on low speed if using an electric whisk, for about 30 seconds, until frothy. (A pinch of cream of tartar or dash of vinegar or lemon juice added now will help the structure of the whites to stiffen.) Then, increase the speed and continue whisking. Soft peak is when you lift the whisk and the peak of whites slightly droops down. Stiff peak is when the peak stands upright.

'Ribbon stage'
For whisked sponges, you need to whisk eggs and sugar thoroughly to build up a thick mass of tiny air bubbles that forms the structure of the cake. Use a large bowl – after 4–5 minutes of whisking on high speed, the initial volume of eggs and sugar will increase five-fold. The ribbon stage occurs when you lift the whisk out of the bowl and the mixture on it falls back on to the surface of the mixture to make a distinct thick, ribbon-like trail.

WHIPPING CREAM
Always use thoroughly chilled cream for whipping, as the coldness prevents the butterfat from separating and the mixture curdling as you whip. If you need to fold the cream into another mixture, whip to soft peaks (see above). For piping, whip to a slightly firmer peak.

LINING A FLAN TIN OR PIE PLATE WITH PASTRY
Set the pastry dough on a lightly floured worktop, dust your rolling pin with flour and gently but firmly roll out to a circle about 8cm larger in diameter than your tin/plate. Roll up the pastry around the rolling pin and lift it over the tin, then unroll the pastry gently, so it drapes over the tin.

Flour your fingers and press the pastry onto the base and up the side of the tin, smoothing out any air pockets. Leave the excess pastry hanging over the rim, or roll the pin over the tin to cut it off.

Gently ease the pastry up the side of the tin, just slightly higher than the rim, to allow it to shrink during baking. Curve your forefinger inside this new rim and press the pastry over your finger so it curves inwards – this makes it easier to unmould. Prick the base of the pastry case well with a fork, then chill for 20 minutes.

Blind baking
This means to bake an unfilled tart so the pastry is cooked before adding the filling. Line the pastry case with the baking paper (cut to size and crumpled up to make it more flexible) and fill with ceramic baking beans or dried beans (see p.16). Place in the heated oven and bake as stated in the recipe (or about 12–15 minutes, until set and firm). Remove the paper and beans, then return the tin to the oven and bake for a further 5–10 minutes, until the pastry is thoroughly cooked and starting to colour (this is vital to avoid a 'soggy bottom').

CAKE 'DONENESS'
For delicate sponge cakes, the most reliable test for doneness is the fingertip test: gently press the top of the sponge, in the centre, with your finger – the cake is ready if the sponge springs back.

If you leave a slight dent, the mixture is still soft – bake for a few minutes more and test again. When done, a sponge will start to shrink from the sides of the tin.

For richer, heavier cakes, fruit cakes and dense chocolate cakes, insert a wooden cocktail stick or fine skewer into the centre of the cake. If the stick or skewer comes out clean, the cake is done. (Note that some cakes, such as brownies, need a bit of stickiness. In specific cases follow the instructions in the recipe to test for doneness.)

COOLING A SPONGE
Always loosen the edges of a sponge with a palette knife before turning out. To avoid a wire rack leaving marks on the top of a sponge cake, cover a clean board with a clean, dry tea towel. Invert the sponge (in its tin) onto the tea towel, then lift off the tin and remove the lining paper. Set the wire rack on top and turn the whole thing over. Carefully remove the board and tea towel and leave the sponge to cool, right side up, on the wire rack.

CUTTING A SPONGE
Make a small, vertical nick or cut in the side of the sponge with the tip of a small sharp knife – this will help you align the layers when sandwiching. Gently but firmly press down on the top of the sponge with the flat of your hand and, using a long serrated knife, carefully saw the sponge horizontally in half.

KNEADING A BREAD DOUGH
Kneading – or working – a dough develops the gluten in the flour to create neat bundles of strands that can stretch around the bubbles of carbon dioxide gas. The dough will then rise slowly, and set in the oven. You can knead by hand or in a stand mixer fitted with a dough hook.

To knead by hand lightly dust the worktop and your fingers with flour, or grease with a teaspoon of oil. Turn out the dough onto the worktop. Hold down one end with your hand and use the other hand to pull and stretch out the dough away from you, as if it were an elastic band. Gather the dough back into a ball again and give it a ¼ turn, then repeat the stretching and gathering-back. As you knead you'll notice the dough starts to feel pliable and then stretchy and very elastic, and silky smooth. Nearly all doughs need 10 minutes of thorough kneading by hand. (Under-kneading can produce a soggy, flat or dense loaf.)

If you're having a hard time kneading a dough made with rye flour (which contains very little gluten), give the dough (and your arms) a break: cover the dough with the upturned bowl and rest for 5–10 minutes, then continue.

To knead in an electric mixer, use a dough hook on the lowest possible speed and knead for about 5 minutes. While it's almost impossible to over-knead by hand (your arms will give out first), you can stretch the gluten beyond repair in a mixer, which means the dough won't rise well at all.

To test if the dough has been kneaded enough, take a small piece and stretch it between your fingers to make a thin, translucent sheet. If it won't stretch out or it tears easily, knead a while longer.

RISING A BREAD DOUGH
Most recipes require the dough to rise until doubled in size. For the best results, provide the dough with a moist and gently warm spot in which to rise. A room temperature of 20–24°C/68–75°F is ideal – if the room is too hot, the yeast will grow too rapidly and the dough will become distorted (and

maybe develop a slight aftertaste); too cool and the yeast develops more slowly (although this can give a richer flavour and chewier crumb and crust). To deliberately slow the rising, mix the dough with cool or even chilled water and leave it to rise in a cool spot or the fridge overnight. With some experimentation you can try slowing the fermentation by using less yeast.

KNOCKING BACK A BREAD DOUGH
Knocking back or punching down the risen dough breaks up the large gas bubbles to make a lot of smaller, finer bubbles that rise more evenly. Use your knuckles to punch down the puffy dough so that it collapses. Some bakers prefer to fold or flop the dough over on itself 2 or 3 times. After knocking back, you'll probably need to shape the dough.

PROVING A BREAD DOUGH
Proving is the last rising prior to baking, which happens after you have shaped a bread dough, leaving the dough to rise until it has about doubled in size again. The time this takes depends on the temperature of the dough (some, like Brioche are chilled before shaping), and how lively your dough is.

However, correct proving is important. If a dough is under-proved, it can suddenly expand in the hot oven and distort; over-proved and the dough can collapse in the heat. To test whether or not the dough is properly proven, gently prod it: if it springs back, it's not quite ready; if it returns to its original state fairly slowly, or if there's a very slight dent, it's ready.

BAKING A LOAF
To bake a loaf with a good crust, make sure the oven is thoroughly heated, so the dough quickly puffs

(called 'oven-spring') and then sets, bakes evenly and forms a good crust. If you're worried about the oven temperature dropping as you load the bread in the oven, heat it slightly higher than the recipe says, then turn it down to the specified temperature as soon as you close the door.

For a crisp crust create a burst of steam in the oven at the start of baking. This keeps the surface of the bread moist, helping the bread rise easily. Once the surface has set, the moisture evaporates, leaving a crisp finish. To do this, put an empty roasting tin on the floor of the oven when you turn it on to heat it. Then, immediately after you've put in the loaf, pour cold water, or throw a handful of ice cubes, into the hot tin. Close the oven door to trap in the steam.

For a crisp base put a baking sheet or baking stone in the oven to heat up. Then carefully transfer your loaf (in a tin or on a sheet of baking paper) on to the hot baking sheet or stone for baking.

To test for doneness, carefully remove the bread from the oven and turn out, upside down, onto one hand (wear oven gloves). Tap the underside of the loaf with your knuckles. If the bread sounds hollow, the loaf is cooked through, but if you get a dull 'thud', put the bread back into the oven – straight onto the oven shelf. Bake for a few more minutes, then test again. (A slightly over-baked loaf will taste far better than an undercooked one.) Cool on a wire rack (not in the tin or on a baking sheet), so that the crust stays crisp.

DECORATING TIPS & TECHNIQUES

Creating beautiful-looking bakes needn't be complicated – the simplest of decorations can look stunning. The tips in this section are here to help you as you perfect your skills. Remember that practice (along with a bit of patience) works wonders – and always make sure the decorations you use are edible.

DUSTING
If you're short of time, or are a baking novice, it's hard to beat a dusting of icing sugar or cocoa on sponge cakes and sweet pastries, and flour on top of bread. Use a small, fine sieve and a light hand. If you want to create a dusted pattern, lay or hold over a simple paper doily or stencil and dust through it. An edible shimmer spray or edible powder lustre over baked biscuits can make them look magical – great for a children's party (always read the labels for allergy information, and to ensure edibility!).

COLOUR
Think about contrasts and combinations: cocoa powder combined with edible gold dust looks amazing on darker surfaces. Edible shimmer sprays come in a wide range of colours and will add fabulous, misty metallic gloss to icing – pick a colour that will give a good contrast. Test and practise on a sheet of paper before you spray your bakes, to check your choices.

METALLIC LEAF
Edible gold or silver leaf can look very dramatic, but do use sparingly. Available in small packs, the leaves are thinner than tissue and easily disintegrate, so treat very gently. Use the tip of a knife to transfer small segments to the finished bake. The leaves will stick better if the icing or frosting is still slightly soft

or damp when you apply them. Try brushing fine edible leaf powder or lustre onto a dark chocolate pastry or biscuit, or to a chocolate decoration, using a small dry cake-decorating brush.

GLAZING
Glazes add a glossy pattiserie-window finish to pastry, breads and tarts. Although egg is the most usual glaze ingredient, even a light brushing of milk can add shine to the top of bread.

To make an egg glaze, lightly beat a whole egg with a fork, and brush it over the top of a pie or loaf of bread before baking for a glossy or shiny finish. Two light coats, rather than one heavy one, will help your bake stay streak-free. Use just the yolk for a deeper golden colour, while a glaze made from frothy egg white and finished with a sprinkling of caster sugar will give a slightly crunchy, sparkling finish.

To make a fruit glaze, from jams or jellies, pick a fruit that works well with your filling. Melt, stirring, the jam with a little water over a low heat until smooth and very hot (but not boiling). If the jam contains seeds or bits of fruit, you may want to sift them out at this point, and gently reheat the smooth liquid. Brush the hot liquid over the filling with a heatproof pastry brush, gently reheating the glaze to re-liquefy if necessary.

PASTRY DECORATION
Pastry decorations can add the 'wow' effect to any pie.

To flute the lid, use the thumb and first finger on one hand to take a small piece of the pastry rim and pinch a bit together, then repeat it at regular intervals all around the

edge. Or, pinch a little of the pastry edge between your thumb and first finger on one hand, while pushing in between them with the first finger of the other hand.

To make lattice and twists, instead of a lid, to top a pie or tart, make sure the pastry is firm and chilled before you start. Roll out the pastry as for the base, then cut narrow strips of even width – use a pizza wheel-cutter or large sharp knife to avoid dragging or tearing the pastry, and a ruler for precision. If the strips are too narrow or too wide, they're more likely to tear – you'll need a bit of trial and error, and patience, when you first start. As you work with each one, keep the rest of the strips covered with cling film so they don't dry out.

To make a lattice, cut the strips to fit the top of the pie, lightly brush the rim with water, then evenly space the strips on top of the filling. For twists, using both hands, gently hold each end of the strip between fingers and thumbs and carefully twist in opposite directions before setting on top of the filling.

Chill well before baking so that the strips don't shrink, and trim off the excess pastry with a sharp knife.

To make leaves, roll out the chilled pastry. Either cut into oval shapes free-hand, use a shaped leaf cutter, or cut the pastry into 3cm-long strips, then across on the diagonal into 7 x 4cm lengths, and mark veins on each with the back of a knife. Remember that cut-out shapes will shrink in the oven, so don't make them too small. Fix each on top of the pastry lid with a dab of water or milk, chill well, then glaze.

Plaited pastry strips need some well-chilled, firm pastry and some practice. Again, use a ruler and pizza cutter for precision. Form the plaits on a baking sheet lined with baking paper and lightly dusted with flour – that way you can transfer them to the fridge easily if they start to soften.

SPREADING BUTTER ICING

First, check that your butter icing, buttercream or frosting is smooth and spreadable. Hold a cupcake in one hand; place a large cake on a rotating cake stand or lazy Susan, or stand the cake on a cake board on an upturned bowl. Use a round-bladed knife, such as a palette knife, to spread the icing.

To decorate a cupcake, put a dollop of icing on the top then, starting at one side, swirl the icing around the top in a continuous movement, pushing the icing almost to the edges.

To decorate a large cake, spread the icing evenly over the top and down the sides, either with a swirled finish or with a smooth, flat finish using a plastic cake scraper. You may wish to cover a sponge cake in a first thin layer of your icing mixture to 'catch the crumbs', then chill it until firm, and finish with a neat covering.

PIPING BUTTER ICING

First, check that the icing is smooth and spreadable. Drop the nozzle you want to use (a star, or plain tube) into the piping bag (see p.18). Twist the bag above the nozzle to prevent the filling oozing out at this point, then set the bag in a jug or tall container, and fold the top of the bag over the rim. Spoon the filling in to the bag no more than ⅔ full. Gather the top edge of the bag together, then twist to push the filling down to the (still twisted) nozzle end. Push out any air pockets as you go. Untwist the nozzle end and squeeze the bag so the filling

reaches and fills the nozzle, then twist the top end again to compact the filling. Ice a little on a plate to have a practice before you begin.

To pipe a spiral hold the bag almost upright about 1cm above the cake. Start at the edge, squeezing the bag with even pressure, and work inwards and upwards in a circular motion to make slightly overlapping rings. To finish, press down lightly, then lift the bag up and away.

To create round 'kisses', hold the bag vertically, squeeze and pull up.

PIPING AND FLOODING BISCUITS

Make up some royal icing to a smooth, thick paste (usually, 100g royal icing sugar to 1 tablespoon of chilled water). The icing should hold its shape and be thick enough to pipe. If it is too thick, add water a couple of drops at a time; if too runny, add more of the royal icing sugar, 1 teaspoon at a time.

Put half your icing into another bowl and cover it tightly with cling film – this will be your flooding icing. Divide the remaining icing into smaller bowls, one for each colour. Cover the bowls when you aren't using them. Using the end of a cocktail stick, add 1 drop of edible food colouring to the icing and mix, adding a drop at a time, until you have the shade you want.

To pipe fine line outlines, fit a No.2 writing nozzle into a small piping bag, spoon the icing into the bag then test the flow speed and shape on a plate. Make sure the biscuit is thoroughly cold or the icing will spread. Keeping the pressure consistent, squeeze the bag to start the icing flow and slowly trace the outline of the biscuit with the piped icing. If you intend to flood to fill in the outline, make sure there are no gaps. Cover

the tip with cling film when you've finished so that you can come back to that colour for detail if needed. Use the other colours to pipe outlines of your design, then fill. Leave the piped icing to dry while you make up the flooding icing.

To flood, divide the remaining icing into small bowls, as before, one for each colour. Add just enough water, a little at a time, to make a smooth, pourable consistency. Add colouring as before. Fill a clean, disposable piping bag with your first colour and snip off the tip, then hold the bag above the area you want to flood and gently squeeze. Use a zig-zag motion and don't overfill the space: the icing will run to fill the area marked by your piping icing. Tap or shake the biscuit to settle the icing, and prick any bubbles with a cocktail stick.

To create 'flood-on-flood' patterns (such as polka dots and hearts), add small dots of flooding icing in a contrasting colour before the colour has set. Use a cocktail stick to create the shapes.

USING ROLLING FONDANT

This soft, flexible paste, designed for covering cakes, and moulding shapes, sets firm as it dries. You can make your own (see p.305) or buy it made in blocks to roll, or as ready-rolled sheets that just need to be set in place, or cut as needed. (Ready-made fondant is often made without gelatine, so suitable for vegetarians.) To cover a cake, roll out the fondant to a circle large enough to cover the top and sides. Drape the fondant over the rolling pin and transfer it to the cake (cover the cake in a thin layer of buttercream or warmed, diluted jam first). Gently smooth out any air pockets and any creases, starting at the top and working down the sides. Cut off any excess.

INDEX

This book is published to accompany the television series entitled *The Great British Bake Off*, broadcast on Channel 4 in 2018

The Great British Bake Off® is a registered trademark of Love Productions Ltd

Series produced for Channel 4 Television by Love Productions

First published in Great Britain in 2018 by Sphere

10 9 8 7 6 5 4 3 2 1

Text and recipes © Love Productions Ltd 2018
Design and recipe photography © Little, Brown Book Group 2018
Additional photography © Love Productions Ltd 2018

Wagon Wheels is a registered trademark of Burton's Foods Ltd

A CIP catalogue record for this book is available from the British Library.

ISBN 978-0-7515-7464-7

New recipes developed and written by: Claire Bassano, Linda Collister and Becca Watson

Editorial Director: Hannah Boursnell
Project Editor: Judy Barratt
Design & Art Direction: Smith & Gilmour
Food Photographer: Susanna Blåvarg
Additional Photography: Smith & Gilmour, pages 1, 2, 3, 6, 7, 8, 14, 19, 27, 37, 49, 58, 60, 73, 80, 102, 123, 130, 144, 165, 169, 170, 172, 180, 182, 193, 198, 200, 209, 210, 225, 229, 238, 275, 280, 290, 295, front and back endpapers; Mark Bourdillon, pages 14, 210
Food Stylists: Lisa Harrison, Emma Marsden and Isla Murray
Assistant Food Stylists: Danya Simons and Evie Harbury
Props Stylist: Olivia Wardle
Production Manager: Abby Marshall
Cover design: Smith & Gilmour

Typeset in Sentinel and Neutraface 2
Printed in Germany

Papers used by Sphere are from well-managed forest and other responsible sources.

WITH THANKS

Love Productions would like to thank the following people:
Producers: Jane Treasure, Claire Emerson, Chloe Avery
Challenge Producers: Tallulah Radula-Scott, Lucy Terrell
Food Team: Georgia Harding, Katy Bigley, Emma Hair.
Home Economist: Becca Watson
Love Executives: Letty Kavanagh, Rupert Frisby, Kieran Smith
Publicist: Amanda Console
Commissioning Editors: Kelly Webb-Lamb, Sarah Lazenby

Thank you to Paul, Prue, Noel and Sandi. And to the Bakers: Anthony, Briony, Daniel, Imelda, Jon, Karen, Kim-Joy, Luke, Manon, Rahul, Ruby and Terry; Chris, Flo, James, Julia, Kate, Liam, Peter, Stacey, Steven, Sophie, Tom and Yan; and Sandy.

Sphere
An imprint of Little, Brown Book Group, Carmelite House, 50 Victoria Embankment, London EC4Y 0DZ

An Hachette UK Company
www.hachette.co.uk
www.littlebrown.co.uk